Scandal and Silence

Contemporary Political Communication

Robert M. Entman, *Scandal and Silence*

Max McCombs, R. Lance Holbert, Spiro Kiousis and Wayne Wanta, *The News and Public Opinion*

Craig Allen Smith, *Presidential Campaign Communication*

Scandal and Silence

Media Responses to Presidential Misconduct

Robert M. Entman

polity

First published in 2012 by Polity Press

Polity Press
65 Bridge Street
Cambridge CB2 1UR, UK

Polity Press
350 Main Street
Malden, MA 02148, USA

ISBN-13: 978-0-7456-4762-3
ISBN-13: 978-0-7456-4763-0(pb)

A catalogue record for this book is available from the British Library.

Typeset in 10.5 on 12 pt Times Ten
by Toppan Best-set Premedia Limited
Printed and bound in Great Britain by MPG Books Group Limited, Bodmin, Cornwall

The publisher has used its best endeavours to ensure that the URLs for external websites referred to in this book are correct and active at the time of going to press. However, the publisher has no responsibility for the websites and can make no guarantee that a site will remain live or that the content is or will remain appropriate.

For further information on Polity, visit our website: www.politybooks.com

*In memory of my beloved father, Bernie Entman (1922–2010),
and for my sister Barbara Synnott and her children
Michael, Katherine and Thomas*

Contents

Figures

Tables

Acknowledgments

This book benefited enormously from assistance from the diligent, intelligent and creative students at the School of Media and Public Affairs (SMPA) of the George Washington University. The most important of these are graduate students Abby Jones, Lauren Martens, Morgan Dibble, Gerard Matthews, Jesse Holcomb, and undergraduates Zack Hutson and Eric Walker. Abby Jones spent the longest time working with me and deserves particular thanks for her extraordinary help on this and other projects. All of these students provided not merely assistance but critique and suggestions, and Morgan also helped in designing the graphic figures for the book. Dongxiao Li of Zhejiang University spent a year at the SMPA writing her dissertation on scandal and media in China, and I benefited from our cross-cultural discussions. Ji-Hyeun Kwan and Matthew Iles were able and helpful research assistants during the 2008–9 academic year, while I was Visiting Professor of Public Policy at Duke. Above all, I'd like to thank Dr. Carole V. Bell who, as a post-doctoral fellow at SMPA during 2010–11, offered indispensable insights and research, along with a sharp critical eye. In addition Carole's help with my teaching duties when I took ill was generous and greatly appreciated. The support of Dr. Kimberly Gross, Associate Director of SMPA, and Frank Sesno, Director, also helped enable the writing of this book in a variety of ways for which I am grateful. The idea of writing a book about media and scandal occurred to me during a stimulating week in 2001 spent as the Stice Lecturer in Social Science at the University of Washington. In the decade since then, I have enjoyed the support, questions and insights of many fine colleagues at NC State University, Duke and GW; they made this a better book.

As always, special thanks and love go to my wife Francie Seymour and to our children Max and Emily. I couldn't have done it without them.

1

High Crimes or Misdemeanors?

To an outside observer, the Washington scandal machine may seem to operate at random. The same media that roundly condemned President George W. Bush for his passivity in the face of Hurricane Katrina (see Bennett, Lawrence & Livingston 2007) failed to get worked up by his inaction as economic calamity loomed in 2008. The same news organizations that endlessly probed the marital psychology of Bill and Hillary Clinton passed over the unconventional aspects of John and Cindy McCain's marriage (see Heilemann & Halperin 2010). And journalists came down hard on 1988 vice presidential nominee Dan Quayle for using family connections to evade Vietnam by entering the National Guard, yet in 2000 barely mentioned George W. Bush's similar record.

If corruption, immorality or incompetence sometimes generate a punishing avalanche of negative publicity, what about the many instances where the media ignore or downplay serious misdeeds? And if in some instances intense attention focuses on private trespasses, how can we account for the more numerous times when politicians enjoy a generous zone of privacy? Over the years, in fact, journalists' responses to transgressions of comparable gravity – or triviality – have varied dramatically. Concentrating on US presidents and aspirants to the White House, the level at which the stakes are highest and the media's watchdog duties most pressing, this book reveals the underlying logic to what might seem arbitrary and capricious journalism.

Although the media's scandal choices do possess an internal logic, the journalistic swings from overkill to neglect are problematic for democracy. Holding governments accountable and reducing the tendency of power to corrupt requires that attention to scandals be *properly calibrated*. As just suggested and the book will show, American media do not, and perhaps cannot, regulate scandal news to consistently match up with the seriousness of official misdeeds. Nor does scandal journalism give similar treatment to equivalent or even identical misconduct from one case to another. Exploring and explaining poorly calibrated scandal news, the inconsistency and the lack of proportional fit between the societal costs of official misbehavior and the intensity of media attention, is this book's mission.

Many have observed that the media often seem to pursue trifling mischief far beyond rational judgment of the its underlying severity, which diverts the attention of the public and politicians alike, while discouraging fundamentally honest, competent potential leaders from entering politics (see Sabato, Stencil & Lichter 2000; Davis 2007). What's far less understood or debated is the watchdogs' frequent hesitation to bark even after they sense trouble. When the media ignore evidence, show only glancing interest or fail to frame the acts as a *scandal*, misdeeds tend to evanesce, often going unattributed and even unrecognized. Seemingly capricious treatment of scandal weakens the disincentives to corrupt behavior that a vigorous free press should maintain.

Perhaps paradoxically, this remains true in the Internet age. Information is more widely and cheaply available, but the fragmentation of the public sphere into more specialized (and polarized) ideological enclaves (see Gitlin 1998; Hindman 2008) means scandalous information about misconduct often cannot reach the critical mass needed to initiate a full-blown scandal. All the Internet, infotainment and social media diverting the audience make it *more* urgent, not less, that scholars and journalists themselves understand the forces that lead the *New York Times*, *Washington Post* and other major print, broadcast and cable news organizations to magnify some scandals while neglecting others. And, not coincidentally, websites run by these leaders of the legacy media also rank among the top 20 devoted to news (Pew Project for Excellence in Journalism 2010), so this focus does not mean ignoring the Internet. As we'll see, at the close of the twenty-first century's first decade, such innovative channels for news as the blogosphere, Facebook and Twitter could not create politically meaningful scandals without assistance from traditional national outlets. These remained the crucial gatekeepers, the ones whose imprimatur lent political heft to scandal.

Justifiably enough, the bulk of scholarly and popular writing on scandal focuses on the malfeasance that actually does materialize into scandal. Yet this concentration allows the media themselves to define the phenomenology of scandal: what the news classifies as scandalous garners most of the scholarly study. Researchers need to cast a wider net, to develop theoretical understanding of both the scandals that spread throughout the political system in a consequential way, and those that barely cause a ripple. When they do happen, the major scandals arise from a self-reinforcing process whereby official misdeeds stimulate news coverage, which begets government reaction; and that response in turn creates fresh newsworthy developments, heightening incentives and opportunities for some politicians and unelected officials to pursue (or exploit) the potential scandal, leading to still more scandal news. Activation of these cascading reactions is necessary if a scandal is to persist long enough to hold responsible officials accountable for misdeeds. As already suggested, even if the high-voltage accusations that yield outsized political effects are those that come to mind when we hear the term "scandal," the book will contend that, in practice, they constitute the exceptions, not the rule.

The forces that determine whether the media provide a sustained scandal narrative are not fully under news organizations' control. After all, no overriding governor patrols the news system to ensure it consistently achieves any particular informational standard. Indeed, journalists lack the time, resources and commercial or political incentives to ensure calibration. What results are those wild swerves from overplaying to underplaying alleged official misconduct.

In recent decades, scandals have of course received considerable and illuminating attention from scholars (Sabato 1991; Lull & Hinerman 1997; Sabato, et al. 2000; Ginsberg & Shefter 2002; Adut 2008; Nyhan 2008; Feldstein 2010). Journalists themselves have analyzed the media's apparent obsession with scandals involving presidents and would-be presidents (Garment 1992; Fallows 1997; Kurtz 1998; Kalb 2001), as have political operatives (Davis 2007; McClellan 2008). Although most of these works hint at the absence of calibration, they don't scrutinize scandals on that basis. As a result, the existing literature misses this most fundamental trait and other politically crucial features of scandal production in the US (and, to some extent, in Western Europe and Latin America – see Thompson 2000; Waisbord 2000; Tumber & Waisbord 2004 and cases therein; Canel & Sanders 2006).

One reason for the gaps in research could be that so much recent scholarship, journalistic self-reflection and history have been shaped by a few iconic outrages, a kind of golden age of disgrace running from Richard Nixon's Watergate (1972–4) through Ronald Reagan's Iran–Contra (1985–7) to Sen. Gary Hart's (D-CO)[1] adulterous self-immolation as a presidential candidate (1987–8). From this vantage point, the Bill Clinton sex scandals (1992–9) appear to be a continuation of post-Watergate scandal politics. This book, however, suggests otherwise. After the Hart affair, the politics of media and scandal in the US underwent a transformation of sorts. These important changes are demonstrated by case studies from the period 1988–2008, spanning the administrations of George H. W. Bush, Bill Clinton and George W. Bush. Careful analysis of scandals – and non-scandals – occurring during these years tells a new story, one that requires adjustments to the most common understanding of American political scandals and the media.

Understanding scandals

We first turn briefly to conceptual matters. Discussions of scandal can become confusing when they fail to distinguish between the underlying unethical, careless or illegal actions, which merely hold the potential of scandal, and the emergence of publicity framing that malfeasance *as* a scandal. Lots of potential scandals remain just that. *Scandal* or *political scandal* will be used to denote individual misconduct by presidents or candidates that the media *do* publicize as an urgent problem for the polity, one that must be investigated and somehow remedied. *Potential scandal* refers to misconduct that the media could reasonably be expected to treat as a scandal because the bad deeds resemble previously publicized scandals in key respects. Typically, we can recognize misconduct that possesses scandal potential by asking how difficult it would be for the accused to acknowledge and explain their own wrongdoing without risking political damage to themselves or allies. Incidentally, it is this peril of admitting and justifying the behavior that usually leads to cover-ups. Taking the risk of denial and deception may appear to be the lesser of evils for miscreants. The misbehavior itself will be described using that term and such synonyms as malfeasance and misconduct. I will do my best to keep the distinctions clear.

Many definitions reflect the imprint of Thompson's (2000) influential book, which emphasizes five traits that distinguish scandal from politics as usual. In summary these are: transgression of moral codes, norms or values; an "element of secrecy" characterizing a violation that makes some outsiders suspicious; disapproval of the act by outsiders; public denunciation of the transgression; and potential damage to the reputation of transgressors (pp. 13–14).[2] Adut (2008) and Nyhan (2008, 2009) advance the discussion by distinguishing two

schools of thought on media and scandal: objectivist and constructivist. Objectivist scholars assume that the degree to which an
official's behavior violates moral expectations or damages the society
matches the extent of scandalous publicity and scandalized public
opinion. This perspective runs counter to what this chapter has
already discussed, the many serious violations that do not engender
major scandals – and trifling ones that do (see also Adut 2008, p. 216;
Nyhan 2009).

In contrast, the constructivists emphasize citizens' reactions to
publicized misconduct, defining scandals as secret transgressions
of social norms that attract publicity and stimulate widespread
indignation. No public indignation, no scandal (see also Esser &
Hartung 2004).

As Nyhan (2009, p. 3) points out, the constructivist standard
stumbles when it concentrates on public reaction without recognizing
the heavy influence of elites' attempts to promote or deflect scandal.
In fact, a key problem with many treatments is their reliance on
public disapproval: if only those scandals that provoke massive public
indignation count, the Monica Lewinsky affair must be excluded
from the category despite having led to the first impeachment of a
president in over 100 years. As surveys and scholars recorded,
substantial majorities of Americans responded to news of Clinton's
sexual escapades with amusement, concern or boredom rather than
anger (Lawrence & Bennett 2000; Zaller 2001).[3] Poll data also suggest
a paucity of public outrage at the revelations of torture in Iraq's Abu
Ghraib prison, although by many measures the matter spawned a
scandal.[4] In other cases, the public's complex and often ambivalent
responses may be difficult to discern or summarize. Relying on public
outrage as a condition for scandal also means omitting the instances
where substantively serious misbehavior never receives sufficient
publicity to stimulate a scandalized response or any widespread
interpretation at all. A robust concept of scandal should incorporate
not just politically damaging, high-publicity variants, but also
those that fail to garner enough time in the spotlight to catch the
public eye.

Furthermore, as Tiffen (1999, pp. 8–11) observes, misconduct (such
as Bill Clinton's infidelity) may be overtly denounced but tacitly
condoned by much of the public. Still other actions generate widely
varying responses among different groups. Particularly in the
polarized political climate characterizing the US during the period
covered by this book, in fact, scandal allegations predictably met with
selective outrage as Democrats disregarded Republicans' charges
and vice versa. For instance, in 2009, some Republicans promoted a

scandal over President Obama's place of birth, claiming he was not a native-born US citizen and thus ineligible for the presidency. Despite the evidence of state records and contemporaneous newspaper announcements of Obama's birth in Hawaii, a poll found 42 percent of Republicans (as opposed to 93 percent of Democrats) accepting his legitimate citizenship (28 percent of Republicans said they believed Obama was born outside the US and 30 percent said they weren't sure).[5]

Nyhan (2009, p. 4; see Nyhan 2011) offers a modified constructivist stance, defining scandal as: "a socially constructed event that takes place when a public figure's actions are *widely interpreted* as contravening established moral, political or procedural norms" (emphasis in original). Whether this interpretation takes hold depends on the "political climate," which can favor or hinder "the efforts of opposing elites to foment scandal." Nyhan's conceptualization represents real progress in that he fully recognizes the heavy dependence of scandal news on elite competition and pressure, rather than on the severity of misbehavior, public outrage or journalistic deficiency. Since about 1990, the objectivist view is rare and most definitions recognize the culturally constructed nature of scandal, along with its entanglement with political competition and use as a political weapon. The present study seeks to enhance understanding by extending these insights through a more comprehensive dissection and modeling of scandal news production.

Themes

Building on prior treatments while teasing out and making explicit journalists' and scholars' implicit assumptions about the scandal process, the book offers a series of somewhat contrarian themes. The first theme reflects the calibration problem: study and critique of media and scandal should focus on understanding the *system* of political communication rather than on news organizations as separate entities charting the course of scandals by themselves. Much writing, especially but not only by journalists and political practitioners, analyzes scandals as if they reflect (often deficient) journalistic ethics and processes, rather than this larger system. The system comprises party organizations and elites, pressure groups and activists, variously competing and cooperating with each other and with news organizations to advance or protect their interests. In turn, the media themselves compete for prestige, political influence and economic survival. Other participants include government institutions, especially Congressional committees and courts, and public opinion. Most of the time, a governmental entity must take action on allegations for any scandal to persist in the news sufficiently long and intensely to leave a noticeable imprint on the political environment.[6]

The occurrence, severity and effects of scandals are influenced by all of these players, some acting strategically and others not. Depending on their self-interests, strategic actors – party operatives, politicians, activists, interest groups – seek either to stoke or to derail a scandal. On the other hand, the mainstream news media do not strategically shape their news reports to achieve some political goal; their strategizing revolves around profit and prestige.[7] The other important non-strategic actor is public opinion, the citizenry's actual, apparent or anticipated level of interest and outrage (cf. Protess, Cook & Doppelt 1991; Ettema & Glasser 1998). Rather than the media's addiction to scandal, it is the outside, strategic actors interacting with typically non-strategic news organizations and citizens that yield any unfortunate excesses of scandal news.

No wonder the system often produces scandals poorly calibrated to the severity of dubious behavior. Yet it is not random or arbitrary. It exhibits discernible patterns identified in the book's second theme: party competition, intersecting with predictable biases in the decision-making processes of news organizations and, to a lesser extent, with public opinion, helps explain proportionality and focus in scandal news. Whether scandals erupt, spread and persist depends far more on the skill of the partisan competitors and on the norms and incentives governing news production than on the degree and nature of the official's offense (see Tiffen 1999, p. 249). A corollary to this point is a direct outgrowth or consequence of the system: when Republicans and Democrats share responsibility for a potentially scandalous situation, chances are slim it will become a major scandal. If any scandal reporting appears despite a bipartisan interest in silence, the publicity is typically too fleeting or confusing to penetrate public consciousness in a timely fashion. As a result, it will be unlikely to influence politics.

This point connects to a third contrarian theme: the metaphor of a "feeding frenzy" rarely applies to scandals.[8] The term implies not only that media indiscriminately crave scandals but also that they are easy for journalists to activate at the hint of political blood in the water, and difficult to stop once started.[9] This book contends that when it comes to scandals involving serious high-level misdeeds, the converse is closer to the truth: full-blown scandals concerning substantively grave misconduct are difficult for media to initiate and virtually impossible for them to sustain on their own.

Most news organizations, most of the time, do not thirst eagerly for this sort of scandalous scoop. Nor do audiences. Related to the misleading depiction of scandal as a primordial instinctive motivation for journalists is the exaggeration of public demand for news and resolution of scandal. In making the undeniable point that the entertainment potential inherent in a scandal story influences journalistic decisions about pursuing it, Waisbord (2004, p. 1095) notes that publics often tire of scandal stories quickly. Even Watergate did not engage the public or most of the media when it first made the news in 1972. It took almost two years for surveys to show unequivocal public support for removing Nixon from office (Lang & Lang 1983). Watergate only ended the way it did because of decisions by Congress and the judiciary to pursue investigations into the matter, not because the public rose up to demand accountability.

Journalists' memoirs testify to the reluctance of most US news organizations to dive into potential scandals that could seriously threaten powerful interests and individuals (Hertsgaard 1989; Rather 1994; Schorr 2008) – unless other influential actors are promoting outrage. Even when important people sponsor a scandal involving the powerful, there's little frenzy at mainstream media organizations. Upper-level news executives and lawyers usually intervene, slowing down the writing and editing process, asking questions, demanding confirmations. This assertion held true even at the *Washington Post* during Watergate (see Woodward & Bernstein 1974; Kalb 2001). Indeed, sometimes news outlets alert the government before publication and succumb to entreaties that they delay or spike the story. For instance, the *New York Times* held, for over a year, James Risen (2006) and Eric Lichtblau's investigation into the George W. Bush administration's surveillance of US citizens in apparent disregard of the Foreign Intelligence Surveillance Act (FISA).

These observations bring us to a fourth theme: it generally seems easiest for media to produce a scandal when the accusations do not pose much danger to existing structures of power and distributions of resources. After all, the greater the peril to powerful individuals or interests, the more formidable the capabilities mobilized to block a scandal will be, and the more cautious members of the mainstream media are likely to be about taking a chance on a story. The more powerful the individuals and interests implicated by the allegations, then – all else being equal – the less, not more, likely they are to spark a major scandal. Similarly, the more serious and widespread the corruption, the lower, not higher, is the probability of a politically meaningful scandal. This means sexual impropriety or financial corruption involving a rank-and-file member of Congress or governor can be more likely to generate scandal news with lasting political consequences *for that individual* than for a presidential candidate. A prototypical example is the widely publicized scandal in 2011 over Democratic Rep. Anthony Weiner's exchange of sexually suggestive pictures and messages with women other than his wife over the Internet. Weiner apparently neither violated the law nor engaged in any physical sexual misconduct, yet his sensationally entertaining story generated considerably more media interest than much of the serious high-level misconduct explored in this book.[10] Further, in this somewhat perverse pecking order of scandal potential, the personal peccadilloes of White House occupants or seekers are more vulnerable to scandalized publicity than are, say, their appointments of regulators who maintain close personal ties (and conflicts of interest) with the industries overseen.

Such a counter-intuitive inverse relationship between the most deeply rooted and societally costly official misconduct on the one hand, and scandalized attention from the media on the other, implies that the most harmful malfeasance often fails to ignite a political scandal. One glaring example is the financial meltdown of 2008, which was not framed as arising from *scandalous* misconduct by high-level government officials. Although there was plenty of indignation, and a few office-holders experienced sporadic harsh criticism (for example, Treasury Secretary Henry Paulson and Federal Reserve Chairman Ben Bernanke), neither they nor anyone else in government became a central villain in an ongoing narrative of scandal. This contrasts with more-scandalizing publicity in the aftermath of Hurricane Katrina (2005), in which FEMA (Federal Emergency Management Agency) Director Michael Brown served as a handy whipping boy. Blame for the far more costly economic crisis was placed on an ambiguous and largely anonymous set of targets like "Wall Street greed" and "executive bonuses" (see Martens 2011).

The dependence of scandal production on party skill and media decision rules also implies a fifth theme: scandalous misbehavior, and sometimes scandal publicity, do *not* necessarily involve secrecy. Some definitions of political scandal turn on the idea that secret misconduct becomes widely known. Yet history suggests that transgression frequently occurs in plain sight, as was true in the case of the 2008 financial crash, when lax regulation, ideologically driven economic reasoning, close relationships between Treasury officials and Wall Street, and other causal factors were all out in the open along with many warning signs (see Stiglitz 2010). It is the timing and framing of bad acts *as a scandal* that matters, not the publicizing of secrets. A scandal can be averted, no matter how serious and open the misconduct, if the misdeeds are framed dishonestly or misleadingly – or virtually ignored – at the time they occur. If it takes weeks, months or years to unearth the lies and cover-up, or to re-interpret an activity as scandalous, editors typically deem the story insufficiently newsworthy to follow up. An important corollary is that, in opposition to the conventional wisdom that "truth always comes out eventually," this book suggests that cover-ups often work.[11] With important exceptions that arise from specific competitive conditions in the scandal process, a scandal delayed is usually a scandal denied. Journalistic lore notwithstanding, American history includes a long series of successful cover-ups and still-born scandals from the time of the founding (Flynt & Eisenbach 2011) through the eras of Franklin Roosevelt, John Kennedy, Lyndon Johnson and Richard Nixon (Feldstein 2010).

Deciding whether to pursue non-timely news of malefaction is one area in which news organizations exercise a degree of autonomous power. Yet, even if journalists do expose past misconduct, governmental entities rarely respond to revelations with sufficient determination to initiate a scandal cascade. An example of this dynamic is the George W. Bush administration's policy on torture in its war on terror. Aspects of the policy, including deaths of detainees, became public in December 2002 (Priest & Gellman 2002; cf. Sifton 2009), more than a year before news broke of practices at the Abu Ghraib prison. Most media and officials ignored the story or discussed the issue of torture as if it were just another policy option, not a scandal.[12]

When Abu Ghraib did become a major story in 2004, it ultimately acquired the label "scandal." But neither the mainstream media, nor the Congress or judiciary, followed up with sufficient vigor to allocate responsibility for the misdeeds beyond a few low-ranking bad apples at the one prison. The buck stopped well short of the White House or even the Pentagon (Rich 2009). Indeed, news organizations were reluctant even to label the actions "torture," preferring "harsh interrogation" or other euphemisms (Bennett, Lawrence & Livingston 2007; on whether the mistreatment of detainees – which led to dozens of deaths – did constitute torture see ACLU 2005).

Five years later, Democrats, in control of the White House and Congress, failed to advance a scandal over investigative findings (Rockefeller 2009) that the Bush administration misled the public about the president's and vice president's personal involvement in approving torture within and beyond the confines of Abu Ghraib.[13] This occurred even though the Obama administration released evidence that some prisoners were tortured less to extract information about pending terrorist attacks, than to induce their corroboration of a link between Saddam Hussein and the 9/11 attacks.[14] In other words, credible information from a government investigation suggested President Bush and Vice President Richard Cheney authorized instances of torture to serve their domestic political interests in justifying the Iraq war (Froomkin 2009; Landay 2009; cf. Risen 2006).[15]

Given the extraordinary challenges facing the country when he took office, President Obama's decision to let this potentially scandalous bygone simply go by might be defensible. We can further stipulate that, when Bush authorized torture (as he confirms in his memoir *Decision Points* [2010]), it was because he sincerely believed the urgency of eliminating the Hussein regime justified manipulative public relations practices and violation of US law (18 USC 2340) and international law (United Nations, *Convention against Torture and Other Cruel, Inhuman or Degrading Treatment or Punishment*). What's relevant here is this: by definition, an independent, functional fourth estate cannot be bound by the same considerations as the government it covers. Yet, with the mainstream media's cooperation, for all intents and purposes, the Bush White House evaded not only a high-magnitude scandal but also a targeted investigation of the two top government officials' responsibility for a torture policy that may have been in some measure politically motivated. This occurred despite ongoing, vociferous protest against the administration's torture policies by civil liberties groups and in the left-leaning and libertarian blogosphere. The latter point suggests the limits on the Internet media's political influence, at least through the first decade of the twenty-first century. Some writing about the Internet evinces irrational exuberance about the potential of the Web, allied with crusading journalists and government investigators, to expose high-level corruption and thrust important truths into the spotlight.[16] In practice, evidence suggests, the traditional media remain crucial gatekeepers, and that is our sixth theme.

The seventh involves rethinking the common scholarly claim that, as they play out, scandals yield larger lessons that clarify a society's moral standards, patrol its moral boundaries and register changing mores. Reflecting this perspective, Lull & Hinerman (1997) describe scandal as a key "outpost for moral thinking and decision-making," and Jacobsson & Löfmarck (2008) write that scandals help delineate areas of moral conflict and consensus (see also Adut 2008). Such conclusions do not mesh very well with the core findings of this book. If scandal coverage in the US is uncalibrated, if trivial misdeeds often get trumped up while perfidious behavior, even when publicized, escapes scandal framing, it would appear difficult for scandals to teach morality.[17] Because the media so frequently evince little determination to get to the bottom of a matter, because they often fail to frame evidence of misbehavior as scandalous, it seems more appropriate to conclude that scandals blur America's rather permeable moral boundaries. Going through presidential scandals of recent decades (and the many latent ones that never erupted) hardly conveys any consistent message about America's moral codes or cleavages.

As a corollary to this premise, the common idea that scandal must involve the breaching of legal or moral dictates demands closer consideration. The Bush administration's response to the damage wrought by Hurricane Katrina in 2005 was frequently labeled a scandal,[18] illustrating not only that malfeasance can be far from secret but that incompetence, inattention and inaction can be framed as scandalous. The category *scandal* is not limited to illegality, dishonesty or immorality. It also includes violation of a society's norms and ideals. Such arguably occurred when President Bush's mismanagement of Katrina seemed to violate norms demanding that presidents respond to natural disasters by expressing compassionate concern and directing urgent efforts to restore order. However, further illustrating the perhaps-inevitable ambiguity of moral lines drawn by scandal narratives, once a threshold of managerial incompetence is crossed, it can raise issues of immorality or even legal transgression.

The plan of the book

In support of the themes laid out above, the book compares high-magnitude presidential scandals between 1988 and 2008 with potential scandals that never materialized. It considers why major scandals arose from President Clinton's conduct with respect to the military draft, marital fidelity and financial investments, when similar alleged misconduct involving other recent presidents or hopefuls never gained traction in the news. It asks why more serious misconduct involving presidential violation of positional norms and ideals, as well as law, failed to ignite scandals, especially during the administration of George W. Bush. More broadly, it asks what theory might account for the media's varied framing of malfeasance – in some cases depicted as scandals, yet in others, equally harmful, virtually ignored. Finally, it explores the implications of a poorly calibrated scandal process for the distribution and accountability of power in US politics and policymaking.

Although this book encompasses three presidential administrations, the bulk of attention falls on cases involving George W. Bush. This focus arises from the book's core purpose: to illuminate the processes by which potential scandals either expand into political significance or deflate with little impact on politics – with special reference to the latter, largely neglected outcome. George W. Bush's repeated success at evading scandal therefore provides important grist for the book's explication of the ways scandals either ignite and persist, or fade quickly. Exposition of problematic episodes in Bush's life and career is necessary precisely because he was so adept at minimizing publicity of them that – unlike for Bill Clinton – few readers would be familiar with the relevant details. For the Clinton administration, most of the scandals that could catch fire, did. We can stipulate that there was quite a lot of high-magnitude scandal publicity surrounding his presidency. I believe concentrating on George W. Bush yields far more insights into the evolution and operation of the scandal process than would rehashing Clinton's many troubles. However, both Clinton and George H. W. Bush do receive scrutiny, along with vice presidents and aspirants to the presidency who were active during the two decades covered here.

The book proceeds as follows. Chapter 2 lays out the theoretical framework, which adapts the cascading network activation model (Entman 2004) to explain scandal production and evasion. The model has been applied mainly to international news (e.g. Chong & Druckman 2007; Entman 2008; Castells 2009; P. B. K. Potter & Baum 2010; Nyhan 2009 uses the term "cascade" but not the model). As a guide to understanding why some framings become dominant and others dormant, the model illuminates the spread or suppression of scandals. In briefest terms, it depicts news production as involving a hierarchy of networks, with political elites contending to control news frames; through feedback paths, media themselves and public responses also contribute to the framing and political effects. The chapter describes each level of the hierarchy and how the networks interact in the scandal process.

Chapter 3 begins building our theoretical understanding of scandal production and suppression by thoroughly airing the sexual scandals, and evidence of extra-marital escapades that did not receive timely publicity, involving Republican and Democratic aspirants for the 1988, 1992 and 1996 election cycles – essentially covering the era before widespread public access to the Internet. All of these were personal indiscretions with little impact on society, but some nonetheless became major political scandals whereas others remained almost (but not quite) private. The cases therefore illuminate the inconsistency aspect of the calibration problem. The chapter does not delve into the Monica Lewinsky affair. Unique among modern sex scandals, it provides little basis for generalizations.[19] Of more interest here is the infidelity coverage before and after. The scandalized treatment of Clinton contrasted markedly with journalists' reluctance to penetrate the privacy and besmirch the moral images of then-Vice President George H. W. Bush; of House Speaker (and presidential hopeful) Newt Gingrich in 1994–6; and of Republican presidential nominee Robert Dole (R-KS) in 1996. People inside the Washington beltway widely suspected all these men of infidelity. But in these three cases, the mainstream media uttered barely a peep until after the information was relevant to voters. A thorough exploration of the varying media responses helps illuminate the lurching gyrations of scandal journalism and the potent effects the variation can have on American political history.

Chapter 4 pushes forward the exploration of sex scandal to the 2008 campaign. With the Internet in full swing as an acknowledged player in the political process, that year offers an opportunity to probe for further effects of online media in scandal politics. Along with their spouses, three candidates contended with and evaded the threat of scandal: former Democratic Senator and 2008 nomination candidate John Edwards (NC), then-Senator Hillary Clinton (NY), and Republican nominee Senator John McCain (AZ). In all of these cases, despite salacious material circulating on the Internet, the mainstream media decided to ignore the matters. The media cooperated in a bipartisan fashion with presidential hopefuls to suppress information of considerable interest and relevance to understanding the nomination horserace (Edwards and Clinton) or fall election (McCain). This also had the effect of obscuring candidates' misrepresentation of themselves and their constituents. The curious failure of the mainstream media even to provide thorough horserace coverage, let alone substantive accountability news, highlights the intellectual incoherence of news organizations' operational definitions of scandal. The squelched scandal around McCain further reveals how skilled political operations can turn the spotlight 180 degrees and convert a scandal of politics into one of journalism.

This chapter also demonstrates that, despite an epic of intense competition among online and traditional media outlets, the latter don't thirst for scandal but often turn a blind eye even when coverage might boost circulation and illuminate social mores. And it reveals that, at least through 2008, information on the Internet made little difference to politics unless the traditional media opened their gates.[20]

Chapter 5 continues the attempt to answer the book's core questions and develop theoretical understanding with an exploration of the potential and actual scandals surrounding the military draft and service records of Dan Quayle – the Republican vice presidential candidate (and later Vice President) under George H. W. Bush in 1988 – Bill Clinton in 1992 and George W. Bush in 2000. These scandals involved violation of norms and ideals governing *societal* as opposed to merely private responsibilities and, as such, in contrast with infidelity, imposed some costs on the society at large. The chapter first examines how and why Quayle's Vietnam-era draft evasion became a scandal whereas Bush's did not. Since both men's military careers were quite similar, the comparison sheds light on non-partisan forces in scandal production. For reasons that display further wrinkles in scandal politics, Clinton was treated more harshly than either Republican.

Chapter 6 turns to the transformation of a potential political scandal involving George W. Bush's alleged misconduct as a National Guardsman into a *journalism* scandal widely known as "Rathergate." Bush's military service did not gain traction in 2000, but the 2004 campaign saw renewed interest, perhaps because the Democratic nominee was John Kerry, a decorated veteran of Vietnam. Ultimately though, the actor framed as scandalously misbehaving was Dan Rather, the CBS anchorman whose investigation of Bush blew up in a fusillade of accusations that his story relied on fraudulent documents. This is one instance where Internet sites and the blogosphere took center-stage in promoting and redirecting scandal. The blogosphere polarizes around party and ideology (Hindman 2008) and proudly engages in digital activism openly intended to impact political outcomes (Aday, Farrell, Lynch, Sides, Kelly & Zuckerman 2010; Karpf 2010), and thus generally fits into partisan networks of scandal sponsors.

Although Republican-leaning websites and bloggers promoted Rathergate, Internet media cannot manufacture presidential scandals or enforce accountability on their own. For malfeasance to cascade throughout the political environment and produce noteworthy effects on national leaders required cooperation from the mainstream media in 2004; even in 2008 they remained the chief gatekeepers of political information. The blogosphere did amplify the scandal, but thanks to Republican skill and the media's motivations and decision-making heuristics, the opprobrium focused on Rather's violation of journalistic norms instead of Bush's violation of presidential ideals.

Chapters 3–6 deal with transgressions that had low to moderate social impact. The limited scope of their effects had little bearing on media depictions. Through intensity of attention and moral denunciation, the publicity of some politicians' violation of norms and ideals conveyed the sense that they posed threats to the political and social order. The lack of attention to others conveyed no information at all to citizens. All of these potential or actual scandals involved some amount of misrepresentation, including in the sense of deception, a point elaborated in the next chapter. Misleading the press and public is an intriguing topic for scandal studies, since the chapters reveal that – contrary to political lore – candidates and officials regularly get away with deceitfulness or cover-ups. Equally important, these chapters illuminate how the media themselves become the object of malfeasance allegations and, in some instances, of full-blown journalistic scandals. As suggested by Rathergate (and by John McCain's assault on the *New York Times* for its insinuation of adultery in 2008, covered in chapter 4), attacking the media offers a robust tactic for squelching presidential scandals. The unpleasantness in these cases also serves as a warning to news organizations about the pitfalls of overly vigorous scandal journalism.

Chapter 7 zeroes in on allegations of financial impropriety that violated the law. If true, these offenses would have had more serious social impacts than those explored in prior chapters. But once again, vast disparities characterize the coverage. Whereas Clinton's Whitewater investments received detailed coverage for years, George W. Bush's Harken Energy investments (and other dicey financial affairs)[21] attracted only sporadic and superficial attention. The failure of the Securities and Exchange Commission (SEC) to fully investigate his apparently illegal insider trading itself contained the seeds of scandal. The contrast between the treatment of Clinton and that of Bush allows us to explore the distinct ways the two political parties operate in the scandal system. The comparison also clarifies not just what scandals look like – which message components constitute a scandal – but also how non-scandals are encoded. Understanding the construction of non-scandals is more difficult and subtle, but for political purposes just as significant as the manifestations of actual scandals.

Chapter 8 focuses on the most serious offenses, those that imposed major social costs. In one case, publicizing the identity of the high-ranking undercover CIA agent Valerie Plame Wilson, the behavior violated the spirit of the law even if, technically speaking, the president has the right to declassify any information. Naming Ms. Wilson arguably damaged national security, as she was one of the key officials working to track and contain the spread of Weapons of Mass Destruction (WMD), particularly with respect to Iraq. Authorized by Bush, Cheney had I. Lewis "Scooter" Libby and others leak her identity to cooperative journalists in retaliation against her husband, Joseph Wilson, who wrote a stinging critique of justifications for the Iraq war (J. C. Wilson 2004; McClellan 2008, ch. 16; see Risen 2006).

Moving against Wilson also served as a warning to those who would challenge the Iraq policy. The second case looks into treatment of the nonexistent Iraqi WMD, in particular the degree to which George W. Bush was framed as dishonestly – as opposed to mistakenly – leading the US into war. We'll see that the media let him off the hook, not because they were deliberately shilling for the administration, but mainly because the Democrats failed to make a scandal of the matter. In illustrating how the scandal process implicates the functioning and dysfunctionality of the entire political communication system, not just the media, the chapter summarizes the book's themes.

Chapter 9 synthesizes the findings, the conceptualization of scandal, and the application of the cascade model. The empirical and theoretical discussion of accountability then moves into the normative benefits to democracy of making scandal production more consistent from case to case. Failing this yields a political process in which some presidents and candidates find themselves saddled with images as sleazy cowards or sinners, while others guilty of interchangeable trespasses hold on to their misleading reputations as moral paragons. When the media publicize the missteps of some but not others, they intervene in political processes and distribution of power in ways problematic for representative democracy. The discussion also assesses the good that would flow from alignment of media coverage with the societal impacts of malfeasance.

2

Analyzing Media and Presidential Scandal

Most citizens who were politically aware in 1973–4 can easily remember images of Watergate: Senator Sam Ervin (D-NC), his bushy eyebrows wagging, interrogating nervous witnesses in his thick Southern drawl; Richard Nixon, at a lectern emblazoned with the presidential seal, defiantly declaring "I am not a crook"; and Nixon jerking both arms aloft, flashing the peace sign before he boarded the helicopter that ferried him from the White House the day he resigned. Nixon's role in the break-in at the Watergate offices of the Democratic National Committee, and in covering up this along with many related and nefarious campaign schemes, imbues America's collective memory with its prototypical scandal. Allegations and evidence of secret, illegal activities that imposed heavy costs on society were thoroughly investigated, heavily publicized and appropriately concluded with punishment for the chief villain.

Watergate has shaped Americans' understanding of presidential scandal (see, for example, Schudson 1992), yet it is a misleading standard. No other president has been forced to resign, and it's not because no other president's misdeeds approached the gravity of Richard Nixon's. Instead, only during Watergate did elites and media together pursue a scandal sufficiently to hold the chief executive fully accountable. More often, harmful misdeeds barely register as scandals, if they register at all. The silence enveloping these undeveloped potential scandals forestalls democratic and legal accountability of the responsible individuals at the top.

This book identifies four dimensions of variation in presidential scandals: social cost, realm of transgression, magnitude of publicity, and political impact. Watergate scored high on all four. The two other mega-scandals after Watergate that arguably approached this status were Iran–Contra (around 1986–7) and the Monica Lewinsky affair (1998–9). Like Watergate, both included highly publicized criminal investigations and Congressional hearings, both led to criminal prosecutions targeting associates of the president, and both tainted the chief executive's reputation and popularity. But the resemblance to Watergate stops there.

Some observers at the time argued the activities encompassed by Iran–Contra were as serious as Watergate, if not more so. By this they meant to suggest that the misdeeds had more detrimental effects on the US public than Watergate, or involved more serious breaches of norms and law. The Reagan administration evaded legislated Congressional strictures on US aid to the Nicaraguan Contra rebels, by using proceeds from illegal arms sales to the officially certified terrorist government of Iran.[1] Yet the magnitude of the Iran–Contra media spectacle was smaller. Little came of Iran–Contra in the long term. History has been incomparably gentler on Reagan than on Nixon (Bunch 2009), as testified by the encomia on the centennial of his birth in 2011 (see, for example, the series of videos produced by the *Washington Post* entitled *Ronald Reagan: Actor, President, Statesman*, 2011). Reagan's vice president, George H. W. Bush, was elected president a couple of years after Iran–Contra, and President Obama awarded him the US Medal of Freedom, the nation's highest civilian honor (February 15, 2011).[2]

Setting aside Iran–Contra, it seems a debatable question whether Nixon's misdeeds exceeded in social cost Lyndon Johnson's or George W. Bush's. Claiming a certainty they knew to be unfounded, both Texans sold avoidable military ventures to the public using distortions of epic proportion. In this way they breached the norms of their position, misrepresented themselves and the citizenry, and damaged the public interest. Both also violated US laws and international law.[3] Although both presidents suffered politically, they did not face anything like the sustained attention to their individual culpability, and the proper government response to it, that Nixon did. Nor did they have to endure lengthy Congressional and criminal investigation aimed at answering the defining questions of Watergate: "What did the president know, and when did he know it?"

In contrast, Bill Clinton did get impeached by the House of Representatives and could have lost office had the Senate convicted him. Yet few would equate Clinton's malfeasance or its social welfare costs with Watergate or Iran–Contra. This point underscores my core argument: there is little relationship between (1) the costs the public must endure from presidential misconduct, and (2) the degree to which a president violates the norms and laws governing his office, on the one hand, and (3) the media's framing of misconduct as a major scandal, or (4) the political consequences for the wrongdoer, on the other. All this also supports my point that Watergate, scoring high on all four scandal dimensions, is *sui generis*: unique rather than prototypical of presidential scandal. And the weaknesses of the interrelationships recapitulate the basic theme: whether misdeeds yield scandal or silence depends on political interactions that are largely untethered to substantive judgment.

The boundary separating scandal from politics as usual is blurry. By looking more closely at variation among potentially scandalous incidents along the four dimensions introduced above, we can trace this frontier to reveal scandal as a matter of degree rather than a binary condition cleanly separable from normal political competition. For our purposes, *misconduct* can be defined as any behavior that violates applicable norms, ideals or laws and thus possesses the potential, based on past experience, to spark scandal publicity. The realm of misconduct runs along a spectrum from the narrowest private to the broadest public sphere. It ranges from breaching norms and ideals governing entirely private conduct, to infringing norms, ideals and laws shaping the society-regarding obligations and professional codes regulating adults in their careers prior to entering politics, to violating laws regulating the behavior of officials exercising (or seeking) governmental authority. Breaking the law while carrying out public duties by definition breaches norms, or at least ideals. The *social cost* of misconduct accounts for the impact of the malfeasance – the scope and depth of its effects on the public's welfare. This dimension gauges the misconduct's negative consequences for the public, *not* the harm to the careers of individuals ensnared in political scandal.

Taxonomy of presidential scandal

Combining social cost and realm of misconduct yields the taxonomy shown in figure 2.1. These two dimensions tend not to be teased out and made explicit in either journalistic decision-making or scholarly exploration. Building upon while refining prior treatments, the taxonomy undergirds the book's themes and its occasionally contrarian analysis of presidential scandal. Social cost is arrayed across the horizontal axis, and arena of the misdeeds on the vertical. The taxonomy could apply to any politician; for most, costs are restricted to family and associates or a limited segment of the public. Since presidents

SOCIAL COSTS

	LIMITED	SUBSTANTIAL	HIGH
GOVERNMENT REALM	$200 haircut (Clinton) Paula Jones harassment (Clinton)	FEMA/Katrina (Bush) Plame/CIA (ch. 8) (Bush)	WMD (ch. 8) (Bush)
SOCIAL REALM	Mistreating employees Avoiding military duties (ch. 6) Draft evasion (ch. 5)	Insider trading (ch. 7)	
PRIVATE REALM	Adultery (chs. 3–4)	Racial slur	

Figure 2.1 Scandal taxonomy based on social costs and realm of misconduct

and aspirants serve the entire US public as constituents, much more of what they do could impose substantial costs on society. The figure includes examples of potential and actual scandals, most dealt with in this book.

The examples in figure 2.1 suggest that potentially scandalous malfeasance usually constitutes some form of *misrepresentation*. The vertical axis illustrates a hierarchy of misrepresentation running from essentially private and (more or less)[4] legal behavior, to public and illegal actions, and from the descriptive and symbolic senses of representation to the substantive (see Pitkin 1967). What can spark political scandal is contradiction between politicians' behavior and their (and their party's) implicit promises to represent citizens in all these senses. Politicians pledge to represent in the sense of embodying and modeling in their private lives – not just rhetorically endorsing – norms and ideals congruent with the dominant culture and their constituents' desires for symbolic and descriptive representation. By ideals, I mean promises and expectations to exceed minimum standards, to embody the best of type. Although constituents understand their representatives are only human, many assume they are and should be better than average – "all-American," conventionally attractive, married with children, professionally successful. The tendency of Americans to rate their own congressperson positively even while scorning the institution of Congress (see Mezey 2008, p. 171) provides evidence for this predilection toward idealization.

That is why behaviors listed on the bottom row of the figure, although private, sometimes become matters of media interest and wider public concern.

The middle row depicts scandals that can arise when politicians violate promises or public assumptions that those elected or appointed to public office behaved in accordance with the norms and ideals pertinent to their pre-political lives and careers. The top row shows scandals that breach expectations for officials to fulfill the norms regulating their governmental responsibilities. These *leadership norms* demand that politicians work energetically, fairly, competently, constitutionally and truthfully to advance constituents' interests, the general public interest, or both. At all three levels, norms encompass obedience to applicable laws. In practice, transgressions at any of these levels can turn into a political scandal of some degree.

On the horizontal axis in figure 2.1, the range of scandal is categorized along a continuum of social effects, from the least cost to the highest. As the bottom row suggests, the costs of adultery are narrowly confined to a tiny segment of society: the politician's family, and perhaps friends and closest associates. If publicized, even such intimate misbehavior can turn into a politically damaging scandal, as such actions violate some constituents' desire for symbolic and descriptive representation – that is, for politicians who embody constituents' moral codes and serve as ideal role models.[5] Further along the spectrum of the bottom row, a fitting example might be a racial slur that the politician utters in what (s)he assumes to be private, picked up by an open microphone and broadcast widely. The costs are depicted as greater because such remarks potentially inflict symbolic or psychological damage (albeit slight) on an entire ethnic group and on the general public interest in racial comity.[6]

Moving to the middle row, violation of social and professional obligations, here too social costs range from minimal to major. In cases where politicians are revealed to have a history of mistreating their employees, despite creating minimal social costs, publicity can create a low-magnitude scandal. A case in point is former eBay CEO Meg Whitman, whose campaign for governor of California sustained damage from such charges in 2010. Running along the spectrum toward greater social costs, the figure suggests deviating from social obligations governing males during the 1960s as an example: registering for the military draft, adhering to Selective Service rules and obeying orders once in uniform. Failing to do so imposed costs on the many men who did not evade the draft or fail to meet their military service obligations.

On the top row are breaches of norms, ideals and laws covering public office. Clinton's fabled $200 Air Force One haircut on the LAX airport tarmac (Entman 2005) and his alleged harassment of Paula Jones did violate official ideals (haircut) or norms and laws (Jones), but neither imposed significant social costs. Hiring cronies or political hacks is an example of more seriously violating official ideals and norms. Every president does it, but perhaps the epitome of this syndrome during the period covered in this book is George W. Bush's appointment of Michael D. Brown, previously the Judges and Stewards Commissioner for the International Arabian Horse Association, to head the Federal Emergency Management Agency (FEMA). The agency bungled the response to Hurricane Katrina in 2005, imposing substantial costs on American society. When presidents breach leadership norms and ideals, it can (but doesn't necessarily) get them into trouble with the press and public for substantive misrepresentation – i.e. incompetent performance (see Bennett et al. 2007 on Katrina).

Breaching norms of attentive management and truth-telling, as critics have said George W. Bush did in some combination when he justified the Iraq war on grounds of the imminent threats posed by Saddam Hussein's Weapons of Mass Destruction (WMD) arsenal, can impose immense social costs, as indicated by placement at the right end of the top row. The Iraq war-related examples show how misconduct that imposes major social costs may shade from norm violation to outright illegality. The Iraq invasion itself arguably placed the US outside of *international* law (Sarat & Hussain 2010), but that particular type of transgression rarely generates presidential scandal in the US. The instructive partial exception of torture at Abu Ghraib prison – illegal under domestic and international law – is considered briefly later.

Notice that many high-magnitude scandals involve failure to fulfill leadership norms and ideals rather than engaging in corruption or other violations of law. Let us call the first type incompetence scandals and the second, corruption scandals. In both situations, the accused will generally initiate a range of defense tactics. Initially the inclination tends to be toward cover-up and denial. If these fail, the next step is to blame subordinates. If those steps don't staunch the scandal, the leader will generally admit to a degree of incompetence and, sometimes, apologize. To my knowledge, in modern times only Clinton actually admitted to breaking the law.

Beyond the two spectra that comprise the taxonomy in figure 2.1 are media magnitude and political effects. *Magnitude* is measured as the duration, prominence and cultural resonance of the *scandal* framing – treatment not merely as a controversy, crisis or issue but as a problem caused by individual misconduct requiring urgent consideration and resolution. High-magnitude scandal coverage lasts for days or weeks, with stories and commentary featuring evocative language (including use of the word *scandal*).

The fourth and final continuum relevant to understanding scandals concerns their *effects on the politician*. Scandals vary in their political impacts from imposing major, lasting reductions of the accused person's influence, to transitory damage, to negligible impacts. Political effect can typically be measured by the degree of erosion in indicators of public regard for the accused. For incumbent presidents, decline in the widely noted job approval rating is one key sign. Where the scandal-tarred politician is running for office, of course, the key measure is the election outcome. Another metric is poll responses that question or affirm the leader's competence, credibility, personal character and trustworthiness, traits that constitute the currency of a leader's political legitimacy and clout (see Thompson 2000, p. 248). Arguably, although Clinton retained office, his moral authority was so sapped by the Whitewater and Lewinsky scandals and his focus so distracted that he accomplished little during his second term (on the way scandals can damage the influence and maneuvering room of leaders, see Thompson 2000, pp. 248, 257). Even though his performance as president received majority approval, his aura of moral misrepresentation was sufficiently toxic for Vice President Al Gore to distance himself from Clinton in the 2000 presidential campaign despite the administration's highly favorable economic legacy, perhaps costing him the presidency (see R. Johnson, Hagen & Jamieson 2004; Vavreck 2009).

The calibration problem inheres in the weak correlations among the four dimensions, especially between the *magnitude* of media attention and the *social costs* imposed by scandalous misdeeds. When the same media that intensely scrutinize a president's guilt in a single incident of alleged sexual harassment (Paula Jones's accusation against Bill Clinton) pass lightly over another president's responsibility for approving revelation of a top-ranking, secret CIA agent's name, thereby undermining her mission (the outing of Valerie Plame Wilson), there's a disconnect. On the other hand, a moderate correlation does exist between the third dimension (media magnitude) and a scandal's political impact. Low-magnitude scandals tend to impose lesser penalties on the accused politician than those of higher magnitude. High-magnitude scandals are both causes and symptoms of damage to the politician's standing.

Figure 2.2 offers hypothetical illustrations of the negligible correlation between the social costs of misconduct and the magnitude

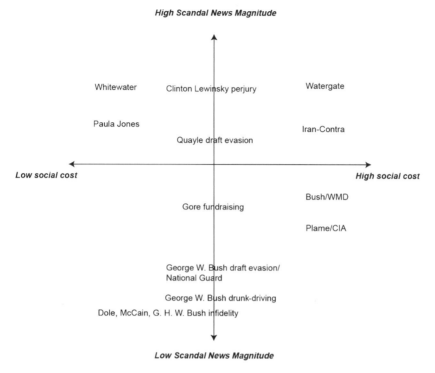

Figure 2.2 Scandal magnitude and cost

of scandal coverage. Readers might quarrel with placements of specific cases, but the graph is not intended to offer definitive classifications. It is designed to clarify the calibration problem: that magnitude of scandal news fails to align with the social costs of alleged offenses. After finishing the book, readers can judge this core theme for themselves.

Failure to frame high-cost misconduct as scandalous usually occurs because journalists cannot impose the scandal frame or elevate substantively damaging malfeasance to high magnitude on their own. News organizations need cooperation from government institutions and officials. The sine qua non is "cooperation" by the politician, who obliges by misbehaving, whether in private, social or government realms. With rare exceptions, journalists require official investigations, reports, leaks or confessions by somebody directly involved for evidence of the misbehavior to publicize. For scandal news to attain significant magnitude, the media need official government actions responding to initial disclosures. This creates continuing news pegs and stories worth pursuing because of their potential political fallout or because they reveal additional malfeasance. Otherwise, the constant flow of new developments in the world unrelated to the scandal soon pushes aside the alleged misdeeds. That can allow malefaction of high social cost to remain under the radar, a political silence instead of a presidential scandal. And for scandals to have important political impacts – as they can whatever the degree of harm to society – the coverage must alter the attitudes and strategic calculations of enough officials and politicians for them to see advantage in attacking (or failing to defend) the alleged wrongdoer.

Altering politics is not the normal outcome of a scandalous revelation. Typically, when a single news outlet reveals malefaction, it doesn't stimulate a self-reinforcing cascade of negative publicity. The usual life cycle of a potential presidential scandal is brief: one outlet publishes allegations, the accused ignores, denies, defends or makes a counter-charge (such as "this is old news" or "this is just partisan politics"), followed by . . . nothing (see Tiffen 1999, p. 255). The scandal story becomes the proverbial tree falling in the empty woods, functionally making no political sound.

Even Watergate languished within this category during the year 1972. While the *Washington Post* heroically probed, most of the major media downplayed it. *All the President's Men* (Woodward & Bernstein 1974) recounts the frustration of *Post* personnel as their hard work yielded little to no follow-up by other media, thus no political effect. Indeed, a survey showed half the public had not even heard of Watergate by November 1972; in other words, it wasn't a significant issue in the election (Lang & Lang 1983). Nixon was re-elected that month in one of history's greatest landslides. The scandal burgeoned because of government action – Washington Judge John Sirica's determined prosecution of the original Watergate burglars and then the Senate Watergate hearings – which renewed media interest early in 1973.

More commonly, scandals fade into silence after a few news cycles because no government entity initiates newsworthy remedial action, and no powerful scandal sponsors keep the drum beating. For instance, Richard Clarke (2004), the government's terrorism czar, chronicled how he spent the eight months after George W. Bush took office in 2001 sounding the alarm about al Qaeda to administration officials, without provoking any interest, let alone urgency. Clarke's tale of what could have been framed as scandalous incompetence received a burst of intense attention from the news media when published in

2004, followed by silence. Another author (Suskind 2006) reported that on August 6, 2001, a month before the September 11 attacks, George W. Bush received a briefing and memo entitled "Bin Laden Determined to Strike in US," explicitly warning that the US was in imminent danger of an al Qaeda assault. Apparently eager to return to his summer vacation, the president reportedly dismissed the CIA briefer, after asking no questions, with the words "OK, you've covered your ass now" (Suskind 2006). Although a commission investigating the 9/11 attacks (National Commission on Terrorist Attacks Upon the United States 2004) was established by Congress against the strong opposition of the Bush administration, it did not yield lasting opprobrium or reputational damage for the high-level officials responsible. Arguably, it didn't even clearly identify them.

The point is not that there should have been a major political scandal over the president's inattention prior to 9/11, but that there could have been one, had political opponents, government entities and media pursued the matter more vigorously. Instead, Bush won election in 2004 based on the public's perception that he was the candidate most competent to protect the US against terrorism, and his foreign policy team – minus Secretary of State Colin Powell, the one powerful official who (privately) voiced early reservations about Iraq – remained in place. Similarly, Al Gore won the popular vote for president in 2000 and became a Nobel Peace Prize winner despite violating campaign finance laws (using his vice presidential office to make fundraising calls); George H. W. Bush won the presidency in 1988 after playing a central role in the Iran–Contra scandal;[7] and the list of scandal dodgers goes on.

Cascading network activation and scandal

We now turn to the main issues: how does America's poorly calibrated process of scandal production work, and how does it affect the democratic process and government accountability? Under what circumstances does the US system of political communication produce scandal cascades, and what forces combine to silence potential scandals? For the purposes of this project, we are concerned primarily with the mainstream national media: the major broadcast and cable news networks (ABC, CBS, NBC, CNN), the two leading news magazines (*Time* and *Newsweek*) and the newspapers with wide national readership among political elites (the *New York Times*, *USA Today* and *Washington Post*). These are the outlets whose decisions directly or (through their sway over the rest of the media) indirectly shape elite perceptions of the political environment and influence the priorities and opinions of the public (see Entman 2004).[8]

Having cast aside Watergate as a model with little value for understanding presidential scandal after the Reagan administration, we turn to the identifying traits of scandal news. Publicizing misdeeds is necessary, but far from sufficient, to create a scandal. A *scandal frame* must be applied, repeatedly and prominently. *Framing* is the act of selecting and highlighting aspects of a perceived reality so as to promote a particular interpretation (see Entman 2004). The frame structures media texts, performing up to four functions: problem definition, causal analysis, moral judgment and endorsement of a remedy (see Entman 2004; Canel & Sanders 2006; Entman, Matthes & Pellicano 2009). In this view, scandal demands a narrative identifying an individual villain as causing the socially significant problem. More specifically, a presidential scandal frame requires that:

- the behavior be defined as a problem impeding or threatening the proper operation of government or society;
- the misdeed be clearly attributed to the individual president, vice president or candidate as a causal agent;
- the misconduct and the responsible leader receive public moral condemnation from legitimate political actors; and
- a remedy involving sanction against the individual be widely demanded or debated.

Personalization of the causal agent is critical to establish newsworthiness. Indeed a typical tactic of those trying to block scandals is to attribute blame to larger, anonymous institutional forces or to obscure underlings operating without their boss's knowledge, rather than an accountable individual. Lower-level officials in the executive branch excite little media interest, and if they are far enough down the chain of command, the president enjoys plausible deniability that he ever knew of their rogue behavior. Scandalous misconduct may involve many individuals, but scandals rarely attain high magnitude in the media if responsibility is diffused over too many bad guys; a central scoundrel is usually necessary and in the cases here, that means the president, vice president or candidates for those positions.

Senator Dan Quayle's national career began with a scandal that can illustrate these four traits of the scandal frame (see chapter 5). George H. W. Bush selected Quayle (R-IN), for the vice presidential nomination in 1988. That was just 13 years after the ignominious US defeat in Vietnam. Much news during the campaign's early days concerned Quayle's leap to the head of a long line for a coveted spot in the Indiana National Guard – time being of the essence for men to avoid getting drafted into the regular Army as soon as they left college. The volume and resonance of attention conveyed that Quayle's past actions posed a *problem* for the society if he were to become vice president. The primary *cause* identified was his own deficient character. His behavior was widely condemned on *moral* grounds. Tied to other unflattering information, and compounded by his maladroit handling of the press, Quayle's image for many Americans became that of an over-privileged hypocrite unfit for national office. As was true of Sarah Palin 20 years later, the partially self-inflicted wounds of a politician new to the national stage generated public calls from activists in both parties for a swift *remedy*: removal from the ticket.

Scandalizing public opinion

In order to apply the cascading network activation model to explaining whether scandal frames are applied to presidential-level malfeasance, we start with the standard definition of an *attitude* described by Chong & Druckman (2007). An attitude summarizes a series of evaluations of an object in relation to a variety of attributes. Individuals give varying weights to different attributes in developing an attitude. For some, a politician's religiosity and business success might weigh very heavily; for others, his status as a father and experienced government official may hold great importance, and religiosity or business record count for little. Perhaps a voter considers only the first two criteria, religiosity and business success, and weighs religiosity four times more heavily than business success. The attitude will thus arise from the person's weighing the religiosity criterion at 80 percent and business success at 20 percent. This simple formulation can be expressed as a more general equation: $\Sigma\ v_i{*}w_i$ where v_i is the evaluation of the object on attribute i, and w_i is the salience weight ($\Sigma\ w_i = 1$) associated with that attribute. The mathematical expression clarifies the concept of an attitude: it's the sum of an individual's assessments of an attitude object on each attribute (s)he believes relevant, with each assessment weighed in accordance with individual value priorities. The total of the weights for all attribute evaluations must equal 1 (i.e., the total of evaluative weights adds up to 100 percent of weights).

For our purposes, the object of the attitude is the political actor publicly accused or potentially accused of scandalous malfeasance. That actor has a series of potential attributes stored in public, elite and journalistic sentiments about him or her, including power/weakness, morality/immorality, competence/incompetence, ideological moderation/extremism and compassion/indifference. Scandal framing highlights evidence for negative attributes, making them more salient to fellow elites as well as members of the public. Alteration of evaluations can arise from increasing the weight of particular attributes and from providing new information that causes people to adjust their perceptions of the attribute's applicability to the politician.

In some cases the best defensive strategy for those accused is to deny any wrongdoing, and thus any problem. This works only when the misdeeds cannot be readily confirmed. If a politician can successfully deny the allegations, there will be little effect on the traits that others attribute to him or her and little alteration in the weights given any perceived attributes. Attitudes will remain the same. More often, defense means shifting the causal analysis so that any potentially scandalous facts reflect little on the most salient, heavily weighted attributes of the accused.

Two measurements of citizens' attitudes toward presidents are widely available – approval of job performance and favorability to the chief executive as a person. These two aren't necessarily correlated. Thus Bill Clinton's personal favorability was decimated by the Lewinsky scandal, but not his job approval. Consider a brief example of the distinct components that go into the public's attitudes toward a president, revealed by the Iran–Contra scandal. Before it broke, in late 1986, President Reagan's approval ratings were robust. Around his 1984 re-election, the Michigan National Election Study found that 83 percent of Americans considered him intelligent, 82 percent moral, 77 percent knowledgeable, and 71 percent a strong leader (Inter-University Consortium for Political and Social Research 1984). When new information came to light concerning the Iran–Contra activities, it raised doubts about Reagan's fulfillment of leadership norms and adherence to law. In terms of the attitude equation, Iran–Contra news created the potential for attitudes about Reagan to shift as new information pertaining to evaluative criteria became available. Reagan's defense strategy revolved around decreasing the weight and apparent applicability of damaging information on legal transgression by raising the weight of leadership norms.

Unable to deny all the facts and calculating that most Americans weigh breach of leadership norms less heavily than breaking the law, President Reagan defended himself by admitting to an overly detached managerial style. With so much positive information already stored in the public mind, he and his advisors apparently decided he could take a hit on management style (see Regan 1988).[9] Reagan deftly shifted blame for misdeeds by admitting in the passive voice that "mistakes were made," removing causal agents (Kramer 1987; cf. Wallison 2003; Longley, Mayer, Schaller & Sloan 2007). Violating norms for competence just happened to keep him in the dark about his subordinates' lawbreaking. If a more negative attribute thus was added to people's information store about the president, Reagan gambled that citizens would on average attach less weight to managerial incompetence than to flouting the law.

Public approval of the president dropped, but not as far as it could have. And it was more amenable to recovering as time allowed new evidence of positive attributes to accumulate. By 1988, when he was leaving office, the National Election Study survey found 73 percent of respondents rated him intelligent (a decline of 10 percentage points from 1984), 77 percent moral (−5 points), 71 percent knowledgeable (−6) and 68 percent a strong leader (−3). The relatively small decline evidences the success of Reagan's defense. Beyond 1988, fleeting memories and a campaign by conservatives promoted a positive collective memory of Reagan's presidency (Halper & Clarke 2005; Cosgrove 2007). His reputation was so thoroughly rehabilitated that Washington's National Airport bears his name, along with government office buildings and schools around the US (see Berkowitz 2001, June 26; Schaller 2006; Bunch 2009).

In the Clinton impeachment saga, his public denial of infidelity with Monica Lewinsky followed by perjury before a grand jury failed to stop the scandal because the DNA evidence was incontrovertible. He defended himself by apologizing for the misdeeds, moving on (as urged by the citizens' group Moveon.org) and directing attention to his competence, energy and compassion in representing the public's interests ("doing the people's business," as he put it). In this way, like Reagan, he sought to reduce the weight of the scandalous facts in citizens' attitudes as time went by. Public approval of Bill Clinton's job performance did recover after Americans fully digested the Monica Lewinsky revelations (Zaller 2001) – though judgments of his moral character never did, and no major Washington edifice bears his name. Clinton's ratings in 2000, when he was about to depart office, were far below Reagan's on morality (77 percent rating Reagan as moral, just 16 percent for Clinton). Clinton did best Reagan on knowledgeability and intelligence (at 86 percent, about 15 points higher than Reagan), but of course the essence of Reagan's defense against Iran–Contra was to denigrate his own level of knowledge and, perhaps by extension, intelligence.[10]

The difference in what we might call the veneration quotient of the two presidents has many sources. Still, it is an illuminating commentary on scandal as a ritual teaching morality given that Reagan's reputation in this sphere so vastly exceeds Clinton's. One flouted Congressional intent on foreign policy and directly or indirectly aided terrorism in Iran and Nicaragua. The other had an extramarital affair with a woman 30 years his junior, then lied about it to a grand jury. It would appear that, through collective memories of scandals, the word *morality* has come largely to connote "presidential adherence to behavioral standards in the private realm" – the arena where (as figure 2.1 shows) misconduct exacts the lowest social costs. As we'll see, however, the media's inconsistent responses to different politicians' sex lives convey moral confusion rather than clarification.

Networks in production of scandals

This book conceives of the competitive process that produces scandals as organized into networks of association. From here on we use the term "sponsors" to denote strategic actors outside the media who, as members of political networks, seek to promote or block scandals. (This use of "network" should not of course be confused with the notion of broadcast or cable television networks).[11] Sponsors are members of networks in the sense that they are in regular communication with others, communication motivated by their pursuit of similar goals.

At the apex of the two major sponsor networks that organize the competition in the US are the Democratic and Republican parties. The Democratic network – which as we shall see is typically less cohesive than its Republican equivalent – encompasses party leaders and members in Congress; state governors and legislators; interest group leaders from the likes of the NAACP, AFL-CIO and the National Organization for Women; political groups like People for the American Way; the political action committees led by presidential hopefuls; and foundations and think tanks such as the Center for American Progress. The Republican network consists of analogous components but appears better funded and more disciplined (Brock 2002; J. Taylor 2006; Westen 2007; Lakoff 2008; Karpf 2010). With partisan news media growing in national reach since the mid-1990s, a few journalists and commentators (e.g. Bill O'Reilly and Sean Hannity at Fox News, Chris Matthews and Lawrence O'Donnell at MSNBC) could be considered members of party-affiliated networks too. The differential capacities of the two partisan networks are illustrated by the comparison between Ronald Reagan and Bill Clinton discussed just above. Reagan enjoyed continued moral authority and personal reputation – even Barack Obama praised his strong leadership[12] – despite the serious official misrepresentations embodied in the Iran–Contra scandal, whereas Bill Clinton's moral standing continued to be tainted over largely private failings.

Membership in the networks does overlap at times, with some organizations and individuals playing both sides of the partisan fence. For their part, news organizations are also informally networked with each other, continually checking each other's reports, using competitors' coverage in making their own news decisions, and worrying about their relative standing in terms of audience share, profitability, prestige and clout.

With respect to scandals, the goal of the partisan sponsors is to control the spread of information along their own and others' networks, hawking politically useful material while blocking the diffusion of any data imperiling their side. In attempting to distribute information on their networks, sponsors connect through internal channels, using digital and interpersonal communication – the Internet, the cocktail circuit, cell phones. When endeavoring to block the spread of scandal news, they strategically work to keep any harmful information inside friendly networks (limiting it as much as possible to interpersonal conversation, gossip or rumor) and thus to minimize its newsworthiness and media attention.

Whether allegations attain high-magnitude publicity and political significance is determined by complex strategic activities and inter-actions within and between the elite networks, news organizations and public opinion. Among elites, responses rest on weighing the political advantages and disadvantages of sponsoring a scandal frame, opposing it or simply keeping quiet. Among mainstream national news organizations, the strategic calculation involves gauging the potential scandal's commercial value (including positive or negative reactions from advertisers and audiences), its service to a watchdog ideal that these organizations and many citizens do cherish, and the risks of harmful or stressful political pressures from elites sponsoring the scandal and those trying to block it. Given all these factors, it is important to keep in mind that the course of political scandals is over-determined, influenced by multiple interactions that are not entirely controllable or even predictable.

Scandal cascades

There is no clear line between merely negative news and scandal news. It could be argued, as does Nyhan (2008), that the line is crossed when media use the word *scandal*, and perhaps when they apply the suffix *gate* (see Waisbord 2004) and repeatedly associate it with the accused politician. In this book, using the word itself is not sufficient to mark a high-magnitude scandal, the kind that triggers a cascade, holding the potential for affecting politics at the time – and historical memory later on.

What marks a scandal cascade? All the variables here are continuous, not binary. The major dependent variable, the one we're trying to explain, is the magnitude of scandalizing publicity. As suggested, scandal news is a matter of degree. The explanatory, independent variables can also vary across a large range. None can be measured with absolute precision. But in order to generate insight, this study assumes that high-magnitude scandal involves nearly all the major national news outlets mentioned earlier giving attention to the accusations in a manner that shares three traits:

1. *Duration*: coverage must continue, at minimum, almost daily for more than a week. This seems as good a rough indicator as any as to whether a scandal reaches the critical mass to penetrate wider public consciousness, shifting political calculations inside the Washington DC beltway and potentially influencing the status of the accused. Such media attention also raises the probability that national polls will be taken to measure public reaction; these responses then influence further action by politicians and journalists.
2. *Prominence*: attention must be highly visible, appearing frequently on page one of newspapers and in commentary on the editorial pages, in the daily and nightly news programs – not just the traditional network news but also the political talk shows on cable and broadcast outlets (MSNBC's *Hardball*, Fox's *O'Reilly Factor*, NBC's Sunday morning *Meet the Press*). Newsmagazines must devote long stories (often with mention on the front covers) to the matter; Jay Leno's and David Letterman's late-night talk, and such infotainment shows as *The Daily Show* and the *Colbert Report* will likely satirize it. After the mid-2000s, it also became appropriate to assume heavy mentions in high-traffic blogs and Twitter streams as indicators of magnitude.
3. *Resonance*: the scandal must be framed as such, not just through the use of that word but through evocative, symbolic language and images that connote the president's or candidate's guilt of misrepresentation causing some degree of harm to Americans. The repeated use of culturally salient words and symbols in covering malfeasance gains attention and comprehension from the

average member of the public. When such messages repeatedly appear in prominent places, survey organizations take note and begin asking questions about the scandal.

Frequently (though not always), negative poll numbers feed a downward spiral of scandal that degrades the accused person's reputation, popularity and influence. That encourages further attacks from opposing politicians, gives pause to allies, and stimulates aggressive questioning from news organizations and blogs, spreading perceptions of even more negative public opinion.[13] Figures 2.3 and 2.4 illustrate the process, including feedback loops from the lower to the higher levels in the network hierarchy. The figures adapt the cascading network activation model (see Entman 2004, 2010c), adding the time dimension and specifying the five levels at which frames develop and spread, all of them necessary to a more fully specified model of scandal in political communication. This rough graphic outline of the process is nothing more than that. Its purpose is to show how framed communications, some chosen strategically by partisan elites, others formed in accordance with unmindful decision

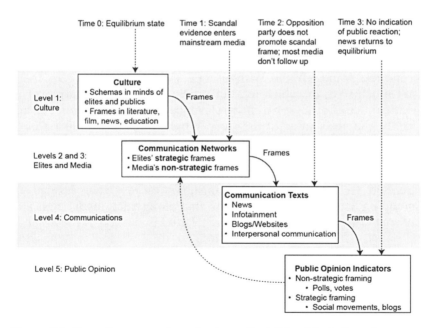

Figure 2.3 Cascading network activation – Path I (political silence)

rules by most citizens and national journalists, stretch over time, operate at multiple levels and work together to produce (or quash) presidential scandals.

The box at the uppermost left marks Time 0, before scandal erupts. The *Culture* denotes the dominant set of schemas in the society. These constrain the cognitions and emotions of most members of a polity and present a menu of framing options and cautions to political actors seeking power. At Time 1, information with scandal potential receives publicity.

As an example, we'll consider the Iran–Contra scandal below. The initial revelations could have been framed either as ordinary news or as scandalous. Let's call these divergent media frames Path I and Path II. Path I is the Path of Political Silence. For all practical purposes, scandals traveling along Path I – as most do – will be politically inconsequential. Information on the misconduct will not be framed in a highly resonant manner and the story will not "gain traction" or "have legs," to use the vernacular. Coverage will not repeatedly affirm the proposition that the president, vice president or aspirant has engaged in misconduct that creates a problem for society. In such instances, moral judgments, an urgency to trace ultimate causal responsibility or to settle on a solution to the problem of misconduct will not feature prominently in the coverage. In a self-extinguishing cycle, the absence of an overtly denounced individual villain reduces the newsworthiness of alleged misdeeds – and as publicity diminishes, so do opportunities for public awareness and indignation to build. This in turn reduces incentives for opposition elites to promote a scandal frame. Without a personalized causal agent, there isn't much basis on which to alter public attitudes toward powerful political actors. The apparent irrelevance to public opinion further shrinks the news value of the story. What makes misconduct a non-scandal is often the lack of scandalized media framing of a guilty actor, rather than secrecy or dearth of evidence that serious malfeasance occurred, although of course many scandals are short-circuited by concealment and misdirection as well. Instead of spreading activation of a scandal frame along elite, media, text and citizen networks (Levels 2 through 5), Path I is marked by the absence or paucity of scandal framing applied to evidence that has the potential to be framed as scandalous.

On the other hand, full scandal framing characterizes Path II, the Path of Political Scandal. It is illustrated in figure 2.4. In response to a new potentially damaging revelation at Time 4, some elites and media organizations identify an individual president, vice president or candidate as a causal agent responsible for behavior that violates

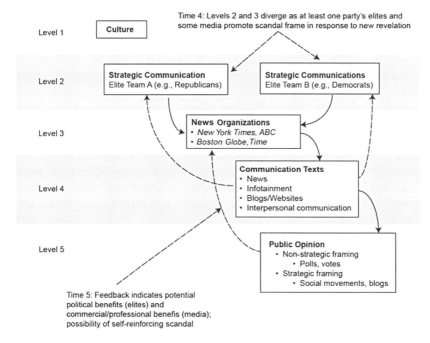

Figure 2.4 Cascading network activation – Path II (scandal cascades)

private moral codes, social norms, or laws and norms applicable to government position. Reports suggest the transgressions symbolically or substantively imperil the wellbeing of society. Coverage will proffer evidence that people should alter the attributes and weights they use in assessing the accused leader. That message is conveyed in part by moral condemnations and demands for swift investigation and remedial action coming from elites and commentators, which at Time 5 alter perceived public opinion.

So far we have laid out the cascade model of scandal production as a descriptive framework. The model also seeks to explain variation in scandal coverage. As already discussed, the intensity of scandal news is not propelled by the substantive seriousness of the politician's offense. Nor do mainstream media exhibit continuous vigilance to unearth and publicize any potential scandal they find. For the purposes of this study, Level 4 is the location of the dependent variable: the magnitude and resonance of the scandal news. Using the variables at the other levels for explanation of this dependent variable, the model includes: at Level 1, *cultural congruence*; Level 2, *elites' strategic skill*; Level 3, *media decision-making heuristics or biases*; and Level 5, *perceived public opinion* in response to scandal publicity. At Levels 2, 3 and 5 as well, *motivations* play a role in determining how elites, journalists and citizens react to potentially scandalizing information. Contrary to the implication of some writings on scandal, motivations to pursue potential scandals are often weak or absent at all three levels.

With respect to Level 1, when charges of misconduct seriously violate standard cultural expectations, it can actually increase the difficulty of promoting scandal, particularly at the presidential level. Although after the 1960s – with the Kennedy assassination and the Vietnam war, followed by Watergate – much of the reverence once accorded the office of the presidency diminished, there remain misdeeds that would be difficult for most (though definitely not all) Americans to believe. For instance, allegations that a president authorized murder of his opponents, sold heroin or sexually abused his children would probably have to surmount enormous hurdles of skepticism.

Beneath these core attributes that the political culture associates with the office rather than any individual politician, and far more pertinent to real-world politics, are schemas Americans (journalists included), develop for individual presidents and major candidates. For our purposes, Level 1 includes the store of attributes most commonly registered for prominent politicians like presidents, vice presidents and candidates for the only two national offices. Since Bill Clinton was already widely stereotyped in the political culture as a scheming opportunist, it was easy to sell the idea that he participated in legally questionable deals as an investor in the Whitewater real estate venture. But allegations that a president like George W. Bush, widely understood as a deeply religious, patriotic and macho supporter of the armed forces, shirked his own military duties clashed with popular schemas of him, making for a tougher sell to the media. Similarly, when the blogosphere briefly lit up in 2010 with unconfirmed (and later denied) allegations that Barack Obama had an affair with Vera Baker, a campaign staffer in 2004, the mainstream media didn't touch it. Whatever his political problems in 2010, Obama had successfully cultivated an image of familial bliss that made the charges virtually unthinkable.

Level 2 taps the two parties' levels of skill at following strategies to pursue or block scandal. A skillful party in this context is one that can get its activists and supporters to follow a unified communication strategy, consistently orchestrating rhetoric and actions to fit the media's needs and limitations. Skill also encompasses politicians' ability to calibrate charm and intimidation in managing their relationships with journalists. Adroit party elites can advance their preferred framing, whether that be spreading a scandal frame or shutting it down. In the US since Watergate, Republicans have generally demonstrated more skill in working the scandal process than Democrats.

The heuristics at Level 3 shape the decisions that news organizations constantly make in response to elite talk or to other sources of evidence. Generally tacit rather than explicit criteria for choice (Tuchman 1978; Gans 1979), they are embedded inside the minds of individual journalists and editors, and within organizational norms and routines. Though far from hard-and-fast rules, these heuristics, which I also term *decision-making biases*, guide journalistic decisions about what and how to report on potential scandal. They include preferences for:

1. process over substance;
2. simplicity over complexity;
3. visually illustrated over non-visual information;
4. popularity and power over unpopularity and weakness (Entman 1989, 2007; Nyhan 2009);
5. party unity over party discord;
6. likeable politicians over unlikeable;
7. stereotype-confirming novelty over incongruous novelty;
8. diffusing elite pressure over publicizing core truths.

Various combinations of these considerations, which are far more important to scandal politics than ideological or partisan bias (see Entman 2007, 2010a), will be explicated and illustrated in the chapters that follow.

At Level 5, public opinion has its effects through channels of political and economic/commercial feedback. When a significant segment of the public is interested in – or, better, outraged at – a politician's misbehavior, it heightens journalists' incentives to cover the matter. It also enhances the perceived rewards for opposing politicians to keep pressing the scandal. Unless elites are highly motivated to sponsor a scandal for other reasons, a lackadaisical reaction from the public tends to send scandals onto Path I, as elites detect little political benefit, and media, little commercial gain. Note here that the actual reactions of the diverse individual Americans who make up the public in public opinion are often difficult to detect and summarize. Therefore what's most relevant is public opinion as *perceived by elites and journalists* rather than individuals' actual sentiments (see Entman 2004).

More generally, when competing over a scandal, elites jockey with each other to frame public opinion data to encourage perceptions favorable for their side, just as they selectively highlight evidence supporting the accused politician's guilt or innocence.

In the ideal-typical case, the two parties compete – one hoping to spread a scandal and the other to block it. The goal of sponsoring elites is to frame the alleged facts so as to increase the audience's interest and outrage. This gives the media commercial reasons to provide more prominent and negative scandal publicity. Sponsors hope this in turn will diminish the target politician's clout. Even if audiences initially seem uninterested, journalists pay attention if they anticipate future effects on public opinion and the political process, particularly where they detect the potential for damage to a prominent leader. Journalists also might pursue the scandal driven in part by their watchdog instincts. This is where the underlying social cost and misrepresentation for which the politician is allegedly responsible can play some role in determining the magnitude of the ensuing scandal. But, as already suggested, these watchdog impulses always compete with all the other forces in the model.

Meanwhile, to discourage the watchdogs from barking, the other party's elites will dispute the facts, or deny they should be framed as scandalous. They will also seek to block scandal by dampening or diverting the public's interest in a scandal frame, dispelling journalists' perceptions of public curiosity or outrage about any malfeasance, while minimizing chances that the scandal will generate political fallout.

All of these forces and levels interact. For instance, if a scandal frame is culturally congruent, it lowers the threshold for the amount of strategic skill and degree of motivation needed to succeed in sponsoring a scandal. Thus, news about Lewinsky, yet another (stereotype-confirming) allegation of Clinton acting sleazy, was easily assimilated by journalists, who knew it would be instantly recognizable to audiences, and those conditions made scandal sponsorship more attractive to even the minimally motivated opponent. On the other hand, as illustrated in chapters 4 and 8, the media's motivations often point away from pursuit of scandal that might otherwise be considered highly attractive given their decision-making biases.

The cascade model in operation

To provide a more detailed illustration – admittedly stylized – of the cascade model's application to scandal journalism, let's return to the Iran–Contra affair. It originates in potentially scandalous information published by a Lebanese newspaper (November 3, 1986). The initial reports suggest that the US government not only negotiated with Iran, a terrorist regime, but also sold it armaments to secure release of American hostages in direct contravention of the law. On Level 2 in figure 2.3, strategic communication ensues. Attempting to frame the situation in ways that reinforce their power,[14] Republicans select framing words and images from the (Time 0) stock of culturally resonant symbols. They brand Reagan as a strong leader, associating him with symbols of resolute patriotism, and of compassion for American hostages being held by Iran-supported militants. After early dismissals, Reagan announces he will get to the bottom of any wrongdoing, thereby identifying others as causal agents and deflecting moral opprobrium (and potential punishment) onto them. This portrayal resonates with journalists who might well believe this a plausible story and, just as important, that it would play favorably with audiences.

Through much of November 1986 (Time 2), Democrats, seemingly intimidated by the president's popularity and skill, and fearing that attacks on the Great Communicator could alienate so-called "Reagan Democrats" (swing voters), hold their fire. Partisan inputs into the national media's processing and framing of information are relatively homogeneous. This is why the Communication Networks box in figure 2.3 (Path of Political Silence) is marked as occupying both Levels 2 (strategic framing by elites) and 3 (non-strategic framing by journalists). That makes for news slanting toward the administration's preferred framing at Level 4, the networks of words and images populating media texts. Journalists accept the line not because they are maneuvering to protect the Grand Old Party (GOP) but because they're following standard news production practices. In this hypothetical case, few sources on reporters' networks are promoting a scandal frame that challenges the White House line, and the news reflects the scarcity of opposition.

By Time 3 (November 20), feedback emerges from the public (Level 5), filtering up the hierarchy, in the form of polls (themselves a frame, not a mirror, of public opinion) and other indicators responding to the frames suffusing early news texts. The dominance of the narrative pushed from the top – Reagan guilty mainly of lax management – is suggested by polls showing Reagan has lost popularity, but retains majority approval. Early discourse apparently has some effect on presidential standing, but changes in the public's evaluative criteria and weights are surprisingly limited, with loyal Republicans dismissing the information altogether and loyal Democrats seeing confirmation of what they already thought. Less politically engaged citizens perhaps barely notice the initial spate of publicity. But for new damaging revelations, news might have returned to the status quo ante.

Note that in separating out these time segments, the model does not presume a strict linear march from one to the next; the periods overlap, merging into each other, and some things happen nearly simultaneously. For analytical purposes, however, making these distinctions clarifies the framing process.

The scandal moves onto Path II (figure 2.4) around November 25, Time 4, when new information surfaces and cover-up efforts falter. A few media organizations publicize charges and evidence that disrupt the previously smooth stream of blame-shifting publicity, and Congress announces it will hold investigative hearings. Around this time, Democrats finally feel safer to begin attacking Reagan, holding him responsible at least for cooperating with investigations into the matter. All this supports a counter-frame that focuses on a less benign causal analysis and the president's less appealing traits. Rather than serving largely as conduits for the frame packaged by the administration, the media now have competitive sources of framing material. This differentiates Levels 2 and 3, and pretty soon what had earlier been (from the Republican perspective) a virtuous circle of positive feedback bolstering their frame becomes a vicious circle.

Fed by the media's biases for popularity and unity, framing of Reagan increasingly offers cognitively accessible and clearly applicable information that could alter the public's evaluative criteria and weights. By early December, Time 5, sharp negative movement in the polls and other data on public reaction (Level 5) mingle with journalists' inside-the-beltway networks of colleagues and political actors (including some Republicans in unguarded moments) who are increasingly speculating about political damage, furthering the flow of scandal narrative.

The process continues, of course. Over time, elites' strategically framed, competitive responses to perceived and anticipated public opinion can, in concert with enterprising journalism, the media's decision-making biases, and uncontrolled – sometimes unexpected – events, reshape the frames reaching the public. This sets off further alterations in public opinion, both apparent and real. In the actual Iran–Contra case, by copping to Reagan's mismanagement of over-zealous subordinates like Oliver North, Robert MacFarlane and John Poindexter – all high-ranking military officers as well as White House foreign policy operatives and central figures in the scandal – the administration managed to reduce the newsworthiness of the facts and pave the way for the media to focus on Congressional hearings as theater or process, with lower-ranking staffers, not Reagan or Vice President Bush, the stars (see Robertson 1989; Chestnut 1996; Fried 1997, p. 68). The hearings sputtered out during summer, 1987, when the previously obscure Colonel Oliver North, who was the Reagan administration's key fall guy, emerged to gained wide *perceived* popularity.[15]

Among the other explanations is cultural congruence. Unlike glowering, ill-at-ease Richard Nixon, the affable, handsome, rhetorically gifted and charismatic Reagan would not easily fit the mold of villain. In two senses, Reagan as villain was culturally incongruent: he was a former movie and television star whose winning persona (he rarely played bad guys) actually enjoyed a place in the popular culture long before he entered politics; and the schema of him as a politician was benign. The Democrats backed down from what would have been a Watergate-like constitutional crisis barely more than a decade after the trauma of Watergate. Nor did they seem to care for aggressively questioning men in uniform like North and Poindexter. Robert Williams (1998, pp. 43–5) shows how Democrats ceded Oliver North advantages that not only helped him establish a heroic image in the media, one that made him a media star among conservatives for the next 25 years or more, but also (by prematurely granting him immunity for his testimony) undermined his criminal prosecution. As to the Democrats' motivations then, it seems safe to infer that even if they ached to inflict political damage on the Republicans, they calculated the political benefits of scandal promotion in these circumstances as substantially lower than the costs and risks.

Notice how the media's own motivations played a role in de-motivating the Democrats: what the media loved was Oliver North at the hearings, the seemingly earnest, patriotic, all-American military man only trying to help his country, standing up against conniving politicians. His was a great story, especially for the visually oriented television and news magazines. The intricacies of Iran–Contra, teasing out who ordered whom to do what and when – these stories were not likely to boost circulation or ratings. Knowing this would be bound to discourage Democrats from pressing the matter further.

As previously suggested, this fading without creating a definitive historical memory, without final determination of causality, accountability and punishment for misdeeds, is perhaps the typical outcome of the presidential scandal process (see R. Williams 1998, p. 248). Iran–Contra initially traveled on Path I, made a transition to Path II for a few weeks, but ultimately, reflecting the skill of the Republicans in handling the media, the timorousness of the Democrats, and both parties' and journalists' sensitivity to perceived public opinion, settled back down onto Path I.

There will be more to say about the levels of the cascading network hierarchy as we go along. The hierarchy might have begun flattening in the early twenty-first century with the spread of online and social media, for instance. Examining hierarchies within each level will also prove fruitful in illuminating the course of certain presidential scandals and non-scandals.

Throughout the book, framing analysis is deployed using the cascading network activation model to examine the paths taken by potential scandals. Some turn into politically meaningful scandals; many others take a path toward silence that renders them politically insignificant. The primary analytical technique used is the content analysis of case studies. Throughout, the general approach to the evaluation of scandal coverage is consistent with that endorsed by Matthes and Kohring (2008) regarding the content analysis of media frames: examining the most concrete, measurable subsidiary attributes of scandal at a granular, usually paragraph level of analysis rather than making broad thematic statements about framing in whole articles.

Accordingly, though customized to each scandal, the consistent thread in analyses throughout the book is a focus on identifying and making connections among the essential elements of scandal production in the cascading network activation model. These include who's speaking – which scandal sponsors dominate the narrative – and what's being said. The latter includes what claims are made about the problematic conduct, to whom individual causal responsibility is assigned, what moral judgments arise from the problem and causal agent, and which treatments or remedies are recommended. Analyzed political effects include the magnitude of media attention and political and public-opinion impacts from the way the scandal plays out.

Conclusion

The cascade model explained above stands in opposition to the scandal process portrayed by scholars who emphasize the contagion of scandals (e.g. Adut 2008; cf. Nyhan 2008, p. 19). Adut writes that the size of scandal is "an increasing function of the social stature of those who are compromised by the publicity of a transgression." So, the higher the rank of the transgressor, the more likely publicized transgression will generate a major scandal. Indeed, Adut suggests a linear relationship between status and the size of the likely scandal, despite his own critique of the objectivist model: "The high status of the offender tends to transform transgressions into scandals mostly inasmuch as it multiplies these effects." What's more, in Adut's view, this particularly holds for those occupying positions of high public trust (Adut 2008, p. 220). In other words, whereas Adut suggests the most powerful are the most vulnerable to large-scale scandal, the cascade model sees more variation across scandal processes and outcomes involving the very highest government officials.[16]

Besides denying that a bad act took place at all – which is often impossible – a president's best strategy, and one that succeeds more often than not, is to keep it from tainting him by deflecting attention. At least in the realms covered by this book, if the stain of scandal spreads to subordinates, it is less because of an ineluctable process of "semiotic association" (Adut 2008, p. 24) than because the top people deliberately channel awareness toward the underlings, as did Reagan. Furthermore, as Robert Williams (1998) discusses with reference to the Savings and Loan (S&L) scandal (1980s), corrupt behavior and indefensible outcomes can reach such intricacy that responsibilities are diffused, making it hard to identify a single culpable villain. This seems the case not only with the earlier financial scandal, but also the US-led global financial meltdown of 2008. Complexity of this sort can lead to scapegoating, as occurred with the S&L scandal, when the "Keating Five" senators (including John McCain) essentially took the rap for structural corruption and incompetence within Congress, the regulatory agencies and the rest of the executive branch. In the extreme, as with the economic crisis of 2008, the pressures for accountability can be so weak that the White House doesn't even need to sacrifice a named scapegoat (see Martens 2011; cf. United States Financial Crisis Inquiry Commission 2011, on the bipartisan reponsibility; and t' Hart and Tindall 2011 on leaders' tactics for squelching scandal in the wake of the crisis).

Therefore, both vulnerability to scandal and contagious spread of the taint are highly contingent phenomena. They depend far more on the scandal sponsors' strategic goals and skills, and the complexities of the misdeeds in question, than on the status of the wrongdoers. Indeed it is the lack of contagion that strikes an observer of Washington scandals after Watergate (see Lowi 2004) – their tendency to stop before they contaminate the most skilled and the most powerful.

The succeeding chapters trace the taxonomy of scandal from private realm misdeeds imposing low social costs, through misconduct in the social realm imposing moderate costs, to malfeasance in the official realm that wreaks major societal damage.

Thompson (2000) suggests most scandals fit into three categories: sex, finance or power, and indeed those discussed in this book do involve transgressions in these areas. The next two chapters examine sexual misbehavior that cost society little and therefore fit into the lower left portion of figure 2.1. These chapters shed particular light on the conceptual and operational incoherence of Washington's journalistic culture when it comes to constructing scandals. These are also the scandals most often condemned by media critics for unwarranted violations of a politician's privacy. Together, chapters 3 and 4 suggest a somewhat different perspective.

Chapters 5 and 6 move on to the middle ground in figure 2.1, concerning as they do violations of norms and ideals that regulate social obligations of everyone – including politicians before they go into politics. As do some but not all transgressions in the social realm, the misconduct imposed costs on society via the future politicians' abusing power to transfer burdens onto those less well connected than they. Chapter 5 explores scandals *and* non-scandals arising from draft evasion during the Vietnam war, actions that contravene norms and ideals for American politicians – such as Dan Quayle, George W. Bush and Bill Clinton – who were young men during the 1960s. Chapter 6 probes the phenomenon of non-scandal in granular detail through its focus on the Bush team's diversion of scandalized attention from the apparent shirking of Vietnam-era National Guard duties by the man who would be president, to the media's violation of journalistic norms.

Moving upward and to the right in figure 2.1, chapter 7 combines financial misconduct with abuse of power that imposed arguably higher costs on society. Credible evidence suggests that George W. Bush may have violated insider trading laws while his father was president. He might have escaped sanction at that time because of his powerful associations, but the chapter focuses on his evasion of the potential scandal that arose when events made his financial history relevant while he himself occupied the White House. Finally, the book focuses on the most costly misconduct, involving George W. Bush and Richard Cheney's activities in prosecuting the Iraq war. Their actions contravened leadership norms, entailing incompetence, corruption or both. Yet neither endured a significant scandal process. At most they suffered minor declines in moral standing, as suggested by the absence in common parlance of a term like "WMDgate."

As even this brief preview suggests, it is no wonder that, contrary to the view in some media scholarship, scandals fail to clarify moral boundaries or social norms. They don't even necessarily engender much normative debate. Nobody orchestrates the scandal production system to convey clear lessons or even to generate line-clarifying debates. Instead the scandal system's outputs are traceable to strategic partisan political action, the media's needs, limitations and decision-making biases, and, to some degree, happenstance and the times. The next two chapters, probing sex scandals, offer empirical support for these observations.

3

Private Lives in the Public Sphere: What Do Journalists Know, and When Do They Tell It?

Most critics of journalism, political observers and citizens say they believe sexual behavior is properly private. After all, the social costs imposed by legal sexual activities of any sort are minimal.[1] Thus one could argue it's inappropriate for media to publicize legal sexual activity. However, a "don't publicize" rule only makes sense if followed in every case. This chapter explores how media frame non-criminal sexual behavior as scandalous for some candidates and not for others. In doing so, news organizations intervene significantly in the distribution of public knowledge, alter political environments and candidate images, and affect the flow of power. Selective publicity can produce what appears to be a valid, socially accepted truth about a politician that is at odds with knowledge available to insiders.

French social theorist Michel Foucault offers useful insights into the ways that obtaining, withholding and distributing knowledge reflect and affect the distribution of power in a society. In his view, the power-inflected nature of knowledge means that the concept *truth* does not denote, as conventionally assumed, a universally valid set of observations on reality. Rather, truth is socially defined. According to Foucault, it should be "understood as a system of ordered procedures for the production, regulation, distribution, circulation, and operation of statements." This chapter argues that truth, whether by Foucault's definition or by the more traditional one, is sporadic in the media's coverage of public officials' sexual private lives. No consistent "system of ordered procedures" governs the production and circulation of statements about the behavior of the powerful in the private realm. Journalists continually make intuitive judgments about what constitutes sufficiently validated and pertinent information to merit public circulation, and what should be restricted. The evidence in this chapter suggests that these "common sense" rules for decision-making are problematic for democracy.[2]

Applying inconsistent tacit rules to decisions on whether to publicize private sexual behavior produces a steeply stratified public sphere (see Habermas 1989; Calhoun 1992) in which only a tiny group of insiders understands the wide extent of sexual hypocrisy and misrepresentation that permeates government. The general public only receives an occasional peek behind the door, usually when an official trips up in a sensationally newsworthy way – when Senator Larry Craig (R-ID) was arrested for soliciting in an airport men's room, Governor Mark Sanford (R-SC) disappeared for a week to tryst with his Argentinean lover, Governor Elliot Spitzer (D-NY) admitted to hiring ultra-expensive prostitutes, and Rep. Anthony Weiner (D-NY) inadvertently posted a lewd picture on a public Twitter feed. But these sorts of behavior in the private realm do not in fact remain entirely private; in most instances, they are well known to Washington elites before generating national publicity.

What journalists generally consider as mere hypocrisy or personal peccadilloes with little connection to official performance – matters legitimately within politicians' zone of privacy – may actually constitute misrepresentation. We can therefore see adultery (whether heterosexual or homosexual) as evidence that politicians: (1) fall short of the symbolic and descriptive representation (Pitkin 1967) that matters deeply to some citizens; (2) exhibit deficient character traits by sexually straying from culturally venerated norms and ideals, and by persistently lying to family and others; and (3) may be guilty of substantive misrepresentation as well through deceiving constituents about their true policy preferences. Despite any journalistic qualms, for many American voters, private-realm sexuality does reflect importantly on character. Political marketing campaigns tend to heavily emphasize evidence of upright personal character, selling candidates via images of happy, adoring families to validate the politician's claims of honesty, integrity and commitments to traditional moral values. Politicians do this because weakly partisan and ideologically non-committal swing voters weigh these criteria heavily in forming their attitudes toward candidates (see W. G. Mayer 2007; Hillygus & Shields 2008). The other two elements, honoring public policy commitments and fulfilling symbolic representational functions, are legitimate concerns for voters and, therefore, journalists.

All this means that if journalists follow inconsistent patterns in conveying what they know, aggressively penetrating one candidate's zone of privacy while leaving another's undisturbed, they are intervening in the distribution of power in ways hidden, unaccountable and undemocratic. To use the basic terms laid out in chapter 2 for scandal framing and attitudes, when media publicize a politician's sexual activities they introduce new information that may shift weights among citizens' evaluative criteria, or register negatively using their existing criteria. In other words, the information could alter attitudes toward a politician. If only one candidate experiences an unfavorable information barrage about his sexual character, it doubly disadvantages him relative to his opponent if, as often appears to happen, the media fail to make similar information regarding the opponent equally available.

Using quantitative and qualitative content analyses of news about the alleged marital infidelity of George H. W. Bush and Bill Clinton, opponents in 1992, this chapter explores how journalists put implicit concepts of truth and relevance into practice when handling information on the private lives of the powerful. Discussions of personal allegations against 1988 Democratic nominee Michael Dukakis, oft-times Republican president aspirant and 1994–8 House Speaker Newt Gingrich, and 1996 Republican nominee Bob Dole round out the story. (Dukakis's travails did not involve sexual behavior but extend the chapter's themes to a different sphere of private behavior.) The Monica Lewinsky scandal is less instructive for this book than the one involving Gennifer Flowers, whose flamboyant denunciations of Clinton threatened his effort for the Democratic nomination in early 1992. The chapter compares treatment of her with that of Jennifer Fitzgerald, one of George H. W. Bush's closest aides and, allegedly, his lover. After demonstrating and explaining significant disparities in news treatments of these leaders' personal behavior before the Internet became a mass medium in its own right, the book moves in chapter 4 to the 2008 campaign. There it considers the more competitive and purportedly transparent media system of the early twenty-first century, with its widely perceived capacity, via blogs and other technologies, to propel public discourse from the bottom up rather than the top down.

Reporting the Bush allegations

Marital fidelity entered the agenda in post-Watergate presidential politics during the prelude to the 1988 campaign, when once-promising Senator Gary Hart's run for the Democratic nomination ended in the wake of media disclosures about his infidelity. It remained a major issue in 1992. Coverage of Bill Clinton's alleged adultery with

Gennifer Flowers and others created continuing image problems. Yet there was another candidate in 1988 and 1992 whose sexual misconduct received only the barest mention, even though Washington insiders had long gossiped about it: George H. W. Bush. He served two terms as vice president, made it through the campaign for the Republican nomination and actually became president: twelve years without significant publicity of these suspicions. What exactly did the media tell their audiences? Keep in mind that during 1992, the depth and credibility of reporters' evidence for Clinton's peccadilloes was not much greater than for George H. W. Bush. There were widely believed rumors among insiders in Little Rock, AK about Clinton, and plenty of whispering about him by Washington insiders, but there was no proof until 1998. Why didn't the media publicize the known facts and widely mongered innuendoes as thoroughly for Bush as for Clinton? Doing so would have allowed those Americans who care about the way their president represents such traditional family values as marital fidelity to cast their appropriate vote in 1992. This chapter suggests that newsmaking choices did not reflect careful deliberation on such journalistic principles as verification of truth, relevance to public duties, and privacy. The alternative explanations advanced here illuminate the problematic decisions media must make in deciding which potential sex scandals they should help to activate and spread through the public sphere.

Campaign '92 offered three news pegs that could have spurred journalists into extensive investigation and reporting on President Bush's marital life: first, *Vanity Fair* ran an interview (May 1992) in which Hillary Clinton alleged that the mainstream press had covered up George H. W. Bush's marital infidelity (Sheehy 1992). Then *Spy* magazine's July/August issue ran the only detailed compilation of the circumstantial evidence indicating Bush's infidelity (Conason 1992; cf. Gitlin 1992). Finally, Susan Trento published a book containing allegations that an ambassador had set up a rendezvous between then-Vice President Bush and his long-time lover in Switzerland (Trento 1992). In response to each of these opportunities, the press ran the other way.

1. Hillary Clinton attacks

Here is an excerpt from the *New York Times'* main mention (April 13, 1992) of the *Vanity Fair* report. It appeared in the middle of a page A-9 continuation of a page-1 story. Ironically the jump head was "In a rough campaign, Bush may get scrutiny to match what Clinton felt" (Rosenthal 1992):

> On a more personal level, long-denied rumors that Mr. Bush had an extramarital affair are already back in play as analysts look ahead to what Mr. [Kevin] Phillips calls "the mother of all dirty campaigns."

> Mrs. Clinton, whose husband has denied a former state employee's assertion that they had a 12-year affair, raised the rumor about Mr. Bush in her *Vanity Fair* interview. Some recent news reports have gone so far as to name the woman said to be involved. In 1987, the Bush team dealt with the issue by having George W. Bush, the President's eldest son, tell *Newsweek* that he had asked his father, and "the answer to the Big A question is 'N.O.'"

The story then switched to a totally unrelated conflict-of-interest issue and continued down that path, exploring it for 13 paragraphs. The entire consideration of the adultery issue is contained in the above quotation. A full-text search of major newspapers, newsmagazines, and *ABC News*[3] reveals that the rest of the mainstream outlets reported Hillary Clinton's charges similarly. They minimized attention to the allegations while ignoring their substance. Most of the news focused on Mrs. Clinton's apology for even raising the issue.

2. Spy *magazine compiles the evidence*

The *Spy* magazine story offered the most complete published synthesis of evidence that Bush had committed adultery – again, evidence that had long circulated in elite Washington circles. Though all of *Spy*'s evidence was circumstantial and far from definitive, it did indicate a significant possibility that Bush was unfaithful to Barbara Bush. Most major media ignored the *Spy* story. Only four available on LexisNexis even mentioned it (*Newsday*, the *Chicago Tribune*, *USA Today* and *Newsweek*). The following is the bulk of *Newsweek*'s coverage. Notice how it derogates *Spy* while acknowledging the previous circulation of the information inside the beltway:

> One of the most gossiped-about political stories of the year will surface later this month in *Spy* magazine, a satirical monthly with a reputation for outrageousness. In a lengthy but not especially convincing cover story, *Spy* says George Bush has had at least three extramarital affairs. Two of the women Bush is alleged to have been involved with (before he became president) have held high-level jobs in his administration. None of the women (*Spy* names only one) admits to having had an affair with the president.

> Numerous sources are quoted in the story, but none of them goes on the record. Still, combined with Hillary Clinton's quote in *Vanity Fair* about an alleged Bush affair, the *Spy* article may force into the open

a topic that has until now been the subject mostly of unsubstantiated whispering among journalists and political insiders.

3. The Swiss tryst

The third opportunity for publicizing the Bush infidelity information came when a book was published in August 1992 quoting a deceased former ambassador to Switzerland about an alleged Bush tryst with his long-time personal aide, Jennifer Fitzgerald (Trento 1992). A large page-1 headline ("Tryst and shout") in the tabloid *New York Post* referring to the allegation prompted two reporters, one from CNN, the other NBC, to ask Bush directly if he had committed adultery. There is more reporting in the wake of this than of the previous openings, but almost all of it is restrained and uninformative. The following is the pertinent part of the *NBC Nightly News* report:

Tom Brokaw:	President Bush today had an angry reaction to a *New York Post* report on his personal life. The newspaper quoted a new book saying an American ambassador, who is now dead, arranged adjoining bedrooms for Bush and a female aide during a visit to Switzerland in 1984. The Ambassador was quoted as saying the two were romantically involved, which has long been an unsubstantiated rumor. Today a CNN reporter asked the President about that story.
Bush:	I'm not gonna take any sleazy questions like that from CNN. I am very disappointed that you would ask such a question of me and I will not respond to it, I haven't responded to it in the past. I'm outraged but nevertheless in this kind of screwy climate we're in, why I expect it. But I don't like it and I'm not gonna respond, other than to say it's a lie.
Brokaw:	Back at the White House this afternoon the question came up again talking with NBC's Stone Phillips.
Bush:	I'm not gonna take any sleaze questions. I told . . . I gave you a little warning. You see you're perpetuating the sleaze by even asking the question, to say nothing of asking it in the Oval Office and I don't think you ought to do that. And I'm not gonna answer the question.

The story offers no hint that any supporting detail on the tryst existed, beyond a single claim by a man who died before the book appeared. This response typified the coverage in the major media. *Time*, for example, reported the entire incident in a single, albeit suggestive, paragraph (*Time* 1992):

[A] CNN reporter threw a question that had rested half-buried like a live grenade from an old war. Had Bush, as Vice President, participated in a "sexual tryst" with a longtime assistant? Unsubstantiated gossip about Bush and Jennifer Fitzgerald had floated among reporters and politicians – including Bush's staff – since the early '80s, then escaped last week through a brassy headline in the *New York Post* based on a brief reference in a new book. "It's a lie," the President responded.

Undisclosed was the specific content of this long-lived unsubstantiated chit-chat; unexplained and unexamined was why it lasted so long or why Bush's *own staff* participated in the gossip.[4] This latter point by itself promised something in the way of substantiation if pursued further. Having Bush's staff gossip about their boss in ways that reached top Washington media outlets offers more evidence that Washington insiders regarded Bush's marital conduct as quite different from the way the president represented it to the American public.

Relative visibility of Flowers and Fitzgerald

In order to take the analysis beyond these three critical incidents, we compare the attention generated by Clinton's and Bush's alleged infidelities in 1992. A large number of news media were searched using the LexisNexis database, including all ABC TV news programs and the *MacNeil/Lehrer News Hour* on PBS; *Time*, *Newsweek* and *US News*; the UPI and Gannett wire services; and 15 major daily newspapers including the *New York Times*, *Washington Post* and *Chicago Tribune*.

For all of 1992 from January 1 through November 3, in those media, the name of Gennifer Flowers, Clinton's alleged lover and accuser (and willing participant in the media circus), appeared in 1,239 stories. The name of Bush's long-time aide and alleged lover, Jennifer Fitzgerald, appeared in 62 stories. Thus Flowers appeared in 20 times more stories than Fitzgerald. The disparity in mentioning the name of the alleged lovers was actually greater than these figures suggest, because Flowers was named more than once in most stories, and her picture shown repeatedly, whereas Fitzgerald tended to be named only once in her stories and was never pictured in mainstream media (a blurry photo appeared in the *New York Post* story mentioned earlier). This disparity is traceable in major part to Flowers's eager (and financially compensated) participation in ginning up the scandal; Fitzgerald denied any misbehavior and wanted no part of a media circus. This contrast between flamboyant public confession of guilt and quiet denial helps explain some of the difference in media coverage, but does not alter the major point: the two politicians experienced greatly different magnitudes of scandal and political consequences for evidence of the similar trespass of conducting a long-term love affair.

During the flurry of attention to the allegation, in the two weeks right after Flowers's charges were made public, her name and Clinton's appeared together in 252 stories, including 22 front-page newspaper stories and 28 items on editorial pages. In the two weeks after Bush was finally asked directly by a reporter whether he had ever been unfaithful (August 11, 1992), he and Fitzgerald were mentioned in 46 stories. Only 2 of these were page-1 stories, and 6, edit-page items. Thus, in the respective two-week periods of most intense attention, not only did a large sample of the major print media mention Flowers in over five times more stories than they did Fitzgerald, but most kept Fitzgerald off the front page.

Notice that 75 percent of the Fitzgerald citations came around the intense two weeks, then disappeared. On the other hand, mentions of Flowers persisted in the news all year. Even during the two weeks when Jennifer Fitzgerald was receiving attention, Gennifer Flowers was actually named more; Flowers appeared in 56 stories, compared with Fitzgerald's 46 during the latter's peak of visibility. Another even starker way to see the contrast is to note that, outside their intense two-week periods of attention, 987 stories include Flowers, whereas only 16 cite Fitzgerald – for a ratio of more than 60 to 1. This is particularly important because it means that audiences received repeated reminders of Flowers throughout the campaign. In fact, Gennifer Flowers made The Freedom Forum's list of "Top-ten campaign names and phrases from the campaign trail" (The Freedom Forum Media Studies Center 1993, pp. 67–8). For the period July 1, 1992 – Nov. 3, 1992, "Gennifer Flowers" ranked ninth; for September 1, 1991 through June 30, 1992, Flowers reached sixth place, just behind "Rodney King" (whose videotaped beating by Los Angeles police sparked riots) and "family values." Many stories also contained allusions to Clinton's infidelity that were impossible to pick up by a keyword search. For example, on October 30, 1992, the *New York Times* reported that Vice President Dan Quayle asked whether Clinton passed "the Tower Test." He was referring to the Senate's rejection of John Tower's nomination for Secretary of Defense on grounds of the senator's alleged womanizing (and drinking). Bush's fidelity issues received very little similarly veiled mention.

Private discourse

As already suggested, although the story lacked eyewitness testimony, the press actually had considerable evidence of infidelity by Bush. The idea was not merely "rumor," defined in the *American Heritage Dictionary* as "unverified information of uncertain origin usually spread by word of mouth; hearsay." Journalists had long talked about Bush's infidelity among themselves as a fact, based on the observations of his staff members and political colleagues, and even Bush himself when his guard was down. The late Clay Felker (former publisher of *Esquire*, *New York* magazine and the *Village Voice*) disclosed that Bush, while serving as UN ambassador, discussed various plans for amorous rendezvous with young women, right in front of Felker, knowing he was a liberal who ran the widely read *New York* magazine. In those days (late 1960s), journalists observed a code of silence on private peccadilloes and Felker honored it.[5] Beyond the lore handed down from senior colleagues who covered Bush during the 1960s, reporters in the 1980s also rested their conclusion on observations of Bush's behavior with Fitzgerald, of her career path, and of Barbara Bush, who publicly indicated emotional estrangement from her husband. Thus the information was not precisely unverified. Its origins were known, and if most of it was hearsay, some was not.

As evidence for the hieratic circulation of data on Bush's love life among the journalistic priesthood, consider this exchange, part of a panel discussion broadcast by C-SPAN on February 18, 1992. Participants were *New York Times* Washington Bureau Chief R. W. "Johnny" Apple, Tim Russert of NBC's Washington Bureau, and Tom Oliphant of the *Boston Globe*:[6]

Russert:	If today, I suddenly got beeped and was told a woman in Washington came forward and said "I . . ."
Apple:	My name is Jennifer Fitzgerald . . .
Russert:	Glad *you* said it.
Apple:	I think you should mention her name.
Russert:	OK, if someone said, "I have had a 20-year affair with George Bush. I met him at this hotel. These are the dates," and on and on. What should we do?
Apple:	The point I made by mentioning the name is that [Fitzgerald] is not a name that is unknown in any newsroom in Washington, any political salon in Washington,

Russert:	Tom, why not?

any Congressional office. It is known everywhere and it
is not used.

Russert: Tom, why not?

Oliphant: It is not used, except when we use it.

Further sign of the circulation among elites of information on Bush's adultery can be found during the 1988 campaign. On October 19, 1988, a rumor spread on Wall Street that the *Washington Post* was about to publish a story that Bush had had a mistress for several years. The same day, the Dow Jones stock average dropped some 43 points or 2 percent (it was at 2137). In its October 20 coverage of the stock market, the *Post* attributed the drop to the financial community's fear that the mistress story could damage the GOP's electoral chances, if highly publicized.[7] This reaction also implies that Wall Street insiders believed the *Post*'s story would be credible and difficult to refute. Barbara Bush even describes the incident in her memoirs (B. Bush 1994, p. 240). Although a junior staff aide to Dukakis, Donna Brazile, tried to interest the press in this quite remarkable financial event, the major media virtually ignored the incident. The *Washington Post* referred deep in the paper only to rumors about Bush's "marital life," the *New York Times* to "damaging" information; CBS briefly alluded to Bush's "personal life" – all in stories focusing mostly on Dukakis's firing of Ms. Brazile for peddling the infidelity story.[8] As with Hillary Clinton's attempt to raise the issue, in the absence of definitive documentary evidence or any other smoking gun, skilled application of Republican pressure redirected a potential scandal, focusing scandalized attention instead on the GOP's adversaries.

Thus the Bush coverage concealed an important empirical reality: regardless of whether the charges against Bush were actually true, Washington and Wall Street elites widely *believed* they might be true. Although they had never been proved by on-the-record witnesses or incriminating photos, there was clearly enough credible evidence to convince such leading journalists as Apple and Russert that Bush could have an adultery problem. In their professional capacity, then, journalists reported as untrue, unsubstantiated or unsupported an allegation whose likely validity was accepted tacitly within their own circles (on the importance and ethical legitimacy of tacit knowledge, see Christians, Ferré & Fackler 1993, pp. 187–9). This assertion is based not just on the earlier discussion but on this author's many informal discussions with top-ranking journalists, including some who knew and covered Bush for years. We have seen that journalists themselves occasionally admitted in public that they spoke about the Bush–Fitzgerald liaison as if it were real. But journalists acted as if their privately held beliefs held insufficient truth value to merit significant reporting – and as if the information that backed their opinions was not relevant enough to be admitted into the wider public domain.

The *Spy* magazine story summarizes the evidence that supported the unpublicized views of Washington insiders (*Spy*, published for about ten years, combined satire and serious investigative reporting; see Carter, Kalogerakis & Anderson 2006). The piece reports, for example, Barbara Bush's response to Gail Sheehy when asked in 1988 why she had stopped dyeing her hair in her mid-forties, letting it go gray. "In a voice tinged with bitterness," wrote Sheehy, Mrs. Bush said that when she stopped coloring her hair, "'George Bush never noticed.'" The Conason piece also includes a verifiable allegation, which no major news medium investigated, that Mrs. Bush lived in the US for much of the time Bush served as ambassador to China, while Jennifer Fitzgerald was in Beijing as his administrative aide. In her memoirs, Barbara does not mention any prolonged separation (B. Bush 1994).

What does remain on the public record is Ms. Fitzgerald's sudden dispatch to the State Department in 1989, after many years of loyal service as a close personal aide, just when Bush at long last attained the presidency. Privately, some journalists traced this otherwise inexplicable act to Bush's fear that his liaison with Fitzgerald could have been exposed under the newly intense scrutiny of the White House press corps. They also suggested she was given the cushy job of deputy protocol chief (which involves wining and dining diplomats throughout the world) in order to cement her loyalty, keeping any bitterness at her banishment from causing her to speak publicly against Bush.[9] The *Spy* piece also offers some written evidence suggesting Bush might have had an affair with a singer as a younger man, along with other provocative material. More tidbits have appeared over the years, including that Bush paid Fitzgerald's salary during the last part of his failed 1980 nomination campaign out of his personal funds, after the rest of the staff was no longer on salary (Blumenthal 1992).

Publicized knowledge: Clinton's infidelity

The contrast between all this merely suggestive information on Bush and the energetically promoted, juicy – and tape-recorded – details supplied by Gennifer Flowers offers a legitimate and strong explanation of the divergence in coverage.[10] The Flowers case provided the kind of dramatic ingredients that news organizations prefer when they cover scandals. Yet the evidence was far from airtight: Flowers was encouraged by Republicans to go public (Blumenthal 1992), for which she admitted being paid an estimated $100,000 or more. It was soon discovered that her tapes were doctored.[11] Bill Clinton firmly denied a sexual relationship with Flowers. Despite doubts about her credibility and motives, she did not fade quickly from sight. In fact, as we have seen, she was mentioned in nearly 1,000 stories by major media even after the initial two-week flurry.

Clinton did virtually (but never quite explicitly) admit to adultery by saying he'd caused "pain" in his marriage, during a *60 Minutes* interview, thus confirming the basic premise. Rumors in Little Rock about his womanizing were rampant,[12] and Clinton admitted in a private meeting with some leading reporters[13] held before the campaign that he went through a period when he and Hillary led essentially separate lives. He pleaded with journalists for understanding, arguing that if he and Hillary had divorced instead of staying married, his affairs would not have been newsworthy at all. It appears the mainstream media did restrain themselves in light of all the tacit knowledge they had about Clinton (Payne & Mercuri 1993). They only went with the story when Flowers played tapes of conversations with Clinton at a press conference. Journalists did not probe rumors of his other affairs until December 1993, when Arkansas state troopers publicly alleged he had engaged in sexual misconduct (Wines 1993). But this restraint also suggests malleable standards of truth-seeking and publishing. The private meeting with top reporters and Clinton's personal plea for journalistic forbearance were not widely reported, and arguably withholding these facts meant censoring data that the public should have known – not just about Clinton, but also about how journalism works.[14]

Flowers became a symbol of Clinton's other infidelities, which journalists believed in based on his admissions on *60 Minutes* and on the kind of tacit knowledge (e.g., circumstantial evidence, rumors and speculation from seemingly credible sources) they possessed about Bush. In this sense, perhaps Clinton would have been well advised to deny any infidelity, as one prominent White House correspondent told me. Journalists apparently viewed Clinton's public near-admission of adultery as licensing the repeated mention of Flowers (Rosenstiel 1993, p. 68), despite the lack of corroboration for, and Clinton's vigorous denial of, her specific claims. Had Clinton simply disavowed adultery and refused to appear on *60 Minutes*, at that time one of the top-rated shows on television – a venue that kept the Flowers drama roiling – the media might have stopped at reporting the denial, as they did for Bush.

Yet it would be paradoxical for journalists to rely on a standard of truth that has at its core the treatment of presumptively false claims as true – as long as their falsity cannot definitively be proven. That is just what they do if they defend their suppression of the Bush story on the grounds that they would have suppressed Clinton's too, if only Clinton too had lied to them. In other words, had Clinton confirmed his bad character by lying, the press would have covered up evidence for his bad character.

Thus the standard for publicizing damaging private information seems incoherent. It appears the criteria for framing scandals in the private realm depend less on consistent rules for producing and circulating statements about politicians' personal lives to the public than on: (a) the manipulative skill and power of those pushing the damaging personal data, and (b) the congruence of the presentational form of the allegations (such as an interview featuring titillating soundbites) with standard operating procedures of news organizations. The incentives and routines that guide journalism are supposed to enhance the credibility of the news as confirmed truth (Tuchman 1978), but may at times contribute to the encryption of facts, and restriction from the public sphere of data that might allow citizens to reach their own decisions on the truth of scandal allegations.

Dukakis, Gingrich and Dole

Three other instances of politically destructive private information, one widely reported without any substantiation, the others barely covered despite much plausible evidence, further illuminate the haphazard oscillations of journalistic gatekeeping on private behavior that might violate certain venerated (if often breached) cultural norms.

1. Shrinking Dukakis's lead

Although it did not involve sex, Democratic presidential candidate Michael Dukakis's experience is revealing in this context because it concerned allegations of embarrassing activities in a realm at least as politically damaging as sexuality. In early August 1988, as Dukakis enjoyed a post-convention "bounce" in the polls, rumors floated that he had been treated for depression by a psychiatrist. The *New York Times* and *Washington Post* had previously investigated the rumor thoroughly and found no basis. Yet they both published front-page stories on this claim, and then ran lead editorials. Paraphrasing, the editorials said essentially "It's OK if a presidential candidate has sought mental health care; that shouldn't matter to voters." However, these items only gave further credence to an apparently groundless accusation.[15]

The Dukakis campaign believed and polls suggest that the psychiatry story shaved their 14-point lead over Bush in half and began their downward spiral (Sabato 1991, pp. 152–6). According to CNN correspondent Ken Bode (1992), the media felt compelled to cover the Dukakis rumors largely for two reasons: (1) one cannot ignore the president; Ronald Reagan put the psychiatry issue at the top of the news by a press conference quip about Dukakis being an "invalid" (referring to his alleged psychiatric problems); (2) competitively, when dozens of news organizations covered the same event and heard Reagan say "invalid," none could suppress the news for fear of being beaten on the story and looking incompetent. But both of these reasons suggest that standards for reportable claims of probabilistic truth are shaped more by the congruence of newsmaking routines with events and utterances, and by deference to power and manipulative skill, than by consistent philosophical or ethical – or even commercial – reasoning.

2. Neglecting Gingrich

At the height of his influence (1994–6), House Speaker Newt Gingrich (R-GA) was widely touted as a strong presidential contender. Indeed, in some reports he was lionized as the most powerful man in Washington, eclipsing President Clinton, even before he officially declared his candidacy. Coverage of Gingrich's private life provides further evidence of journalism's uncalibrated circulation of scandal information. The infidelity charges against Gingrich briefly surfaced in the mainstream media twice. First, the *Washington Post* (Russakoff & Balz 1994) reported in December 1994 that Gingrich "was having extramarital affairs when he was running for Congress the first time, according to four campaign aides." The *Post* quoted Gingrich's explanation: "In the 1970s, things happened – period. . . . I start with an assumption that all human beings sin and that all human beings are in fact human. . . . So all I'll say is that I've led a human life" (Russakoff & Balz 1994). Note that this admission to the *Washington Post* comes at least as close as Clinton did on *60 Minutes* to confessing adultery. Perhaps because the admission appeared in a far less prominent place, deep in the second part of a four-part newspaper series, the media's reaction to Gingrich's *mea culpa* in 1994 was entirely different. The *Post* story received no follow-up in the mainstream press (including the *Post* itself).

More data on Gingrich came in another *Vanity Fair* article (Sheehy 1995), quoting a respected Republican activist, Anne Manning, who said she and Gingrich had an affair in the 1970s, while he was married to his first wife. Manning was named in just 22 stories in the major media over the following month, none on the front page and none on ABC, CBS or NBC. A typical example of the treatment comes from *USA Today* ("Arts, humanities cut by a third in Senate" 1995, p. 4A), printed in the midst of other short items:

> GINGRICH ALLEGATION: Claims that House Speaker Newt Gingrich had an extramarital affair during his first marriage were called "just a bunch of tabloid psychobabble" by Gingrich aide Tony Blankley. Asked about the report in the September issue of *Vanity Fair*, Blankley said, "The subject matter is too low on the food chain" for comment. In the article, Anne Manning claims she had an affair with Gingrich in 1977. She says she's coming forward now because "'he should be stopped before it's too late.'"

In the same piece, two other former Gingrich aides indicated they witnessed the politician *in flagrante* with other women. Perhaps most tellingly, the Sheehy article also quoted Gingrich's then-current (second) wife, Marianne, saying she would "'just go on the air the next day and undermine it all'" if Newt announced his candidacy for president. (Marianne was one woman with whom Gingrich had an affair while married to his first wife.) Thus his own wife clearly implied that she would spill the beans on the Speaker's later escapades, those that happened while he was married to her. (Speaker Gingrich did not deny Marianne's quote, though he claimed it did not mean what it plainly implied.)

Given Gingrich's earlier near-confirmation, Blankley was dissembling. Indeed, *Newsweek* (August 21, 1995) wrote that "Stories about his infidelity weren't exactly startling news." Such claims reveal journalism's frequent confusion about the boundary between knowledge that circulates in Washington power circles and information that penetrates the public consciousness. Few Americans could have known of all the credible data suggesting the most influential politician in America at the time, one who publicly represented himself as a defender of traditional family values and went on as Speaker to lead the charge in the Clinton impeachment, had been flouting those values since early adulthood. *Time* (August 21, 1995) did report that Gingrich "spends far more time with Calista Bistek, a former Congressional aide, and Arianna Huffington, who hosted a $50,000-

a-plate dinner for him, than with his second wife Marianne, who has never actually moved to Washington and who has been candid about their marriage's being 'on and off.' " In this way the magazine obliquely signaled to sophisticated readers, those who could crack the code, that the Speaker's infidelity continued. Bistek later became Gingrich's third wife.

Observers of press behavior might argue that Gingrich was not officially running for president in the mid-1990s, and that at most this material was relevant only to his constituents in Georgia. Yet Gingrich was in the news every day, unlike any other member of Congress. As the same journalists who barely mentioned or ignored Gingrich's private behavior often proclaimed, he was the "leader of the Republican revolution," an official whose power in 1995 may have eclipsed that of the president, and he himself hungered for the White House. In 1995, Newt Gingrich's constituency was as much a national one as Clinton's. During the succeeding years, Gingrich was spoken of as a presidential contender and appeared frequently as a Republican spokesperson within the mainstream media. For instance, his name appeared in over 150 stories or editorial-page pieces in 2010 – an average of 1 almost every other day. In comparison, Gov. Tim Pawlenty (R-MN), also widely expected to run for president, was mentioned in about 50 *Times* items. Gingrich and Pawlenty did seek the 2012 Republican presidential nomination. As a coda to all this, when Gingrich finally married a third time, much of the coverage in matter-of-fact fashion noted his long-time extra-marital liaison with the woman – as if everyone already knew about it. And, of course, everyone in the Washington elite did.[16] Gingrich offered the following justification of his moral relativism:

> There's no question at times of my life, partially driven by how pas-sionately I felt about this country, that I worked far too hard and things happened in my life that were not appropriate. And what I can tell you is that when I did things that were wrong, I wasn't trapped in situation ethics, I was doing things that were wrong, and yet, I was doing them.[17]

3. Covering up for Dole

In 1996, Robert Dole, Senate Republican leader and then GOP presi-dential nominee, was frequently criticized for not hammering Clinton harder on the moral character issue. After all, Dole was a middle American with an image of rectitude, a World War II hero who sus-tained and overcame severe injuries. It turns out there was a story that Dole desperately feared would come out, so much so that he avoided most one-on-one interviews because of anxiety that he'd be asked about the topic: adultery. Dole divorced his first wife, and later famously married Washington insider (and eventual senator and presidential candidate) Elizabeth Dole. He was unfaithful to his first wife and he did not want any probing into his less than perfect marital behavior. His campaign viewed publicity for this indiscretion as a "mortal threat" to his chances. Legendary *Washington Post* reporter Bob Woodward had the goods on the affair and argued, according to a *Newsweek* story ("Don't look now" 1996, November 18) appearing after the election, that "Dole had made trust and character an issue, and thus adultery, even from the distant past, was relevant. Most of the editors, however, accepted the distinction between public trust and private actions. The *Post* and its owners, the Graham family, did not want to get into the business of investigating the dalliances of presidential candidates." So the story never ran. The *Post*'s decision came after Dole's campaign manager and his wife Elizabeth pleaded with the top executives at the paper, including owner Katherine Graham, not to run the story (see Thomas & Breslau 1996; Thomas, Breslau, Rosenberg, Kaufman & Kennerly 1997). The *Post*'s claim, as relayed by this *Newsweek* story, that it didn't want to get into the business of investigating presidential candidates' sex lives is somewhat difficult to square with the way that paper actually coerced Gary Hart to drop his pursuit of the presidency in 1988 by threatening to publish a new adultery allegation (*Newsweek* itself took the lead in pursuing the Clinton–Lewinsky story [Kalb 2001]).

Leonard Downie, who was executive editor of the *Post* in 1996, explained the Dole decision in a book, which reports that journalists at the *Post* debated the issue for weeks (Downie & Kaiser 2003, pp. 56–62). Bob Woodward wrote a 2,500-word memo arguing that: "Withholding the story breaks the contract with the reader . . . Not everyone has to agree on relevance. . . . Any decision not to publish a story we know is true and many believe politically relevant is rooted in a subjectivity that goes beyond an editor's normal role" (Downie & Kaiser 2003, p. 59). Downie and Kaiser, however, defend the *Post*'s handling. They say the truth about Dole did come out eventually. They draw this conclusion (2003, p. 62) because of the following sequence: the *National Enquirer* ran a piece in October 1996, followed by the *New York Daily News*. These led a reporter to ask Dole about the matter directly. The senator responded, "You're worse than they [*Enquirer* and *Daily News*] are." This is not even a non-denial denial; it's just a non-denial. The *Post* then mentioned the matter deep in a story on October 26, 1996. Downie and Kaiser write, "The whole matter was handled inside a routine news story; no headline referred to it." In other words, the *Post* decide to publish after all, but only in a passing manner that restricted the audience for the report to the kind of Washington insiders who read deeply into the continuation page of routine political stories.

There's little doubt Dole's age and the datedness of the behavior played into the media's choices here. Dole, one of the oldest presidential nominees ever, was by 1996 well beyond his playboy days. The same was not quite true of George H. W. Bush, whose alleged dalliances occurred from his early years at the UN right up through his vice presidency (i.e. until around 1988 when he won the presidency). Nor could the Clinton campaign very well push the adultery issue against Dole, especially after the media had repulsed Hillary's attack on Bush Senior in 1992. Susan Paterno (1997) reports that other motivations in the media's decisions included their fear of negative audience reaction and their assessment that his degree of hypocrisy did not reach the (unspecified) threshold to warrant exposure. In addition, Paterno says, journalists were generally fond of the Kansas senator; whereas many hated Clinton, with Dole, "there was nobody to push [the story] and do a drumbeat." This explanation refers, in my terms, to journalists' decision bias favoring politicians they tend to personally like over ones they do not.

So the mainstream media's decisions to leave Dole's old indiscretions out of the campaign narrative made a certain sense, but note the troubling by-product: withholding this information meant misleading coverage on the purported mystery of why Dole's campaign was downplaying character attacks on Clinton. Throughout the campaign, the press ran stories quoting observers who questioned why Dole was not disparaging Clinton's character. After all, as Republican nominee for vice president in 1976, Dole was well known for aggressive attacks on the "Democrat Party." But there was no mystery inside the beltway about his timid tactics twenty years later.

Nonetheless, mainstream news organizations withheld the information until after the campaign. Only then did both *Newsweek* (cited above) and *Time* publish this explanation for something their reports during the campaign treated as inexplicable. Judging by these accounts, as well as Downie and Kaiser's, journalists at other mainstream media outlets also knew of Dole's pre-divorce affair, and understood that fear of having to face questions about it lay behind Dole's restraint in playing the character card. Beyond the relevance of Dole's long-ago adultery to his qualifications for the presidency, about which there was legitimate debate, was another reason to report it: not doing so meant disingenuously covering the horserace, treating Dole's uncharacteristically faint tactics as inexplicable when journalists knew the likely explanation. In refusing to tell the public outside Washington, the mainstream media intervened covertly in the play of power and outcomes of democracy.

Explaining disparities

These cases suggest that decisions on publishable scandal claims were made ad hoc, in the unexamined and uncontrolled rough-and-tumble of deadline-driven, competitive pack journalism, with potentially serious costs for democracy. In these cases, journalism failed to reveal the facts, which are that many if not most Washington journalists believed that Clinton, George H. W. Bush, Gingrich and Dole were all guilty of extra-marital affairs, though this was only proved beyond any doubt for Clinton. And the coverage omitted deeper, epistemological facts: that truth itself is a slippery, hard-to-know thing, conveyed by news imperfectly if not haphazardly, through inclusions *and* silences. In Foucault's terms, the case suggests journalists fall short in the production of truth. To follow Foucault's guidelines for truth, the media would need to act according to *consistent* rules for authentication and relevance. Instead, they followed an operational practice, largely unexamined as to its implicit epistemology or impacts. This section describes the forces that combined in opening and closing the gate to high-publicity sex scandals in the mainstream media (the next chapter explores this area in the epoch of the 24/7 news cycle and the Internet and finds little change in the basic dynamics). The omissions in the Bush, Gingrich and Dole coverage were over-determined, wrought by multiple forces, as were the inclusions in the Clinton and Dukakis sagas. What they were *not* determined by, apparently, was the substantive strength of the evidence, or by the relevance of the charges to citizen deliberation or misrepresentation – or by any consistent standard.

1. Compatibility with media decision biases

Although the profession lacks codified or even articulated standards (Tuchman 1978; Gans 1979), journalism's operational criteria for publishing factual claims on the sexual lives of the powerful seem to be: (1) allegations of scandalous misconduct made by someone willing to speak for attribution; and (2) charges congruent with journalists' preferences for story packages that are simple while being novel yet stereotype-consistent. These are necessary, though not always sufficient, for the information to receive high-magnitude attention on network TV news reports, cable news talk and infotainment, and in the blogosphere and print media. Only such widely publicized stories influence politics; a brief item published inside even a prominent newspaper, or a series of pieces exclusively online, rarely make a dent in public consciousness or the political process.

Attention from broadcast and cable news, with their particular need for simplicity and visual appeal (mentioned in chapter 2 as important media decision biases), seems necessary to trigger the process by which presidential scandal accusations can reach critical mass and ramify through the levels of the political communication system in a self-reinforcing cascade. This is likely because elites, and journalists themselves, believe television remains the medium that can move a public that relies less and less on newspapers. Elites seem further to believe, perhaps justifiably, that television will affect other elites' perceptions and anticipations of public opinion, thereby altering allies' and adversaries' political calculations. Such effects on the political environment in turn affect news production decisions heavily inflected by the process bias, which leads national political journalists to spend much of their time assessing and conveying who's up and who's down in the political game.

If the story does not appear prominently and repeatedly on TV, if it only appears in print, particularly if limited to inside pages of the newspapers – even the *Times* or *Post* – it matters little to politics or public opinion. Appearance in magazines, a lower-status newspaper, books or the blogosphere is even less likely to trigger or sustain a scandal. Level 3 of the hierarchical system of networks illustrated in figures 2.3 and 2.4 (chapter 2) – the news media – itself is arranged in a steep hierarchy that looks something like figure 3.1. Although this figure is impressionistic and hypothetical, and would be nearly impossible to confirm empirically, its point is to help readers roughly visualize the argument here.

Although appearance in the *New York Times* or *Washington Post*, papers read by most national political editors, pundits and reporters, is probably a necessary condition for unleashing major scandals, it is not sufficient. The most influential media actors are in this view not the *Times* and *Post*, as is usually thought, but the traditional broadcast news operations, which still commanded the broadest national news audiences as late as 2010,[18] and the major cable news operations. Also important in sustaining and occasionally sparking a scandal are the AP wire, the two weekly newsmagazines (*Time* and *Newsweek*) and NPR.[19] At the fourth tier of the news organization hierarchy (again, this is just a rough approximation) are the fine regional newspapers like the *Boston Globe*, the major political monthlies, and popular

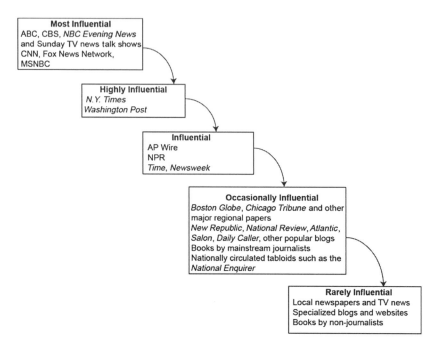

Figure 3.1 Hierarchy of influence within Level 3 (networks of news organizations)

blogs and websites, along with books written by journalists affiliated with mainstream media or other credible organizations. Unlike the organizations at the top three levels, their stories are less likely to stimulate coverage by other media.

As happened with the *Globe*'s scoop on George W. Bush's failure to show up for National Guard service in Massachusetts (chapter 6), this inability to strike a nerve with the upper-tier media can mean the originating outlet itself quickly loses interest. In the current cases, reporting on George H. W. Bush, Gingrich and Dole in monthly magazines and books, or in the back pages of more influential sources like the *Post*, could not ignite a scandal cascade. At the lowest level for presidential scandals are local media outlets that serve mainly to spread ideas activated at the levels above them to geographically or ideologically narrow audiences.

Even within each outlet the hierarchy is fairly steep: a *Washington Post* story on page A-18 is far less likely to generate attention from other news organizations or elites than a story on the front page (see Entman, Livingston & Kim 2009). Hence the prominent play is important to whether a potential scandal ignites a cascading flow of accusations, responses and follow-up measures from official agencies. The editorial and op-ed pages enjoy more autonomy than the objectivity-bound and process-biased news pages. As will be demonstrated further in chapters 7 and 8, this means they are more likely to mention scandals otherwise ignored by the core scandal-producing media. But research for this book and elsewhere has found that there isn't necessarily much relationship between reasoning and facts displayed in editorials and op-eds, on the one hand, and news decisions, on the other (Hallin 1986; Entman 2004).

Books or magazine articles written by journalists affiliated with major national media who are members of the close-knit intermedia networks in Washington have the best chance of influencing scandal production. Examples would include Bob Woodward's inside chronicles of the Bush and Obama White Houses (see Woodward 2002, 2010) or the muckraking investigations of Seymour Hersh in the *New Yorker*. Writings by those outside the clan seem to hold less sway (see Bennett et al. 2007).

Journalists like long-time *Post* editor Leonard Downie seem to believe that a brief mention on the inside pages of a newspaper is equivalent to multiple stories on page one, in the sense that both discharge journalists' duties to make facts available to the public. However, prominence and repetition are crucial to elite perceptions that a wide swath of the general public might take notice. Elite perceptions that the scope of conflict will expand (see Schattschneider 1960), that publics beyond the beltway could learn of and react to scandal accusations against presidents and candidates, prime leaders' motivations to extend the scandal. If politicians believe the public will react, they may sense an opportunity to mobilize for promoting a scandal cascade – or a need to organize their defenses. Promoting the scandal means talking and acting in ways that continue to generate fresh news, for instance by holding hearings, calling for criminal investigations or leaking documents. Defense entails pressuring or threatening news organizations (as did Clinton and Dole), creating distractions (as with McCain [chapter 4] and Rathergate [chapter 6]), or making arguments against the legitimacy of, or public interest in, the charges (see Benoit 2006).

So, for example, Gennifer Flowers had dramatic audiotapes of conversations with Bill Clinton, professional public relations advice – and her own compelling physical presence and demeanor as a former TV newscaster and nightclub singer. Judging by the public reaction, she looked the part of a woman who would break up a marriage, and she fulfilled dramatic conventions and stereotypes of a mistress scorned and left behind by her married lover. All this made her charges irresistible for TV and cable news, which in turn gave it political potential as outlined just above, while heightening the interest of print media as well. Thus, because prominent play on TV could have affected the nomination contest, Flowers's story became an important political process or horserace story for all of journalism (see Rosenstiel 1993).

2. The crucial role of the process bias

The TV-driven dynamic is further propelled by the dominance of the game schema, the mainstream media's treatment of politics as predominantly a contest for official power. Reporting about personal misconduct is calibrated according to the circular logic of the "damage control" story, a central feature of horserace journalism. George H. W. Bush's story had neither witnesses nor visual interest; TV coverage was predictably desultory. It thus held little significance for the horserace, which confirmed the print media's inclination to drop the story without ever really covering it. Gingrich's and Dole's stories, too, lacked dramatic visuals. As described by Rosenstiel:

> Since journalists feel unable or unwilling to judge for themselves what areas of inquiry are legitimate, they publish material they consider improper on the grounds that this information will shape the outcome of the race. Gennifer Flowers was a story not because it was true – that was not established – but because it had become a political liability for Clinton.

The damage control story stars a politician fighting against sensational claims that threaten his political standing. The jeopardy and the fight make the allegations even more newsworthy, and a scandal cascade can ensue. The quality of the evidence can become less relevant once a catalytic story emerges to imperil the politician's standing. Many journalists appear genuinely distressed at the way this works. The ability of blogs and social media to amplify and keep rumors circulating – and thus conceivably further affect the horserace – could, however, cause some slippage in the mainstream media's control, as will be shown in a different way by the Rathergate scandal.

3. Differential partisan skill and resources for managing news

Systematic differences between the press operations of the GOP and the Democrats may give Republicans more power to circumscribe investigative zeal. Among the factors that seem to provide Republicans more consistent clout than Democrats in repelling media invasions of their standard-bearers' privacy are their rhetorical unity (Jarvis 2005); their seemingly better grasp of the way emotional appeals trump analytical reasoning (Westen 2007; Lakoff 2008); tireless repetition of the conventional wisdom that the national press exhibits liberal bias (Entman 2010c), which keeps journalists on the defensive; aggressive use of "opposition research" and willingness to sponsor witnesses like Gennifer Flowers and Paula Jones (whose lawsuit ultimately yielded the Monica Lewinsky scandal); their dominance of the radio talk shows, influential molders of perceived public opinion (see Page 1996; Jamieson & Cappella 2008); and their possession, unlike the Democrats, of cable news outlet, Fox News, completely devoted to promoting their party's power. Obviously these Republican advantages do not protect against all negative news, particularly for politicians below the presidential level, but the cases discussed here suggest they do help when journalists enter the sensitive realm of presidential candidates' private lives.

4. Motivations to protect and rationalize journalism's own power

Preserving their insider status and defending their self-concepts may also drive journalists' responses to potential sex scandals. Knowledge about the private lives of Washington's history-makers elevates journalists in some senses to the same social plane as the upmost political elite. Part of the media's power, from which journalists likely derive at least unconscious satisfaction, lies in withholding information and exchanging it only among peers. Unfortunately, knowing more salacious detail than they report may corrode journalists' sense of connection to the public at large. Like a secret handshake, keeping a cache of data cements journalists' membership in the inner circle (see Bennett et al. 2007).

The irony is that maintaining a (sporadically breached) barrier between politicians' personal behavior and public persona does not truly protect their privacy. Politicians' peccadilloes are rarely secret. Rather, their personal vices are often known or suspected by those in their closest communities: the Washington insiders (including most national journalists). Journalists, then, can remain privy to the inside gossip and lore of Washington, feel important and sophisticated, while their audiences remain outside, in the dark. It was much easier in any case for journalists to rationalize protecting the secret of their belief in George H. W. Bush's infidelity than to admit having kept it. Every Washington reporter I interviewed contrived excuses for not reporting on Bush. These sounded very much like all guilt-driven rationalizations for failing to admit infidelity: it didn't really mean anything, it happened long ago, they (audiences) really don't want to know, they're better off not knowing.

Other forces can override these internal, psychic incentives. Yet in most cases (Dukakis, Clinton in 1992 and 1993, the three brief moments of Bush–Fitzgerald attention in 1992, Gingrich), reports originating outside the elite Washington press corps broke the story. Only then did insiders even mention the matters (Sabato 1991; Patterson 1993, p. 166; Rosenstiel 1993, ch. 3). For Dole, as noted, the figurative oath of silence among national journalists prevailed until after the election. Focusing on 2008 campaign events, the next chapter probes more thoroughly this phenomenon of mainstream journalism's occasional, largely inadvertent collusion with politicians – in this case Hillary Clinton, John McCain and John Edwards – to suppress sexual scandals.

5. Political pressure from the audience

The final force in this equation is the public. Journalists and news organizations always feel their credibility on the line, and there are powerful commercial and career incentives to protect it. In the Bush case, not only were national news organizations, always fearful of reproach for liberal bias, chary of antagonizing Republicans; by publicizing the Bush infidelity claims in 1992, the media might also have undermined their credibility among Democrats, who might have asked why evidence about Bush's apparent adultery was suppressed in 1987–8, when Gary Hart's relationship with Donna Rice received sufficient publicity to knock the senator out of politics. At first Hart defiantly denied a sexual liaison. The *Washington Post* then threatened him privately that it would run a story confirming Hart's affair with yet another woman if he stayed in the campaign. The Democratic frontrunner withdrew (Germond & Witcover 1989, chs. 12 & 13). The outcome of the *Post*'s unpublished threat against Hart reveals that the media's decisions on truth and relevance can occasionally exert independent power not merely over the discourse, but over the course of American politics.[20] With outrage awaiting from the right ("Liberal bias!"), indignation from the left ("Why didn't you tell us in 1988?"), exposing Bush's alleged infidelity in 1992 must have seemed a decidedly unappetizing prospect. Hence the irony: the mass audience themselves may wield significant power to censor the truth claims that will reach them, at least the public as it is imagined and worried over by news organizations.

Contrary to widespread assumptions among observers of journalism and politics, the Internet does not necessarily augment the public's ability to overcome this paradox. The next chapter indicates that the contributions of the blogosphere and Internet news sites to the performance of the scandal process in the twenty-first century – or at least to piercing the veil between public persona and the private realm – are weaker than many imagine.

4

Secret Sins of 2008:
The McCain, Edwards and
Clinton Families' Values

The media's reluctance to publicize the allegations about Bush Senior and Robert Dole in 1996 was no aberration. Twelve years later, despite the promise of the Internet and social media to create a new age of transparency, Campaign 2008 saw three potential sex scandals involving candidates for the presidency that failed to penetrate the wider public sphere in a timely fashion. News about John Edwards's rather spectacular sexual misadventure only entered public consciousness in August 2008, even though it had been exposed by the tabloid *National Enquirer* and subject to intense discussion in the blogosphere. And only well after the election did more than a handful of citizens learn – from *Game Change* (Heilemann & Halperin 2010), a best-selling chronicle of the campaign – that the McCain and Clinton campaigns both had to fend off threats of destructive sex scandals. The authors, two well-known political reporters with extraordinary insider access, did not share the news with their regular audiences in 2008.[1] Nor, even when the book was published, did the rest of the media have much to say about the sexual revelations.

Once again, it seems, the media violated the frequent assumption that they thirst insatiably for scandal, particularly when it comes to sex. The notion that the Internet makes it far more difficult for politicians to conceal information is also challenged by these non-scandals of 2008. This chapter shows that, far from pouncing on the sensational whiff of sexual misconduct involving the top-tier presidential candidates, mainstream media, with an instructive exception, bent over backwards to avoid publicizing the allegations.

Moreover, an arguably disingenuous puzzlement characterized coverage of this campaign, much as it did in the news of Robert Dole in 1996. The mainstream media avoided the scandals to such a degree that they did not tell audiences why the *New York Times* did, ever so gingerly, raise the infidelity issue with respect to McCain; in fact the *Times* itself put up a weak defense when accused of liberal bias in the aftermath of their 85-word foray into adultery coverage, as detailed below. Similarly, major news organizations did not explain why Edwards precipitously dropped out of the nomination race even though insiders knew that the *Enquirer*'s reporting on his sex scandal had a strong ring of truth. Nor did they expose why Hillary Clinton didn't obtain the enthusiastic endorsements from the Democratic establishment that might have been expected, or why Democratic Senate leader Harry Reid in particular encouraged Barack Obama to challenge the heir apparent. One could argue that this treatment constituted a kind of journalistic scandal akin to that arising from the much-maligned Bush National Guard memos (chapter 6).

John McCain – and his wife

That coverage of high-level impropriety by the traditional mainstream national media was restrained yet essential to scandal production in the early twenty-first century is apparent in the aborted coverage of the McCain affair. On February 21, 2008, as he was heading toward increasingly certain victory in the Republican primaries, the *New York Times* published a story questioning McCain's claims to represent the public interest in fighting against the inside influence of special interests and lobbyists (Rutenberg, Thompson, Kirkpatrick & Labaton 2008). The second paragraph of the story read:

> A female lobbyist had been turning up with him at fund-raisers, visiting his offices and accompanying him on a client's corporate jet. Convinced the relationship had become romantic, some of his top advisers intervened to protect the candidate from himself – instructing staff members to block the woman's access, privately warning her away and repeatedly confronting him, several people involved in the campaign said on the condition of anonymity.

In the fourth paragraph the story noted: "Mr. McCain, 71, and the lobbyist, Vicki Iseman, 40, both say they never had a romantic relationship." The rest of this 3,100-word investigative story offers evidence that, whatever McCain's personal relationship with Iseman was, the senator worked cooperatively with interest groups and lobbyists who had business before the Senate Committee he chaired. A *Washington Post* story (February 21, 2008) of about 1,000 words laid out essentially the same tale of McCain's actions belying his carefully constructed image as a maverick, but without the riveting allusion to adultery.

Because of its fears the media would pry open a "Pandora's Box," the campaign spent several weeks "living in terror" and in a "frenzy" (Heilemann & Halperin 2010, p. 308) about what they knew to be a forthcoming story in the *New York Times* linking the senator with lobbyist Vicki Iseman. According to *Game Change*, "no single issue was consuming more of the staff's time or psychic energy than the Iseman problem – and nothing was weighing more heavily on the candidate's mind." The book reports that the candidate called advisors "Umpteen times a day" to ask "What's happening with the *Times*?" McCain finally spoke with *Times* executive editor Bill Keller. If the authors of *Game Change* are to be believed, Keller's first words were to ask whether allegations of adultery with Iseman were true, and McCain responded: "I have never betrayed the public trust by doing anything like that."

Contrary to the campaign's confident public face, the night the story was finally posted on the Web (February 20, 2008), *Game Change* reports that McCain said "he was sure the campaign was over," that he wouldn't be the nominee. At that point his advisor Steve Schmidt pledged that "someone's going to get crushed on this, and it's going to be the *New York Times*" (p. 315). Backed by the networks of conservative blogs and commentators, McCain's campaign launched a heavy assault on the *New York Times* for unethical journalism.

What's noteworthy for our purposes is that, guided by McCain's campaign, the media reframed the problematic behavior from John McCain's inappropriately close (and in one case possibly romantic) relationships with interest-group lobbyists having business before his Senate Committee and elsewhere, to the *New York Times'* violating the tenets of good journalism. The *Times'* sin boiled down to insinuating without providing proof (though never actually charging) that the candidate had committed adultery. Literally, the paper only reported that McCain's people were "convinced the relationship [with Iseman] had become romantic," not that the senator was having sexual relations with her. Thus elites and journalists had to use the inside knowledge that dared not speak its name in order to jump from the *Times'* report of aides' fears about a romantic involvement to claiming the paper had improperly smeared McCain for adultery. The context used by mainstream national journalists was only much later provided to the public by *Game Change*. The *Times* offered no smoking gun or immediate news peg, so critics charged that the article was a hatchet job, especially given that his sexual habits were irrelevant to McCain's public duties. Even Democrats denounced the *Times'* piece. The *Times* limited its defense largely to stressing that the article focused on the contrast between McCain's image as an outsider and his actual practice as a Washington politician who maintained close relationships with lobbyists pleading their own narrow interests before the Senate.

A simple analysis of coverage in the *Times* and *Post* as well as *USA Today* for the month following the initial publications on February 21 reveals how a potential political scandal turned into a media scandal. As was true with Rathergate (chapter 6), an imperiled candidate never had to answer substantive questions about the allegations. Instead, his campaign successfully guided attention to the *Times'* alleged professional and ethical deficiencies, diverting it from McCain's possible misrepresentation of himself in two senses: as uniquely independent from special-interest Washington politics, and as appropriately embodying his Republican Party's family values brand.

The three papers carried a total of 21 items mentioning the imbroglio. Of these, 18 contained attacks on the *New York Times*, and only 5 of these critical stories also offered some defense of the *Times*. The overall amount of space devoted to assailing the *Times* is many times that provided to defending it.

As to the infidelity, 11 of the 21 stories employed only euphemisms, of which the most common was "inappropriate relationship" used in a context where readers who hadn't caught the original *Times* story could easily conclude that the suspicions revolved around the self-proclaimed maverick McCain's being only metaphorically in bed with lobbyists. The *Post* was particularly prone to this evasion, perhaps because their own February 21 story on the same topic steered entirely clear of the sex angle, even though it actually mentioned the *Times'* story (which had been posted on the Internet the previous evening).

The analysis also assessed whether stories provided contextual information relevant to judging the credibility of any allegations that McCain might have strayed beyond marital bounds. None did. Not even the *New York Times* felt it necessary, or perhaps possible, to zero in on those aspects of McCain's history and current life that might enable readers to judge for themselves whether his advisors had good reason to worry that McCain truly was in bed with at least one lobbyist.

The contextual information includes the publicly acknowledged fact that John and Cindy McCain lived apart for most of his time in the Senate. She raised their children largely alone in Arizona, and McCain neglected to fly home after two of her three miscarriages. Presumably most Washington reporters knew of an incident described in a critical biography of McCain (Schecter 2008). In an exchange witnessed by three reporters and two aides (Doug Cole and Wes Gullett):[2] "At one point, Cindy playfully twirled McCain's hair and said, 'You're getting a little thin up there.' McCain's face reddened, and he responded, 'At least I don't plaster on the makeup like a trollop, you cunt'" (Schecter 2008, pp. 49–50). Heilemann and Halperin (2010, pp. 307, 310) reported that incident along with other critical information that provides a fuller accounting of the McCain marriage. This included detailed allegations that Cindy McCain herself had a long-term lover in Arizona, and a description of John McCain's love life as a potential Pandora's Box and "can of worms" for his campaign (Heilemann & Halperin 2010, ch. 17). McCain also acknowledged committing infidelities during his first marriage, which ended in 1980. McCain, then 42, had met 24-year-old heiress Cindy Hensley the previous year. The *Los Angeles Times* reported "the nature and timing of his divorce from Carol Shepp alienated key friends – and his version doesn't always match that in court documents" (see Serrano & Vartabedian 2008).

Furthermore, in the press conference McCain called to defend himself and reframe the problem, he neither was asked nor offered whether he had sex with Vicki Iseman. He was asked whether he had a "romantic" relationship with her and he said "No," asserting she was merely a friend. Even assuming McCain was truthful here, he might also have been relying on semantics (as Clinton was notoriously wont to do). The question was a relative softball. As the vernacular affirmed, a person could easily have sex with a friend absent a romantic relationship, and therefore truthfully answer the reporter's question in the negative. Relationships characterized by "friends with benefits," and "no strings attached," became sufficiently common that those phrases provided the titles of two Hollywood films released in 2011 ("Are 'No Strings Attached' and 'Friends With Benefits' the same movie?" 2010). Romantic or not, sexual intercourse with someone other than his wife would still qualify McCain as an adulterer. Alert journalists might have suspected that they were being manipulated, that McCain's best strategy was to blame the *Times* rather than answer tough questions, but news organizations cooperated with him.

Before probing this further, we should look back at McCain's reported response to Bill Keller, the *Times* editor. According to *Game*

Change, McCain said that he'd "never betrayed the public trust by doing anything like that." Assuming these were McCain's actual words (as the book's authors assure us in their explanatory preface), they were cleverly evasive. The sentence could be read as arguing that "doing anything like that" – adultery with a lobbyist – would not in fact constitute a violation of the public trust. It could also be read as saying something like "If I did anything like that (have sex with a lobbyist), it wouldn't sway my decisions on the lobbyist's policy issues." In other words, "I could have sex with a lobbyist without compromising my official responsibilities." Of course McCain meant for the phrase to be read as an equation of a violation of the public trust with "doing anything like" adultery, and a denial of such infringement. But the sentence remains ambiguous.

I lay all this out not because it proves anything about Vicki Iseman's relationship to McCain, or because I think it was vital to inform voters about John McCain's sex life, but because it provides a context that was both widely known in Washington and relevant to assessing the likelihood that the *Times*' insinuation was plausible. Remember, the paper only says McCain's aides were worried that he was becoming romantically involved, not that he was committing adultery. Perhaps their knowledge of McCain's personal history fed the aides' concerns – as did the aides' understanding that Washington insiders knew this context too. It would be reasonable for aides to believe, as did the authors of *Game Change*, that (like many political couples) Cindy and John McCain led largely separate marital lives. If these ideas were widely circulating in Arizona and among Washington insiders like the *Game Change* authors, it also seems likely John was aware of widespread perceptions that Cindy wandered outside their marriage. Knowing this insider perception also made it more plausible that John felt entitled to freedom from the traditional constraints of marriage. And this entire context would help explain why aides would worry that McCain's public appearances and occasional plane flights with Iseman might start tongues wagging. Similar behavior by a senator with a different personal history might pose less danger to that politician's image.

The aides' concern was relevant to voters not only because it penetrated behind the public "maverick" persona to the backstage reality, but also because McCain's open hobnobbing with lobbyists could undermine public confidence in his judgment by raising appearances of impropriety. Those concerns would later become more salient in light of the reportedly reckless manner in which he chose a running mate (as described by *Game Change*). Incidentally, the core claim that aides were worried about McCain's image being breached and asked Iseman to stay away from McCain was supported by both the *Post*'s and the *Times*' original stories, a detail that got lost in the controversy over the latter paper's adultery allusion (Birnbaum & Shear 2008; Rutenberg et al. 2008).

Game Change was itself widely criticized for quoting and relying on unnamed sources. Even if the book's assertions cannot be definitively confirmed (a point that could also be made about many descriptions of history and many anonymously sourced news stories), they can be taken as reflecting Washington's insider culture. It seems unlikely that the two reporters would risk their reputations and livelihoods by filling their book with quotes and observations that other journalists or political elites could readily refute. Although the book received a lot of criticism, the claims about the McCain (and Clinton) marriages were not refuted, or even widely attacked, on factual grounds.

In any case, focusing on the *Times*' purported misbehavior steered journalists' attention away from the more substantively important evidence that McCain was serially unfaithful to his vows of fighting for the little guy against the special interests. The irony is that, in denouncing the *Times* for sloppiness or bias, the rest of the main-stream media were themselves committing mediocre journalism. They omitted information they knew to be relevant to explaining the *Times*' reporting and to judging the truth of the adultery innuendo. And they concentrated more on the alleged journalistic scandal than on the substantive potential scandal involving McCain's taking favors from organizations with business before the Senate committee he chaired. In this instance, then, media slanted the news to favor McCain.

With this information, it becomes harder to lambaste the *Times*. However, once the scandal focused on journalistic rather than official misconduct, the purportedly villainous news outlet had trouble defending itself. In theory, the *Times* could have responded by pointing out the context known to Washington DC denizens (and mentioned in *Game Change*). In practice, the *Times* knew that pressure and attacks for being biased against McCain and Republicans would only have redoubled at such a response. Americans had essentially no opportunity to deliberate over the substance of the *Times* story. The *Times* itself didn't explain the context of its investigation and more or less stood back and took its lumps from critics. Nor did the *Times*' competitors come to its defense. The rest of the mainstream media left their adversary twisting slowly in the wind or joined in condem-nation (Taranto 2008). That itself suggests a limitation to the media's dedication to examining different versions of truth. In this case, given what Heilemann and Halperin report, it is also evidence for a mechanism that overrides the process/game schema (or what I call decision bias), encouraging journalists – many of whom, like the *Game Change* authors, knew of the internal deliberations about the *Times* story in the McCain camp (Ambinder 2008) – to hold back on this aspect of the horserace narrative.

Consequently, even an attentive audience member would have little basis to conclude anything but that the nation's leading newspaper made an unsubstantiated charge, violating professional standards of neutrality and perhaps letting personal views bias their reporting. However, as a purely empirical matter, the notion that the *Times* or other major media exploit rumors about Republican sexual peccadilloes while letting Democrats off the hook cannot be squared with the record, from Gary Hart and Bill Clinton to Elliot Spitzer (governor of New York and long-shot presidential hopeful who resigned from office when caught using expensive prostitutes in 2008). And in forbearing from clarifying the McCain matter, they reinforced the Republican Party's continued "ownership" of the trait of morality. Given the findings in this and the previous chapter, there is little or no evidence buttressing the continuing ability of Republicans to brand themselves as exemplars of morality in comparison with the randy, unconventional Democrats. That superior moral image remains a significant factor in the public's judgment of the two parties (Hayes 2005).

With respect to the Clintons, the potential scandal might seem even more newsworthy than the McCains'. News about Bill's renewed philandering fits the stereotyped novelty bias, and it explains one great mystery of 2008: why Hillary received relatively little support from the party establishment. From *Game Change*, we learned that some important Democratic insiders dreaded that mainstream media would swarm over a new Clinton marital saga, dissolving any Hillary candidacy in multiple spasms of distracting melodrama. No wonder Senate Majority Leader Harry Reid and other party titans neither coalesced around the heir apparent nor pressed the upstart Obama to wait his turn. Yet again, the media looked the other way. They held off reporting the horserace as well as they might have, and in doing so passed up great opportunities for sensational scandal.

Analyzing media coverage of *Game Change*

The 2010 publication of *Game Change*, with its plenitude of sensational disclosures and potential political scandals involving presidential and vice presidential candidates, afforded another opportunity to evaluate how the media scandal machine actually works. For a work of non-fiction, the book was a blockbuster; it was among the top ten on the *New York Times'* list of best-sellers for 13 straight weeks, and had a first print-run of 150,000. To see how the media covered the book's revelations about the McCain and Clinton marriages, a search was conducted in LexisNexis of the *New York Times*, *Washington Post*, ABC, CBS and NBC (evening news and Sunday morning news talk shows), and *Newsweek* magazine, over the period April 15, 2009 – April 14, 2010. Since the book was published in January, 2010, this period captures all the coverage surrounding its publication. Using the search terms *Game Change* and *Halperin*, the name of the book and one author, virtually all mentions of the book in these major news outlets were retrieved.

Since a primary goal was to find how the media responded to the book's revelations about the McCain and Clinton campaigns' worries over and strategies for handling infidelity issues, compared to other potentially scandalous disclosures, the numbers of mentions for each key political player were tallied: Barack Obama (131 mentions), Sarah Palin (71), John McCain (40), Hillary Clinton (32), Bill Clinton (29), Joe Biden (15) and Cindy McCain (4). Curiously, the bulk of the publicity focused on an unfortunate word choice by Senate Democratic Leader Harry Reid, reported by the book as praising Obama for not speaking in "Negro dialect." In the sample, the phrase "Negro dialect" appeared 20 times, and Harry Reid's name was mentioned 120 times, far more than anyone else's including every presidential and vice presidential candidate except Obama.

None of the sampled media mentioned the book's revelations about John McCain and his Pandora's Box. One did include a brief mention of Cindy's "long-term boyfriend" – in a *Times* book review of *Game Change*. Bill Clinton's sexual peccadilloes as a factor in Hillary's campaign were alluded to four times: in *Post* and *Times* book reviews, on ABC *This Week*, and on NBC *Nightly News*. All of the references were very brief and oblique; none clarified the role of Bill's philandering in Hillary's failure to win the nomination.[3]

The evidence so far suggests that by 2008 – contrary to the critics of the press's sensationalism – mainstream news organizations shifted toward downplaying most sexual allegations against the highest-level politicians unless supported by solid evidence. Perhaps journalists became more reluctant to fully investigate marital misconduct after the ongoing sex scandals around Clinton came to irritate more than interest some audience members. Many journalists agreed the Lewinsky scandal was a low point for the profession (Kalb 2001). This is certainly a defensible stand, and such normative matters will be taken up in the book's conclusion.

Covering (up) John Edwards

John Edwards offers another example of a presidential hopeful's marital infidelity remaining essentially unknown and politically irrelevant despite circulating widely online and among the Washington elite. This section focuses on what we might call the "pre-journalism stage," where information available outside the beltway is limited to the low-credibility tabloid media and Internet sites. The Edwards case further supports the finding that the Internet media are not yet game changers themselves. Through the 2008 campaign, it remained true that a scandal didn't exist until the mainstream national media picked it up. And those outlets hesitated to seize on presidential-level sex scandal, even one as sensational as that of former vice presidential nominee Edwards. As shown by their diffident approach to McCain, the major media seemed far more eager to turn the spotlight on one of their own, to develop a potential media scandal rather than a sex scandal. News organizations might well judge that media scandals sell better than sex scandals, especially if the sexual malfeasance lacks definitive proof. In addition, criticizing a national media outlet would likely generate less political pressure from angry elites, advertisers and party loyalists than attacking a presidential candidate, especially in a time of intense partisan polarization.

The sexual suspicions surrounding former presidential candidate John Edwards were first detailed in the widely circulated supermarket tabloid the *National Enquirer* on October 10, 2007, after which the story was readily available on the Internet and the affair easily accessible to national political reporters. Yet when Edwards "abruptly ended his presidential campaign," as the *Times* put it (January 30, 2008), there was no hint in that paper, the *Post* or *USA Today* that the threat of sex scandal might have influenced this decision. The tawdry Edwards saga went public only when the *Enquirer* published incriminating pictures of Edwards at a hotel where his lover was staying with their child. Finally, with its third story, the *Enquirer* entered the mainstream (see Perel 2011 for an inside account of the *Enquirer*'s probing into Edwards's affair; see also Hoyt 2008).

In one sense, the intense publicity given to the sorry sex life of a Democratic *ex*-presidential candidate raises questions of partisan calibration when compared with the media's failure to clearly inform the public about the possible infidelity, poor judgment and conflict of interest involving the Republican Party's actual 2008 nominee. In another sense, however, what might seem inexplicably arbitrary or politically biased – the thorough humiliation and destruction of privacy experienced by Edwards's family, set against the relatively gentle treatment received by McCain's – actually reveals the main-stream media's disinclination to pursue presidential sex scandals unless other forces in the system promote that choice. Among those forces, the blogosphere and websites by themselves remained a minor influence, because mainstream reporters and editors seemed readily to converge on a judgment that they should often ignore whatever is circulating there. Of course this could change in ways that are not predictable, as traditional newspaper and broadcast news outlets lose dominance or transform themselves into online hybrids. As of the 2008 election, though, the mainstream media still ruled (and dominated the traffic to online news sites, see Hindman 2008; on the eroding but still dominant broadcast news audience, see Pew Project for Excellence in Journalism 2011).

Conveniently, *New York* magazine assembled a time-line tracing the development of the Edwards story. It took nearly a year for the information that began circulating on the Internet to break into the mainstream news cycle. Had Edwards avoided Rielle Hunter's Beverly Hills hotel room, it might never have come out at all, or when it finally did hit the mainstream might have been a minor story, one more easily – though only temporarily – denounced and denied ("John Edwards's docudrama: the anatomy of innuendo (updated)" 2007). As with Clinton, the DNA doomed him to exposure. The point here is that Edwards was able to postpone even this explosive sex scandal in all its tawdry prurience – a serious presidential candidate tangled up with an offbeat, New Age lover and their love child, hush money, videotaped sex and much more – for the better part of a year, despite insiders' knowledge.

The first appearance of the rumor was in the conservative *New York Post*'s page-6 gossip column (August 27, 2007). It read: "WHICH political candidate enjoys visiting New York because he has a girlfriend who lives downtown? The pol tells her he'll marry her when his current wife [Elizabeth, stricken with advanced breast cancer] is out of the picture." This item was then subject of comment on the *Huffington Post*, an aggregator of blogs and producer of some original writing. A month later (September 26) the *Huffington Post* reported the disappearance of campaign videos from John Edwards's website: videos shot by Rielle Hunter, who, it was later revealed, had become Edwards's campaign videographer – and lover. The next day, the liberal-left blog *Daily Kos* criticized the story for spreading malicious rumor. Then on October 10, the *National Enquirer* ran a story under the headline "Presidential cheating scandal! Alleged affair could wreck John Edwards' campaign bid" (2007). The Edwards campaign said the story was "false, absolute nonsense," although even this denial didn't get any attention from the mainstream outlets.

On the same day, the *Huffington Post* reported that Hunter's video company received over $100,000 for the campaign videos and identified her as a well-known participant in the New York party scene who once dated the novelist Jay McInerney and even inspired a major character in one of his books (McInerney 1988). Also that day, conservative talking head Ann Coulter mentioned the *Enquirer* story on MSNBC, leading to another denunciation from *Daily Kos*. The next day, *Slate* online magazine's Mickey Kaus, a prominent member of the punditocracy, published "Emerging Edwards scandal?" criticizing the mainstream media for "strenuously trying to not report" on the allegations. Also on October 11, Jezebel.com offered "Is John Edwards cheating on his cancer-stricken wife?" and Wonkette.com, "Did John Edwards sleep with this lady?"

October 11 was when *New York* magazine's website compiled the above chronology, which went on to predict that within a week "growing Internet buzz" and coverage by tabloids would lead a respected mainstream media outlet to break the story. What actually happened was a question from an AP reporter that Edwards answered by saying the allegation was "completely untrue, ridiculous . . . just false." This response was published, according to a LexisNexis search, only by two conservative papers, the *New York Daily News* (October 12, 2007, p. 13) and *Washington Times* (October 12, 2007, p. A09).

New York magazine's website prognostication, in October 2007, that the mainstream media would certainly break the story soon, was in keeping with the conventional misunderstanding of scandal dynamics analyzed by this book. It also pointed to the tendency for some observers to exaggerate the blogosphere's role in politics. To become politically meaningful, sex charges must receive prominent play on the major network news shows, and spawn front-page coverage in the *New York Times* and other leading papers, the wire services, and cable TV talk and infotainment shows. Rarely if ever does material originating in a blog or elsewhere on the Internet create political consequences by itself. The Edwards case also suggests, again, that the mainstream do not jump all over sex scandals, even when it involves a top-tier presidential candidate and a love child. In this case, the candidate dropped out under pressure from his staff, who knew the story was true.[4] Still the major media ignored the sex angle – as was true of the way they puzzled over Bob Dole's campaign tactics – and covered Edwards's sudden withdrawal as a surprise. Ignoring the story had political consequences even after Edwards was no longer actively contending for president. By only "suspending" his campaign, he stayed in the race for the vice presidency and orchestrated an elaborate, well-publicized courtship ritual that had both Obama and Hillary Clinton seeking his presumably valuable endorsement as they fought out the rest of the primary season. The media covered this ritual without providing the context of Edwards's looming marital implosion.

One might view the media's decision to collaborate with Edwards in covering up his affair as ethically defensible (on grounds that included sparing his cancer-stricken wife Elizabeth public humiliation). But the key point is that this case reveals how the mainstream media retain the power, despite the blogosphere's infinite rumor-mongering capacity, to make a scandal a real factor in politics. At least as of 2008, by tacitly agreeing to keep relevant information out of their own channels, the mainstream media still had the ability to protect a politician's campaign (in Edwards's case, his drive for another vice presidential nomination) as they did for George H. W. Bush and Robert Dole back in the 1990s, before the blogosphere came into being.

The Internet's role in the production of scandal

Having dissected the aborted sex scandals of 2008 – scandals blocked despite the sensational evidence and gossip circulating through the Internet – we turn to the Internet's role in scandal more generally through a case study of ProPublica, a Pulitzer Prize-winning investigative journalism organization that publishes on the Internet. This analysis is needed in part since even the most insightful writers sometimes overestimate the transparency and ready access to information afforded by the Internet and associated digital technologies (Sifry 2004; Trippi 2004; Castells 2009; Sifry 2009). Take the vision described by Micah Sifry, co-founder of the Personal Democracy Forum and senior technology advisor to the Sunlight Foundation, for example:

> We are heading toward a world in which one-click universal disclosure, real-time reporting by both professionals and amateurs, dazzling data visualizations that tell compelling new stories, and the people's ability to watch their government from below (what the French call sousveillance) are becoming commonplace. Despite the detour of the Bush

years, citizens will have more opportunity at all levels of government to take an active part in understanding and participating in the democratic decisions that affect their lives. (Sifry 2009, p. 43)

In this "see-through society," as Sifry calls it, we are all watchdogs and there is little space for malefactors to hide. This portrait has clear implications for the dominant account of scandal politics, with its assumption – rooted in the Watergate experience – that truth eventually comes out and cover-ups don't work. If that truism held in the 1970s, before the Internet, it should hold even more thoroughly in the twenty-first century. As a matter of fact, Feldstein (2010, pp. 195–7 and ch. 12) suggests, cover-ups of major corruption often worked quite well before and after the Watergate break-in during the 1970s. Fast-forward about 40 years and scandalous information circulating online remained functionally invisible to the political process until the traditional media spread it to their mass audiences – and to elites, who rightly assumed scandal charges only count politically if those mass media switch on their spotlights.

This last point warrants a broader examination in an age of sometimes unfettered Internet optimism. By most measures, the direct impact of the blogosphere on the production of the news most Americans consume remained modest through the century's first decade. Few major news stories originated in the blogosphere or other new media, as Hindman (2008) and others have noted. Even in 2010, Pew Research found that "most of what the public learns is still overwhelmingly driven by traditional media – particularly newspapers" (Pew Project for Excellence in Journalism 2010). Furthermore, despite the significant inroads made by a handful of websites like *Huffington Post*, the blogosphere remained dependent on mainstream outlets for content. At Yahoo News, the leading website in terms of traffic, almost all of the news – 99 percent – was aggregated from elsewhere, primarily wire services like the AP (Pew Project for Excellence in Journalism 2010). Similarly, statistician Nate Silver's (2011) analysis of which news outlets are most often cited online traced the majority of references relating to original reporting by traditional, legacy media sources. With AP newswire leading the pack, the top five sources were exclusively comprised of major traditional news media, including the *New York Times*, Reuters, the *Wall Street Journal* and Bloomberg News. These findings provide further support for Hindman's hypothesis of a hierarchical web dominated by a few powerful voices. As the Federal Communication Commission (FCC) concluded in its assessment of the news market, the Internet brought an abundance of outlets and choice, but this "growing number of web outlets relies on a relatively fixed, or declining, pool of original reporting provided by traditional media" (FCC 2011, p. 123).

These conclusions are consistent with our analysis of the diffusion of potential scandal stories through traditional versus online/new media sources. Further on this point, a content analysis of mentions of investigative stories tracked but not necessarily originated by ProPublica itself, over a six-month period, suggests that only rarely do online stories garner significant national attention and become scandals characterized by both high-magnitude publicity and substantial political impact (see chapter 2).[5] ProPublica defines the universe of scandals based on three main criteria, which are generally consistent with, but not sufficient for, this book's definition of scandal. Their criteria include: (1) a clearly identifiable alleged act of wrongdoing by a person with power; (2) that alleged wrongdoing violates the public trust or harms the public; and (3) the track record of the source or sources making the allegation must be sufficiently credible ("ProPublica journalism in the public interest: how we do it" 2010).

Consistent with the book's focus, this section only considers investigations involving wrongdoing by national political figures or executive-branch federal agencies as major potential scandals of general interest to the mainstream media. According to these criteria, a total of ten potential national scandals were tracked by ProPublica over the six months from November 2009 to April 2010. Of these, two – a controversy regarding Republican National Committee (RNC) officials' use of donor funds to attend a bondage-themed nightclub in Los Angeles, and the problematic track records of contractors receiving economic stimulus funds – began online rather than in the traditional, mainstream media.

Only the RNC story involving (sub-presidential) sex and money generated substantial coverage in the mainstream national media.[6] Within the three-week period after the story broke in the online news site the *Daily Caller*, a total of 14 stories related to the affair ran on the three major networks, and 36 in the *New York Times* and *Washington Post*. The low-social-impact RNC scandal received significantly more coverage than ProPublica's investigation of stimulus appropriations, which found that some of the funds were awarded to contractors with serious violations in such areas as worker safety and hiring practices. The potential impact of these violations on the public welfare was substantial – taxpayer dollars were going to firms that discriminate, put workers at risk, do shoddy work or even fail to provide important services (Grabell 2009, 2010). ProPublica's initial investigative report ran in May 2009 and a follow-up appeared in

January 2010. Despite the gravity of the problems, during the six months studied, only 2 stories in the major national media outlets searched (ABC, NBC, CBS evening news and Sunday talk shows, and *USA Today*, the *New York Times* and the *Washington Post*) addressed the issue.

This lack of attention reflects a larger tendency. Despite awards and elite media connections, ProPublica's exposés rarely affected politics. According to LexisNexis, during the period studied, only two broadcast stories and 14 newspaper articles in network news and national newspapers even mentioned the organization by name in conjunction with any of its investigations; 5 other stories mentioned ProPublica in the context of its Pulitzer Prize, the first for an online news organization.[7] Even ProPublica's award-winning reports (Fink 2009) on the life-and-death challenges of delivering medical treatment during Hurricane Katrina attracted little or no attention before the Pulitzer announcements. Between publication in August 2009 and the Prize announcement on April 13, 2010, the investigation wasn't followed up on or even mentioned in any of the top 9 national news outlets (though the *New York Times* ran 2 stories on related subjects, including one examining root causes of the difficulties hospitals faced during Katrina).

According to the evidence here, rather than stimulating a scandal cascade, most online stories fail to trigger the media and government actions and reactions necessary for political impact and accountability. Even when the online world is abuzz with thousands of posts, if the matter doesn't cross over to the traditional media – and very few do – it does not become a politically meaningful scandal. For a scandal to take life, a scandal frame must be applied, repeatedly and prominently, characterizing the behavior in question as problematic, assigning blame at the individual level, and receiving moral condemnation from a range of respected actors. On a national level, when it comes to those in power, such sustained and cohesive condemnation demands credible evidence. This must usually come either from government inquiries, reports and leaks; from confessions by miscreants; or from journalistic investigative reporting. The latter remained largely the province of the traditional mainstream media, although they all mounted substantial web presences by the twenty-first century, developing blogs, Facebook pages and Twitter feeds, thereby becoming a hybrid of traditional and new media.

Despite the limited role that new independent media organizations played in investigative reporting, changes in the media landscape during the first decade of the 2000s did begin to influence the way that scandals and other political stories developed. Through their ability to provide feedback and occasionally original information directly to the gatekeepers at the traditional media, ordinary citizens gained potential to become more involved in the scandal process. News editors reported that traffic statistics and real-time reader responses to 140-character "tweets" sent out by their staffs affected editorial decisions (Brady 2009).[8] By 2010, social media became key components of the information environment in which gatekeepers decided what's worth reporting. Through calling friends' attention to scandal reports via Twitter, Facebook and the like, citizens could spread interest and heighten pressure from audiences for mainstream media to keep digging into a nascent scandal. The influence of hits, links, votes and other measurable forms of reader/citizen activity within the media (and scandal) ecology and the multidirectional relationship between elite blogs and mainstream media has been noted by researchers (e.g., Wallsten 2007). Digital media also served as a source of story ideas for traditional outlets (Pew Project for Excellence in Journalism 2006). For example, in 2011, the online sexual exploits and photos of former congressmen Chris Lee (R-NY) and Anthony Weiner (D-NY) first appeared in the online outlets Gawker.com and BigGovernment.com respectively, before traditional media investigated and covered the story for the wider public.

On occasion, online political communication can stimulate attention from the mainstream media, which then mobilizes citizen involvement that in turn stimulates still more media interest. The classic example occurred in 2006, when Senator George Allen (R-VA) addressed an Indian-American videographer with an archaic racial slur during a campaign stop. Footage of his "Macaca" gaffe went viral through YouTube. Then, Karpf (2010, pp. 156–7) notes, "the DailyKos [liberal blog] community acted as an amplifier of sorts." In addition to spreading the story and keeping it alive, the online community also mobilized the opposition to Allen: "reacting to the same latest intrigues that were covered by the mainstream media, but adding an infusion of vital campaign cash" to Allen's opponent.

Conversely, citizen engagement through new media can help to mute a burgeoning scandal. Researchers in the UK tracked the development of a scandal from initiation to a quiet close, following the complex, multiparty back-and-forth between old, new and "renewed" media – old media that incorporate new media forms. Chadwick's case study (2010) of the Gordon Brown "Bullygate" affair, in which the British Prime Minister was accused of harrying his staff, finds that activists within the social media contributed to the eventual muting of the potential scandal by quickly and effectively discrediting its key source. This experience illustrates the Internet's ability to enable "non-elite activists to use digital practices to intervene in, and sometimes contest, television and press coverage of politics" (Chadwick 2010, p. 9). However, the truth of the accusation was never definitively refuted so the activists' influence might or might not have advanced government accountability for what would be in any case misconduct with low social impact.

Just as low-circulation magazines like the *New Republic* or *National Review* were long able to influence the agendas, themes and memes of the mass-circulation national media, so in the twenty-first century did a few popular blogs and other websites unaffiliated with traditional media organizations come to play an occasional role. In essence, the webscape expanded the cascade system to include some new outlets that can help activate and spread (or block) information along the network hierarchy. A small, fairly stable group of A-list and institutional blogs and websites (Adamic & Glance 2005; Wallsten 2007) dominated audiences' attention, garnering the bulk of traditional media notice, and receiving most links and mentions (Karpf 2008; Hindman 2008). These outfits added a degree of diversity to the competition for coverage in the mainstream media. But the major national media outlets that this book explores remained into the twenty-first century the ones whose news decisions determined the scandals (and other agenda items) that most consistently and significantly influenced politics.

As a final illustration of this conclusion, consider two more aborted sex scandals. One involved former Vice President Al Gore. Shortly after announcing the dissolution of his marriage, Gore was hit by allegations, once again in the *National Enquirer*, of committing a "sex attack" on a masseuse he'd hired at a Portland, Oregon, hotel ("Portland DA: criminal prosecution possible in the Al Gore sex scandal" 2010, June 23). Although charges were never filed against him, there was considerable evidence that something untoward might well have happened. This included the late hour and length of time that the woman spent in Gore's room, along with other women making similar allegations. This sensational story did not ignite a scandal cascade and was covered briefly and dismissively by the mainstream media even while attracting salacious attention in the blogosphere. Some observers might explain the Gore non-scandal by reference to liberal media bias, though – as this book shows – that inference ignores a lot of evidence.

And consider another explosive still-born sex scandal that could have harmed conservative Republicans. It involved the no. 3 man at the CIA, Dusty Foggo, along with the CIA director. Foggo's alleged corruption included acting as sexual procurer for

Rep. Charlie Wilson (R-TX) and others, and organizing intimate poker and drinking parties at the Watergate (of all places in Washington), allegedly including prostitutes. More importantly, Foggo steered CIA contracts to politically connected companies that paid kickbacks to Rep. Randy "Duke" Cunningham (R-CA). And he was appointed over many more senior people by his close friend, former Congressman Porter Goss (R-AL), when the latter became CIA director. Goss himself resigned suddenly in May 2006, around the time Foggo was named as a suspect (Think Progress 2006; Stern, Kammer, Calbraith & Condon 2007). As reported by CNN.com, Goss refused to explain his sudden departure to the media, saying it would remain "just one of those mysteries" ("Goss: CIA resignation 'one of those mysteries,'" 2006, May 6). Despite the sensational elements – malfeasance atop the CIA, booze and prostitutes at the Watergate, bribery of congressmen – the story faded quickly, with little notice from mainstream media. A search in LexisNexis reveals that the major network news operations mentioned the case in about 20 sentences over the two years or so it played out in the courts. It never came close to attaining sufficient magnitude to be perceptible by ordinary citizens.[9] Yet it featured about as many sensational elements as could be imagined for a scandal narrative, and also revealed costly corruption at the heart of the CIA, an important bulwark of national defense and homeland security.

The Gore and Foggo non-scandals illustrate two primary points of this chapter: mainstream media were not eager to exploit every sex scandal, even some really juicy ones; and, at least when it came to those with great power and influence – as opposed to backbench Congress members such as Weiner and Lee – the Internet made little difference to the transparency of official misbehavior in the private realm. Many observers of American politics might approve this situation, and we'll return to the normative issues in the conclusion of the book. Note that the public can have ambivalent reactions to evidence of malfeasance (Canel & Sanders 2006, p. 82), rather than – as implied by much of the writing on scandal – eagerly seeking it. In the Foggo matter, after 9/11 we might expect public opposition to any undermining of the CIA's credibility, along with hesitancy on the part of opposition party elites. So neither ordinary citizens, nor news executives, nor national security elites had strong motivations to pursue this scandal. Low motivation among key players in the scandal process can trump evidence, sensationalism, relevance to the political horserace and other attractions of reporting scandal. This point suggests again the need to deploy multi-factor explanations of why some misdeeds ignite and others sputter out.

One of these factors is the realm in which the alleged misconduct occurs. In fact, Foggo's malfeasance involved more than merely sexual escapades. It concerned official corruption of the national security apparatus, yet still did not excite much media interest. In chapters 3 and 4 we've seen that, despite widespread impressions to the contrary, scandals of misconduct in the private realm do not necessarily throw mainstream media into a frenzy, even when the revelations could be sensational, surprising and revealing. Many will see this finding as a good thing for privacy rights and for democracy; the book will return to these normative assessments in the conclusion. We now turn our attention to the social and governmental arenas, where the stakes for democracy are clearer.

5

Dodging Scandals – and the Draft

In 1988, Republican vice presidential candidate Dan Quayle's avoidance of the Vietnam war sparked a scandal from which his reputation never quite recovered. Although George W. Bush had used similar maneuvers to avoid active service in Vietnam, his actions never even threatened to became a scandal during the 2000 presidential campaign. After discussing the differences between two Republican scandals, one potential and one actual, we add Democrat Bill Clinton's draft evasion and explain why it was covered more like Quayle's in 1988 than Bush's in 2000. Chapter 6 then considers the Rathergate controversy of 2004, which arose when Bush's avoidance of Vietnam finally received prominent press scrutiny. The transmogrification of a scandal arising from a future president's power abuse and norm violation to one centering on then-CBS anchorman Dan Rather puts the finest possible point on the political consequences of uncalibrated scandal production.

Quayle, Bush and Clinton were born within eight months of each other between 1946 and 1947. That made them eligible for the military draft in the late 1960s, at the height of the Vietnam war. Quayle and Bush, scions of wealthy, powerful conservative families and supporters of the war, each used family connections to leap over long waiting lists and land a spot in the National Guard. This was hardly unusual; most other sons of the elite did the same (T. C. Wilson 1995; Bates 1996). Nonetheless, service in the Guard during Vietnam was not what it would become during the Iraq war 40 years later. In 1968, entering the Guard offered nearly a 100 percent guarantee of *not* being sent to fight overseas. Being in the Guard protected men from being drafted into the active military. Of the more than 2 million military personnel who served in Vietnam, fewer than 9,000 were Guard members (0.0045 percent), and their death rate was a third that of the regular service (Leebaert 2003, p. 351).[1] The publicity that enveloped Quayle but not Bush for using the Guard to avoid Vietnam involved violating social norms and ideals for men of their generation and exploiting the power of their families to garner slots in the Guard. Only Quayle was tagged with misrepresenting himself as a hawkish, conventional American patriot despite a record befitting a stereotypical antiwar draft dodger. All of this raised questions about Quayle's moral fiber, diminishing his political capital. Bush's avoidance of such questions was equally consequential for his career in politics. Because both are Republicans, partisan differences do not enter the equation, enabling us to focus more precisely on the other forces. Contrasting the media's treatment of them to that of Clinton helps fill in the puzzle.

A fruitful way to reveal the rhetorical choices that connote "scandal" in the media and that differentiate the treatments of Quayle and Bush is through a framing analysis (see, e.g., Entman 1991, 1993, 2004; Reese, Gandy & Grant 2001; Entman et al. 2008; Matthes & Kohring 2008). Word choice is vital in determining whether private behavior and character will be interpreted as scandalous. Different words can activate quite distinctive mental associations, or in some cases no associations at all. Framing in the media can determine how likely people are to notice, understand, react emotionally, remember and alter their evaluative criteria and weights in response to unfavorable information about politicians.

Biographical facts about the military service records of candidates can be more or less neutral, depending on the mental associations that the frame encourages through repeating particular words and images. With sufficient attention, framed as scandalous, such personal behavior can generate significant political effects (Quayle); granted less attention, framed as unremarkable biographical data, the same behavior can yield no political effects (Bush). The frame can make military experience more or less relevant to judgments of politicians' characters, their fulfillment of relevant norms and ideals for American political leaders, and fitness to symbolically and descriptively represent the larger citizenry. The analysis illustrates how similar sets of facts for the two men primed different considerations for evaluations, through framing that highlighted negative information on attributes for Quayle which were equally applicable but far less available to shape evaluations of Bush (for a discussion of priming and candidate evaluation, see Iyengar, Peters & Kinder 1982; Iyengar & Kinder 1987; Iyengar 1990).[2]

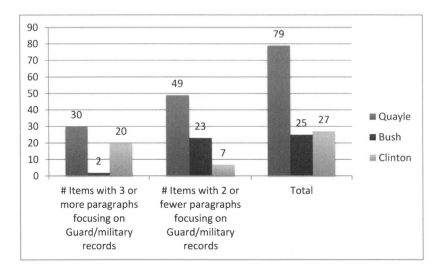

Figure 5.1 Draft dodging and presidential campaigns – comparing the magnitude of coverage

Quayle vs. Bush

As in prior chapters, our dependent variable is the magnitude of scandal coverage, which comprises the prominence, magnitude and cultural resonance of the framing. As shown in figure 5.1, the *New York Times*[3] ran three times more stories mentioning Quayle's National Guard Service in 1988 than it published referring to Bush's in 2000. The numbers are based on a LexisNexis search in the *Times* to retrieve all items using the terms *Quayle* (1988) or *Bush* (2000) within 100 words of *National Guard*. These figures understate the disparity since the sheer number of words and amount of space devoted to Quayle's military record dwarfs that devoted to Bush. (Clinton will be discussed shortly.) In fact, whereas 30 items made Quayle's Guard record a major or primary topic, Bush's was a subject of only two such stories ("primary topic" meant the item contained at least three paragraphs focusing on a candidate's Guard service). Most (23 of 25) pieces mentioning Bush merely included passing references, blandly stating such facts as that he "served in the Air National Guard and was not called to Vietnam," whereas many stories and editorial items on Quayle concentrated largely on his military record.

The headlines demonstrate the thorough difference in the framing of individual stories. For instance, compare these page-1 headlines in the *Times*: "Reopening an old wound; Quayle's Guard duty in Vietnam war era puts the focus on again" (August 23, 1988, by E. J. Dionne, Jr.), and "The 2000 campaign: support of the military; military backs ex-Guard pilot [Bush] over Pvt. Gore" (September 21, 2000, by Steven Lee Myers). Such treatment made it far more likely that the public would notice and remember aspects of Quayle's military service that could activate unfavorable mental associations and evaluations.

This brings us to the resonance of the framing. The differences in culturally potent terminology are clear. Quayle's coverage contained many more words likely to trigger unfavorable mental associations among Americans, suggesting he fell short of the public's ideal image for leaders, and violated normative social obligations for his generation. The analysis searched within stories mentioning *National Guard* for the words *Vietnam* and *draft*, and their co-occurrence with *avoid* and *dodge*. For most Americans of voting age in 1988, these terms had powerful connotations, and their presence or absence would likely register in their thinking about a candidate. By 2000, the terms lost some of their zing as citizens born after the baby boom entered the electorate, but judging by the emotion the Vietnam Memorial continued to generate, and by other facets of contemporary public discourse (including the campaign strategies of presidential candidates John Kerry [2004] and John McCain [2008]), they remained evocative into the twenty-fifth century. Figure 5.2 shows that Quayle received far more coverage that linked his name to the draft and Vietnam, and in particular to avoiding or dodging them, than did Bush. Quayle was six times more likely to be covered in ways reminding audiences of the connection between serving in the National Guard and the context in which he and Bush joined: a war in Vietnam for which young men were being drafted – and from which the Guard shielded them.

During 1968–70, Bush did learn to fly the Air National Guard's (ANG's) F-102, an aircraft originally put into service in 1953 that was being withdrawn from use in Vietnam by the time he was trained on it, though it was indubitably fast and dangerous to fly. According to the Internet site www.aerospaceweb.org, which defends Bush's military service, "the Air Force lacked sufficient pilots of its own for duty in Vietnam but was unable to activate ANG units since Presidents Johnson and Nixon had decided not to do so for political reasons." So the regular Air Force needed pilots for Vietnam, and Bush could have piloted a fighter jet in Southeast Asia rather than Texas – had he chosen to enlist in the Air Force instead of the Guard.

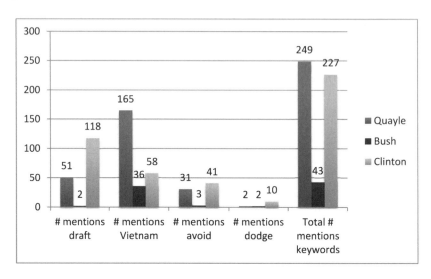

Figure 5.2 Comparative framing of candidates' draft avoidance

The comparison uses absolute counts because these are more appropriate to measure scandal magnitude than percentages. The total counts reflect the likelihood that audiences would be exposed to repeated reminders of the association between Bush or Quayle and scandalous misrepresentation. Given that Bush, as a presidential candidate, received far more attention than vice presidential nominee Quayle, the distance between them in the absolute counts becomes even more telling. Looking only at percentages of the stories that did allude to the candidates' military service: whereas the 79 Quayle items mentioned *Vietnam* an average of 2 times (165 mentions/79), the 25 Bush pieces average 1.5 mentions of Vietnam (39/25). Especially striking is that the concept of a *draft* is virtually absent from Bush's coverage, reflecting the matter-of-fact and glancing nature of the coverage devoted to Bush's military record. The very word *draft* only appears twice in the *Times*' coverage, compared with 51 times in the Quayle pieces. For American baby boomers and their families, that word in particular is highly resonant, because this large group had to grapple with Vietnam-era military conscription and the possibility of combat service and death. Audiences received few opportunities to learn or recall the link between Bush's National Guard service and his avoidance of a draft that often led to these perils.

As these figures suggest, Quayle was subject to a political scandal over his military record, and Bush was not. This was the case even though they both started in college, and remained throughout their political careers, as hawkish defenders of the Vietnam war and denouncers of the counter-culture, thus were equally hypocritical, opportunistic in using their family's power, and guilty of misrepresentation and violating social ideals. (See again figure 2.1, the middle row pertaining to violation of norms and ideals in the social realm.) Among the consequences of the disparate treatment is that George W. Bush's moral authority was little diminished by life choices he made that were essentially identical to those of Quayle, whose moral standing was damaged. Comparing Feeling Thermometers for Quayle and Bush in their respective initial election years suggests how much more negative Quayle's image was. Asked in the NES surveys to rate their feelings on a 0 to 100 degree thermometer, with 100 representing the warmest, most positive feelings, 0 the coldest and most negative, and 50 neutral, average responses were 56.6 for Bush, 46.0 for Quayle.

Substantively, using the criteria outlined in chapter 2, the Bush and Quayle infractions with regard to military service imposed only moderate social costs, though the matter is complicated.[4] Regardless, the essential point remains: the facts were roughly analogous, so, in theory, both cases had similar potential to become scandals. Before suggesting some explanations for the differences in their media *magnitude* and *political impact*, I want to restate the importance of differentiating *social effects* and *realm of behavior* from these other two traits. The disparities between the Quayle and Bush coverage are not inexplicable, irrational or random. In fact, the scandal process as this book has modeled it explains why the disproportion arose. Aside from any empirical or theoretical issue, though, is a normative one. The problem is that, from the vantage point of a citizen, the media are malfunctioning when they cover potential scandals of similar gravity in such varied ways. If the avoidance of active military service in Vietnam by a life-long, self-proclaimed patriotic war hawk amounts to scandalous misbehavior for one candidate, then the same should hold for others.

In creating a scandal around one candidate but not another when both engaged in comparable actions, the political communication system intervened, *without public awareness*, let alone public debate, in the very course of American history. Recalling that the 2000 election was decided by about 500 votes in Florida, where many retired military personnel live, it does not seem too much of a leap to suggest that framing Bush similarly to Quayle on this matter could

Table 5.1 Voter priorities in the 2000 presidential election

Issues	Voters (%)		
	Total	**Gore voters**	**Bush voters**
"Moral/ethical values"	35	17	55
"Jobs / the economy"	26	36	16
"Education"	25	31	20
"Social Security"	21	25	16

have put Democratic candidate Al Gore in the White House. (Gore himself served in Vietnam, albeit briefly.) Consider a *Los Angeles Times* exit poll on Election Day 2000 that asked: "Which issues, if any, were most important to you in deciding how you would vote for president today?" Up to two responses were recorded for each person; the four most common are displayed in table 5.1.

These numbers indicate that many found Bush's brand as the candidate representing moral/ethical values a compelling reason to vote for him. Recall also the Republicans' ownership of the *morality* trait (Hayes 2005). In addition, a *Newsweek* poll (Oct. 18–20, 2000) of 1,007 Americans showed 63 percent rating Bush "honest and ethical," as compared with 52 percent for Gore ("White House 2000: comparing the candidates" 2000). Had the media treated Bush in 2000 as they did Quayle in 1988, coverage would have raised questions about Bush's violating norms and ideals for those politicians who represent themselves as patriotic advocates of muscular military intervention. If deeper probing had raised doubts about his honesty and ethics for even a few hundred Floridians, Bush's narrow Electoral College victory might just have evaporated.

The media affected not merely election campaign outcomes, but the moral authority and credibility of the candidates once in office. The issue at this point is not whether the media did the right thing with Quayle and not with Bush. Rather, it's the way the scandal process exercises such unrecognized and inconsistent power over political history.

The worst-case scenario: Clinton

The relative slant against Quayle as compared with Bush cannot be ascribed to ideological or partisan bias, as becomes clearer by adding

Clinton to the equation. Clinton didn't serve in the National Guard, whereas Quayle and Bush did. Despite this, searching for Clinton's name within 100 words of *National Guard* still yielded 34 items (see figure 5.1), more than generated by the Bush search ($n = 25$) – even though this artificially parallel search criterion greatly understates the attention given the former Arkansas governor's military (or non-military) record. In fact, a separate search shows that the *Times* mentioned Clinton's draft avoidance more often than Bush's *during the 2000 campaign*, even though Clinton was about to retire – illustrating how firmly implanted and central the idea of Clinton as a draft evader had become in the journalistic and perhaps public's schema of him. In figure 5.2, we see the *Times* tagged Clinton in 1992 with the nastily resonant term "draft dodger" 5 times as often as it did Quayle in 1988. Even in this truncated selection of Clinton coverage, the term *draft* appears twice as much as in the Quayle and Bush depictions combined, reflecting that, for obvious reasons, the Clinton scandal was denominated more as a "draft" scandal than a "National Guard" scandal. All in all, if Quayle's was not a pretty picture, Clinton's was downright ugly.

To move beyond this use, for the sake of parallelism, of stories that mentioned the three candidates in conjunction with the National Guard, a new search in the *Times* was conducted for *Clinton*, *Quayle* and *Bush*, each within a paragraph of the words *Vietnam* or *draft*. This different search yielded 345 initial items for Clinton, 77 for Quayle, and 71 for Bush in their respective campaigns (numbers exclude brief entries in the News Summary lists). One gauge of the relative emphasis on their military-related records is a simple average of items per day. For Bush and Clinton, the campaign spanned January 1 – November 15 (one week after election day), or 319 days. Because Quayle received no substantial attention in *Times* campaign coverage before being named vice presidential nominee on August 17, 1988, his campaign lasted 90 days. The 345 items on Clinton run over 319 days yield a per-day average of 1.08. During Quayle's relatively brief 90 days on the national stage, his 77 items generate an average of 0.86. For Bush, 71 items ran, an average of 0.22 per day. By this measure, Quayle's military record received 4 times more scrutiny than Bush's, and Clinton's 5 times more.[5] Whether in absolute volume or as a daily average, the *Times* showed the least interest in Bush's military service.

Examination of the NES data in 1992 and 2000 suggests the impact of the distinctive media coverage of the potential military service scandals on public opinion. When participants were asked to rate the candidates on several traits, Bush was seen as significantly more moral than Clinton. The NES surveys for 2000 saw Bush rated as moral by 72.6% of respondents (the trait described the candidate "extremely well," said 20.9%, and "quite well," 51.7%). In 1992 Clinton was rated as moral by 48.5% of respondents ("extremely well," 5.5%; "quite well," 43.0%). Although Clinton contended in 1992 with sex and finance-related scandals as well as the draft-evasion story, it seems reasonable to infer that the disparity in morality ratings reflects in some measure the paucity of moral condemnation for Bush over draft evasion and its prevalence for Clinton.

Of course there are substantive differences between Clinton and the other two candidates. Clinton refused to serve in the National Guard, even though he already had political ambitions and knew he could damage himself by not having a military record. Like millions of college graduates, Clinton instead avoided the draft and military service entirely, by using all the loopholes available to educated people, the same ones exploited by virtually the entire elite of that generation – by members and leaders of Congress and of the major news organizations, academia and corporations.[6]

Media decision rules and cultural resonance shape scandal

Scandal framing is over-determined, shaped by many forces acting simultaneously. Even if we discuss how a particular independent variable has an important effect, then, no single cause is sufficient or even necessary; other forces are almost always operating and contributing to the outcome as well. That said, what might explain the media's lack of interest in Bush's avoidance of Vietnam, especially given their close attention to Quayle's and Clinton's?

As previously discussed, the cascade model explains scandalizing publicity by tracing the interactions among independent variables at four different levels of the political communication system: Level 1, where the variable of interest is *cultural congruence*; Level 2, *partisan elites' strategic skill*; Level 3, *media decision-making heuristics*; and Level 5, *public opinion*. Level 4 is where the dependent variable – magnitude and resonance of scandal framing – resides. As suggested in the cascade diagrams (figures 2.3 and 2.4), feedback loops connect these levels so the causal relationships are reciprocal and complicated, and the outcomes over-determined.

In this chapter we concentrate on Level 3, the heuristics or decision biases (Entman 2010a) that structure news organizations' production choices when confronted with evidence of scandalous misconduct and conflicting elite pressures to publicize or suppress it. Each of the heuristics applies more generally to the media's framing practices and power and explains why they often yield uncalibrated scandal coverage. The plausibility of this explanation emphasizing decision-making biases has already been tested by the sex scandals of chapters 3 and 4, so this chapter continues assembling evidence that similar norms and practices persistently converge in scandal production – and evasion.

Stereotype-confirming novelty

It is a truism, but a somewhat misleading one, that news is novelty. More precisely, news is novel embodiment of an existing stereotype, fulfillment of conventional expectations. If the news is too novel, too dissonant with established understandings, it becomes difficult for journalists to process or audiences to understand. That Quayle, a neophyte on the national political scene who had a lightweight reputation in Washington, and then Clinton, the purportedly slick opportunist, evaded Vietnam was news that fit right into the images mainstream national journalists had of these two politicians. Quayle and Clinton were also the first baby boomers eligible for Vietnam service to run for national office (in 1988 and 1992, respectively). By 2000 the novelty value had worn off. Vietnam was by then 25 years in the past,[7] and the idea that prominent boomers maneuvered to protect themselves against the draft was old hat. The draft evasion spasms in 1988 and then 1992 were enough to inoculate journalists against finding much novelty in yet another boomer's thin military credentials. Add to this Bush's careful cultivation of a cowboy image. He even bought a rural "ranch" in advance of his presidential campaign, although he never rode horses or raised livestock (and then purchased a home in a gated Dallas community for his post-presidential residence) (Peretz 2005; Spillius 2007). The picture of a draft dodger didn't accord with Bush's image as a patriotic man's man who backed the military in all things. Although it might seem counter-intuitive to journalists who see themselves as seeking out contradiction between image and reality, the opposite impulse tends to dominate – at least when it comes to scandal involving the most powerful politicians. New information that requires journalists – and their audiences – to rethink their understandings is less likely to attract publicity than novel confirmations of existing images.

Likeability

Journalists develop personal feelings toward the powerful folks they cover, and these affect the coverage. George H. W. Bush was by

2000 a fondly remembered elder statesman who had spent the previous eight years cultivating national journalists, and his son George W. was affable and charming in his good old boy manner (as brilliantly captured in the HBO documentary, *Journeys with George*, Pelosi & Lubarsky 2002; see also Jamieson & Waldman 2002; Bucy & Grabe 2008). He was easy enough to like. Even though his family owned a newspaper chain and was powerful back in Indiana, Quayle did not benefit from connections to a Washington dynasty; nor did he have the common touch that Bush had perfected in his years as the public face of the Texas Rangers baseball team. For his part, Clinton attracted a degree of personal venom unusual among the Washington press corps (Conason & Lyons 2000). For instance, in 1992 I had a conversation about Clinton with the late R. W. "Johnny" Apple of the *New York Times*, then a leader among national political reporters and soon to serve as the *Times'* Washington Bureau chief. Apple said, "Bill Clinton is the biggest liar I've ever covered." When I reminded him he'd covered Lyndon Johnson (Vietnam) and Richard Nixon (Watergate), Apple didn't have an answer. His faulty memory hints at the strength of his negative emotions with respect to Clinton.

How does likeability translate into a benefit of the doubt? When charges arise or evidence emerges of some potentially scandalous act, the White House press corps, or a candidate's traveling press pack, can choose to question the politician directly, repeatedly and aggressively. This is the sort of interrogation that can help initiate and sustain a scandal cascade. But it seems that warm personal feelings may deter reporters from high-energy inquiries (see Bennett et al. 2007 on the importance of good personal relationships to journalists inside the Washington DC beltway).

George W. Bush was never pressed personally about exploiting his family's connections, or the apparent misrepresentation embodied in a war hawk's avoiding active service. Being liked seems to correlate with reporters demanding less often that the politician himself respond, remaining content to pepper the press spokesperson with questions. Or if reporters do get to confront the politician in person, they avoid engaging in the kind of vitriolic follow-up queries that make for good copy, good television, bad atmospherics and defensive sound bites and body language. Thus can scandal frames be influenced by journalists' personal relationships with and sentiments toward the powerful. Much as they genuflect before the altar of truth-seeking, evidence suggests journalists (like most other people) subordinate this goal when under pressure from the powerful (Entman 2004; Bennett et al. 2007).

Pressure relief over truth-seeking

Indeed, the preference for relieving pressure over pursuing truth, a quite human trait, appears to be another of the media's standing decision biases or rules. Al Gore's Vietnam service, though brief, might ironically have worked to protect Bush, precisely because it was so cognitively accessible as a counter-frame. Focusing on Bush's draft evasion could create pressure on journalists because the contrast to Gore was so obvious. When Quayle ran with George H. W. Bush in 1988, there was no such disparity: Democratic presidential candidate Michael Dukakis had served in peacetime, and the son of vice presidential candidate Lloyd Bentsen served in the very same National Guard "champagne" outfit as George W. Bush.

Another example of this norm of trading truth for pressure reduction and its effect on scandal is the great reluctance of mainstream media to apply the word *torture* (or torture *scandal*) to practices codified as such in international treaties and carried out during the Bush administration. Labeling the US treatment of prisoners as torture would have appeared to favor one side, the Democrats, in the framing dispute between them and Republicans over anti-terrorism policies. The problem is that accepting the sanitizing, if less judgmental-sounding, terms (*harsh* or *enhanced* interrogation) preferred by Bush and his defenders also boosted one side – Bush's. Choosing between a resonant term likely to evoke a network of mental associations being promoted by one side and a more neutral-sounding term preferred by another poses a real dilemma for journalists.

One solution would be simply alternating use of the terms. In practice, however, framing contests are fought over precisely this terminological battleground and if one side wins, its preferred language will by definition predominate. *Torture* lost out because of the relative weakness and political ineptitude of those supporting that frame, along with its cultural incongruity, the dissonance with many Americans' image of their country in believing that the US might violate international law to unjustifiably harm human beings (Bennett et al. 2007, pp. 72–107). In a parallel way, one reason *draft* virtually disappeared from the media's lexicon during Bush's 2000 campaign was his team's greater skill in pressuring media, compared to Gore's (see Jamieson & Waldman 2002). As for Clinton in 1992, facing the senior Bush, a genuine World War II hero, it was hardly a fair fight. Clinton did maneuver to avoid military service of any kind during Vietnam, and given the cultural disrepute of 1960s antiwar protestors like Clinton, all he could hope to do was change the subject.

He could not attack George H. W. Bush; nor could he explain within the constraints of news formats the moral reasoning that led him and so many others of his generation to oppose military service during Vietnam.

More generally then, the scandal process can yield paradoxes of counter-framing: Journalists, anticipating or experiencing a predominance of pressure from one of the elite teams, seek (probably unconsciously) to construct a frame that forestalls negative reactions from the team that can make things the most unpleasant. If we assume news organizations try to minimize confrontations with valuable sources and to avoid such sanctions as refusals to grant interviews, they will likely go easiest on the side that threatens the most pressure. Better to provoke the party that reacts with mild annoyance than the one with vociferous anger. In this way, news organizations inadvertently exercise political power even as they also respond to it. Given what's postulated here – that the mainstream media are more concerned with minimizing pressure than clarifying truth – a key Republican advantage in scandal-framing contests with Democrats may be the GOP's successful cultivation of the notion of a liberal, pro-Democratic bias permeating the media. This widely diffused stereotype of the mainstream media (Entman 2010a) would predictably make news personnel skittish and defensive – more vulnerable to pressure from the conservative side when scandals threaten (Watts, Domke, Shah & Fan 1999; Jamieson & Waldman 2002; Alterman 2003).

Lacking a record that could be defended with simple, culturally resonant symbols, Clinton compounded his vulnerability by his notorious habit of splitting hairs and appearing evasive when questioned about this, as he had previously done regarding infidelity with Gennifer Flowers. The media pounced, reinforced by information from an energetic network of Republican sponsors (Conason & Lyons 2000; Brock 2002). The ensuing scandal cascade cemented an impression of Clinton on this particular dimension of character and morality that not only stuck, but also, arguably, created a standard that allowed George W. Bush to escape similar scrutiny. That is, Bush simply said he'd served in the Guard during Vietnam. He did not evade military service altogether, and that was enough, along with the other factors discussed, to stave off significant investigation or repeated questioning in 2000.

Popularity and power

The media are also more likely to pounce on threatening news when they sense a politician's vulnerability to a collapse of public support (see Entman 1989, ch. 3). And they are more apt to give a popular politician a pass when bad news comes up. Bush had the popularity bias working for him. He was widely perceived as reasonably popular and electable throughout 2000. Although he lost the popular vote narrowly in November, more trial-heat polls throughout the campaign showed him ahead of Gore than behind.[8] Ironically enough, his father's campaign suffered in 1988 because vice presidential nominee Quayle was aggressively and personally questioned on such matters. George H. W. Bush was seen as an unpopular political weakling, a likely loser, and that fed more aggressive treatment than his choice of Quayle would otherwise have received. Given the ultimate outcome, it might be hard to believe, but Michael Dukakis held a double-digit lead over Bush at the start of the 1988 Republican National Convention when the Quayle story broke. Then, once the story passed a threshold at which the media sensed the potential of precipitous decline in a politically weak candidate's (Bush's) popularity, momentum developed and a self-reinforcing scandal cascade ensued. The threat to the Republican ticket's political standing made it seem fair for news organizations to insist upon direct and repeated questioning of the candidate himself, in this case Quayle. A look back at the images and sounds of Dan Quayle trying to explain his National Guard career to a clamorous press gaggle offers a master class in ways a candidate can undermine himself via non-verbal communication.

The very act of responding to insinuating questions about one's character damages one's image by repeating the framing words in close juxtaposition with the candidate's name and face, activating negative mental associations (see Lakoff 2004). This makes the story even more newsworthy, contributing to the downward spiral. The George H. W. Bush campaign's brilliantly orchestrated series of attacks on Dukakis's personal character and values in the fall of 1988 (discussed briefly in chapter 3), coupled with the maladroit Massachusetts governor's responses, turned the polls around and yielded a decisive loss for Dukakis in November (Jamieson 1993). Clinton won in 1992 despite the draft evasion scandal because George H. W. Bush, running again with Quayle, ran a lackluster campaign whereas Clinton successfully portrayed the incumbent as a poor manager of the economy (see Vavreck 2009).

Cultural congruence and symbolism

George W. Bush was lucky or smart enough to have learned to pilot a jet in the Guard rather than sitting around an office, as did Quayle. This lent culturally resonant symbolic associations to Bush's service

not available for Quayle, even though neither man performed significant war-time military service for the United States. The George W.
Bush campaign circulated snapshots of Bush getting his lieutenant
bars pinned on by his father, of a helmeted Bush sitting in a fighter
jet's cockpit, and of the younger Bush in uniform squatting jauntily
next to an aircraft. These closely resembled images of a genuine Air
Force pilot. In some campaign material and quotes, Bush and his
family members even claimed that he *was* an Air Force fighter pilot
(Ivins 2000, p. 14; Corn 2003, p. 23). In fact, as discussed in the next
chapter, there is considerable evidence that Bush failed even to
execute the minimal duties he was assigned in the Guard, and by
some standards went AWOL. The main point here, though, is that
availability of the resonant visual images of Bush-as-pilot trumped
the kind of verbal defense to which Dan Quayle was limited in
defending *his* Guard service. What's more, Clinton had to defend
himself from an even weaker position by comparison – hence his far
more negative portrayal.

Conclusion

These case studies suggest that the scandal system can yield highly
unbalanced coverage, even in national campaign news, which the
scholarly literature asserts is usually balanced (D'Alessio & Allen
2000). One reason for the different finding here is that the present
case study is diachronic: it compares the framing of similarly situated
candidates at different times. Scholars typically study campaign news
synchronically, comparing candidates competing in the same election,
but this is not necessarily possible or revealing in studies of scandal
(see Entman et al. 2008). In 1988 for instance, the military record of
the Democratic vice presidential candidate bore no resemblance to
Quayle's. Senator Lloyd Bentsen (D-TX) was a quarter-century older
than Quayle and served in World War II. Comparing the treatment
of their military records would be pointless.

But the diachronic comparisons of this chapter illuminate the
scandal process. In the scandal typology of figure 2.1, when George
W. Bush, Dan Quayle and Bill Clinton evaded the Vietnam-era draft,
their misconduct fell right in the middle. Their actions affected a
segment of the public, the men who presumably went to Vietnam
instead of them (and their loved ones). The acts also transgressed
norms of patriotic fair play that governed the social obligations of
all young adult males during the Vietnam era. Yet, only two of the
three suffered politically damaging scandals because of their evasive

maneuvers. Although changes from 1988 to 1992 to 2000 contributed to the differences, the findings lend further support to the core theme of this book: the media fail to calibrate scandal not only to the underlying seriousness of the offense, but also across time and over similar misconduct.

6

Rathergate: From a Scandal of Politics to a Scandal of Journalism

On September 9, 2004, CBS's *Sixty Minutes II* broadcast an explosive story anchored by Dan Rather. It featured former Lt. Governor Ben Barnes (D-TX) confessing that, in 1968, he intervened to help George W. Bush jump over a long waiting list into the Texas Air National Guard. The report went on to allege that Bush had failed to perform his Guard duties, and that he was protected from punishment by his powerful political connections. The Guard story appeared only a couple of weeks after Democrat John Kerry's presidential hopes had been damaged by charges from the Swift Boat Veterans for Truth, a pro-Bush group, claiming that the senator did not deserve all his Vietnam combat medals. Since Kerry did at least see combat in Vietnam, however, allegations that Bush didn't even perform his minimal stateside obligations could have posed a serious political threat. By the time the dispute was over, Bush had deflected any peril so thoroughly that the scandal came to be known as Rathergate (or, sometimes, Memogate).

Not only did this scandal receive the "gate" honorific that embodies and reinforces media magnitude (see Waisbord 2004), but the label reveals the dominant focus: Dan Rather's purportedly deficient journalistic ethics in quoting possibly fraudulent memos from Bush's commanding officer. Yet the preponderance of evidence points to the essential accuracy of the Rather story (Corn 2003; R. Baker 2004; Rimer 2004; Alter 2005; Mapes 2005). Indeed, there is little evidence supporting Bush's version of events. More importantly, the White House never even disputed one key allegation published by the *Boston Globe* just a day before the *60 Minutes* story aired (see W. Robinson 2004). The media's almost total neglect of this "smoking gun" provides the core puzzle for this chapter: how could most of the media establishment cooperate in transforming Bush's well-documented, albeit decades-past, failure to fulfill his military obligations into a poorly documented scandal over journalistic malfeasance?

The *Globe*'s story showed George Bush failed to serve out the final nine months of his six-year obligation in the Massachusetts Guard, as ordered when he obtained permission to leave Texas for the Harvard Business School. Guard rules required that Bush serve 24 months of active duty for failing to report in Massachusetts, but no action was taken against him. According to the *Globe*: "Twice during his Guard service – first when he joined in May 1968, and again before he transferred out of his unit in mid-1973 to attend Harvard Business School – Bush signed documents pledging to meet training commitments or face a punitive call-up to active duty." The *Globe*'s story included several former military officers supporting the paper's interpretation of the evidence. White House spokesman Dan Bartlett admitted to the *Globe* that he "misspoke" in claiming that Bush finished up his service at a Boston-area Air Force Reserve base. Bartlett fell back on the assertion that if Bush hadn't fulfilled his obligations, he wouldn't have been honorably discharged.

In fact, the most common defense over the years whenever the Guard issue surfaced, employed by Bush and his spokespersons, was that his honorable discharge proved he fulfilled his duties (see Ivins 2000; Hatfield 2001; Corn 2003; I. Williams 2004). This argument begs the central question that spawned the scandal in the first place: did the Guard accord Bush special treatment, especially by failing to discipline him for violating orders and rules? Aside from the failure to complete his Guard service in Massachusetts as ordered, much evidence suggested Bush did not attend drills and fulfill assignments while he was in an Alabama Guard unit, where he had transferred in order to work on a political campaign. His shaky record in Alabama was the subject of the disputed memo. Rather than a defense, his receiving an honorable discharge despite serial transgressions would appear to constitute compelling evidence of special treatment and abuse of power.

Rathergate enshrined in history the falsity of the CBS report. Ironically, however, this chapter shows that the alleged sins of Rather's original reporting on Bush's National Guard service were exhibited in media coverage of the Rathergate controversy itself. These shortcomings included: failing to authenticate evidence; sloppiness with facts; credulously accepting the claims of sources with political motivations and failing to disclose those biases to the audience; quoting sources, in this case Rather himself, misleadingly out of context to suggest a conclusion reached prior to any open-minded investigation; and repeating unconfirmed canards conforming to long-held stereotypes. News of Rathergate converged on the idea that CBS committed scandalous journalistic malpractice despite journalists' inability to confirm that the memos were fake. Still less did they verify Bush's own labored, inconsistent claims about his Guard record.

Willingness to repeat the story of CBS malfeasance without concrete proof or even clarity about the underlying veracity of the original story further illustrates the importance of the target's power, position and backing in shaping scandal. In comparison with President Bush, CBS news producers and even star anchor Dan Rather were relatively powerless and isolated.

Within two weeks, CBS announced appointment of an investigative panel, and the network and Rather apologized. The notion that the documents were likely forged became implanted in political lore, and remained so for years afterward. Lisa Myers asked on NBC, for instance, how CBS could "get it so wrong" and asserted without qualification that "the typeface on the documents could only have been done on a modern word processor," a claim she didn't authenticate (Hunter 2004).

Judging by this case, outright falsehoods or misleading partial truths can become enshrined in conventional wisdom with virtually no dissent. None of this excuses CBS's problematic journalism. Story producer Mary Mapes admits misgivings about rushing the report to air on September 9, when it had originally been scheduled for late September, allowing more time for vetting. (She asserts that higher-ups at CBS ordered the early airdate to boost ratings.) Mapes's contacting the Kerry campaign to alert them about the upcoming story was clearly inappropriate (though such friendly mixing between journalists and partisans is hardly unprecedented).[1] Her reliance on Colonel Bill Burkett, who supplied the memos, even though she had doubts about his trustworthiness, was also a serious mistake. Indeed, if *60 Minutes* had omitted the memos and simply combined their Ben Barnes interview with a rehash of the previous day's *Boston Globe* story on Bush's never-denied failure to complete his service in Massachusetts, there never would have been a journalistic scandal. But CBS did use the memos, and that decision spawned Rathergate.

Reporting on the *60 Minutes II* report

Before turning to the quantitative content analytical data, consider how this extract from ABC *Nightline* (which on September 20 devoted the entire show to the memo controversy) itself exhibits the weaknesses commonly attributed to the original Rather story. Initially, Rather himself was quoted in a way suggesting his repudiation of the story's substance when he was actually admitting only its procedural failings:

Chris Bury (introducing the program):	. . . Today, CBS admitted that it could not authenticate those controversial documents that questioned the National Guard service of President Bush. Dan Rather apologized for a mistake in judgment. The network said it had been deliberately misled by the man who provided the documents to a "60 Minutes" producer. That man, a retired official in the Texas National Guard, apparently had an ax to grind. He has a long history of political antagonism toward George W. Bush.
(Off Camera) JIM WOOTEN, ABC NEWS:	(Voice Over) After 12 days, nearly 18,000 minutes, with the clock ticking down on its credibility, on the reputation and future of its most-celebrated anchorman, today's mea culpa from CBS News has sharpened and escalated the country's long-running debate about ideological bias in broadcast journalism.
DAN RATHER:	It was a mistake. CBS News deeply regrets it.
JIM WOOTEN:	(Voice Over) And for Dan Rather, it may have become a matter of survival. As the famous face out front on a report whose authenticity has now crumbled, does he personally answer for what he has described as the deceit and deception of its primary source?
DAN RATHER:	I want to say personally and directly, I'm sorry.
JIM WOOTEN:	(Voice Over) Or does his on-air apology tonight mitigate his and his network's problems? Further, does the CBS acknowledgment that mistakes were made reinforce the argument that all the networks are overly eager to broadcast stories that reflect badly on conservatives in general and in this campaign, on President Bush?

Wooten ignored (and presumably didn't know of) the *Globe* report, never refuted by the White House, which rendered the disputed memoranda moot. Again, whatever his prior record, Bush failed to show up for duty in Massachusetts and not only escaped sanction but received an honorable discharge. As discussed further below, Wooten's neglect parallels that of most mainstream journalists and can be traced to the non-self-activating nature of scandal cascades in combination with Democrats' failure to exploit the smoking gun.

Beyond that, Wooten's suggestion of liberal ideological motives comes just a couple weeks after the very same networks gave considerable and politically damaging attention to spurious claims by conservative allies of Bush that John Kerry did not deserve his Vietnam combat medals (Montopoli, Roth & Lang 2004).

The Swift Boat Veterans were led by John O'Neill, a Republican attorney in a firm closely allied to Bush interests. Beyond partisanship, he had an ax to grind, a longstanding personal and ideological feud with Kerry going back nearly four decades to the senator's time as leader of Vietnam Veterans Against the War.[2] Even assuming the Swift Boat group was right that Kerry's wounds were too superficial to merit three Purple Hearts, and that he did not deserve his medals for courage under fire – an assumption that ignores the official military records – the fact remains that Kerry served in Vietnam. In comparison, Bush evaded combat by joining the National Guard – and checking the "No" box on the application form under the question asking whether he was willing to serve overseas (Romano & Lardner 1999; Rimer 2004).[3] And as noted in chapter 5, the regular Air Force actually needed men to fly fighter jets in Vietnam, had Bush desired to serve.

As evidence for the damage to Kerry from the Swift Boat allegations, a 2004 Gallup Poll / CNN question repeatedly asked whether Bush and Kerry were honest and trustworthy. Around August 1, 2004, before the Swift Boat attacks, the two were tied with just under 50 percent of respondents rating them favorably on this score. By early September, Kerry's honesty rating was about 15 percentage points lower than Bush's. Bush's honesty ratings were stable throughout the autumn, unaffected by the Guard story. By late October, Kerry's ratings recovered somewhat but Bush still held a 5-point margin over Kerry (47–42 percent) in the proportion of respondents calling the candidate honest and trustworthy. Kerry's rating as a strong and decisive leader also suffered a sharp drop in August 2004.[4] Presumably, if the Guard story had stuck, Bush's ratings on honesty and on leadership could have suffered, rather than remaining superior to Kerry's.

The Wooten report does go on to quote Dan Rather to this effect: "What I'm saying is that we shouldn't have used the documents in support of the story." However, Wooten does not clarify the exact meaning of this isolated sentence: Rather was saying they did not need the disputed memos to make their case and therefore should not have used them. The story's main points had plenty of other support, and the White House offered no substantive evidence to the contrary. Even ignoring the *Globe*'s report that Bush failed to join a

Massachusetts Guard outfit as ordered, the CBS story shows Ben Barnes admitting he helped Bush get special treatment to join the Guard.[5] Bush has never explained his swift ascendance to the head of the 500-person queue, aside from claiming he personally did not ask for special favors, which is something of a *non sequitur* since the record shows others asked for him. There is substantial evidence that many other scions of privilege obtained similar help, including the son of the Democrats' 1988 vice presidential nominee, Sen. Lloyd Bentsen (Romano & Lardner 1999; Ivins 2000; Corn 2003; I. Williams 2004; Mapes 2005; Isikoff & Corn 2006), so Barnes's testimony is credible. Even if the memos were forged (for which the evidence is weaker than that supporting their validity, as Baker 2004, Jacoby 2004, Rimer 2004, Mapes 2005 and Blumenthal 2007, among many others, argue), the scandal did not rest on them alone, nor on the adequacy of Bush's Texas and Alabama performance. A life-saving accelerated entry into the Guard obtained through family connections was enough to taint Dan Quayle's image, as discussed in the previous chapter.

Ignoring the smoking gun

To explore the mainstream media's coverage of Bush's failure to fulfill his commitment to serve in the Massachusetts Air National Guard, a LexisNexis search of all US newspapers and wires was conducted for the week after the *Globe* story was published.[6] Only 3 stories mentioning the *Globe*'s scoop appeared,[7] even though the *60 Minutes* piece ran just a day later and offered an obvious news peg for follow-up.

A search of reporting on the Bush – National Guard controversy for a longer period, by ABC and NBC, reveals 17 and 13 stories respectively, between September 9, 2004 (the day of the CBS broadcast) and March 12, 2009.[8] Just one of these mentioned the Massachusetts angle, in a single misleading sentence (from Chris Bury on *Nightline*, September 9, 2004): "Yesterday, the *Boston Globe* claimed he fell well short of meeting his military obligation by not reporting to Air Force officials in Massachusetts, when he attended Harvard Business School." Yet, this was no mere disputed claim of a shortfall. The White House did not deny the *Globe*'s assertion that "Bush never signed up with a Boston-area unit" or that Bush failed entirely to report to the Massachusetts Air National Guard as per his orders.

Few ABC or NBC stories even noted that, just as the memos were under question, so too did questions remain about Bush's service. The mentions were just that: brief references lacking detail. For instance, on ABC *World News Tonight* a correspondent merely alluded to the underlying factual issues: "And finally this document debacle has almost completely overshadowed questions about George Bush's service in the National Guard. Questions that remain unanswered. Dan Harris, ABC News, New York." CBS itself only ran one story mentioning the Massachusetts Guard. On its low-rated morning show, Bill Plante noted: "Bush also failed to join a reserve unit in Massachusetts when he moved there, despite having signed an agreement to do so or face involuntary active duty."

A search of *Newsweek* archives on LexisNexis for the words *Dan Rather* and *George W. Bush* yielded eight stories. This is how *Newsweek*'s cover story (September 20) dealt with the Massachusetts angle: "Bush performed ground duties in Alabama, his biographers say, before enrolling in Harvard Business School. Though he technically had another year to serve, he was honorably discharged" (Fineman & Isikoff 2004). Bush's failure to report for duty in Massachusetts is glossed as a technicality though he was in violation of two orders and should have been ordered to active duty for this transgression. Only in an opinion piece published online, but not in the magazine, did *Newsweek* offer substantive analysis on this aspect of Bush's service (Clift 2004, September 24):

> The controversy over the memos overshadowed what is known about Bush's Guard service, or lack thereof. First, Bush needed political pull to land a coveted spot in the Texas Guard. Former Texas House speaker Ben Barnes, a Democrat, told Rather that he helped Bush at the request of a Bush family friend, that he did it for countless other well-connected young men and that he regretted it. Secondly, we know Bush didn't show up in Alabama when he was supposed to. There's a $50,000 reward for anybody who can vouch for him, and nobody has stepped forward. Third, the *Boston Globe* revealed that Bush never reported for Guard duty in Boston as promised when he attended Harvard Business School. Lastly, Killian's secretary, Marian Carr Knox, says the content of the disputed memos is true even if the memos were forged.[9]

This did not derail the print magazine's emphasis on the memos and CBS's miscues – nor did it prevent the endorsement of the pro-Bush frame: the story was "discredited," the documents "apparently bogus." *Newsweek*, in another web-only item, refers to CBS's "now discredited story about President George W. Bush's National Guard service" and to "apparently bogus documents involving Bush's National Guard service" (Isikoff & Hosenball 2004). Another magazine item (Hosenball, Isikoff & Gesalman 2004, p. 6) raises further questions about the documents and includes a Kerry campaign official saying "the CBS docs are probably forgeries." (This quote from Kerry's own staffer offers another demonstration of the Democrats' failure to skillfully orchestrate a scandal cascade.) By the next week another *Newsweek* web item referred simply to "forged documents related to Bush's Vietnam-era military service" (Roberts 2004).

In nearly 3,500 words, *Time*'s September 27 cover story (Gibbs et al. 2004) on the matter included less than a half-sentence on the substance of the National Guard issue (Bush's inadequate service), and even that bit misled. It suggested the controversy involved Bush's "five years" in the Guard, obscuring Bush's failure to meet his obligation to serve for six years.[10] Another story devoted mostly to cataloguing problems in the *60 Minutes* vetting process briefly quoted Dan Rather's core defense (as did most other outlets) but then inserted a most puzzling coda:

> "Those who have criticized aspects of our story have never criticized the heart of it . . . that George Bush received preferential treatment to get into the National Guard and, once accepted, failed to satisfy the requirements of his service," Rather said. That may be true and important, but it is the kind of thing better left unsaid by the subject of a media inquisition.

In other words, the story suggests Rather would have been smart not to defend the truth and importance of his report, no matter how true and important it was. The last three sentences read: "As for Bush's military records, they still contain glaring holes. But that has been largely forgotten in the recent excitement. Says a senior Administration official of the focus on CBS's predicament: 'This is the gift that keeps on giving'" (Ripley et al. 2004). So the story ended, with postmodern detachment from the fact that this very story further contributed to making Rather "the subject of a media inquisition" and to gifting Bush with plausible deniability.

Even the *Boston Globe* ignored its own smoking gun story once the media frame converged on Rathergate rather than the substantive issue. It devoted far more column inches to the journalistic controversy than to the evidence on Bush's Guard record. This nicely illustrates the self-fulfilling dynamics in scandal cascades: once a particular frame spreads and becomes a dominant schema, it becomes difficult for journalists to reframe. After all, the main story, the framed newsworthy problem, truly did become the questionable memos and allegedly biased or sloppy journalism, and the *Globe* itself apparently felt compelled to focus on that dimension – the one driving the campaign horserace and political fallout.

Accepting the Bush frame

This section assesses the morphing of a potential Bush/Guard scandal into the Rather/Memo scandal through content analysis of the two competing frames. The Guard frame defines the primary newsworthy problem as the allegations regarding Bush's service record in the National Guard. The Memo frame concentrates on the alleged problems in CBS's reporting of the story that included the memo. Stories were classified as dominated either by the Guard or Rather/Memo frame or by a mixture, based on their headlines and first three paragraphs. This content analysis included two months of coverage in the *New York Times*, *Washington Post*, *USA Today* and *Washington Times*, starting January 5, 2005, the date CBS issued its 226-page Thornburgh/Boccardi report on the controversy.[11] Stories retrieved were all those including the words *Bush* and *National Guard* in the headline or lead paragraphs. Table 6.1 displays the data.

The results indicate that the vast majority of stories focused heavily or exclusively on the document controversy rather than on the substantive scandal allegations. Notably, the three mainstream, avowedly non-ideological papers' coverage did not substantially diverge from that of the overtly conservative *Washington Times*.

Another measure of the scandal's reconstruction involved coding the adjectives that modified the words *document* or *memo* and appeared within the 59 newspaper stories retrieved for the first analysis. The analysis recorded which of three connotations was conveyed: outright falsehood/fabrication; uncertainty (e.g., *disputed* or *unauthenticated*); or possible validity (e.g., *possibly authentic*). The adjectives were only coded as applying if the surrounding context indicated they were meant to characterize the Killian memo and

Table 6.1 Media framing of the Bush/Guard vs. Rather/Memogate scandal

Source	Frames (%)			Total stories
	Bush/Guard	**Mixed/ambiguous**	**Rather/Memo**	
NY Times	10.5	5.3	84.2	19
Wash. Post	5	15	80	20
USA Today	0	10	90	10
Wash. Times	10	20	70	10
% of all stories	6.8	11.9	81.4	59

Table 6.2 Adjectives describing the Rather National Guard memo in newspapers

	False (%)	Questionable (%)	True (%)	Total mentions
NY Times	11.5	69.2	19.2	26
Wash. Post	38.6	47.4	14.0	57
USA Today	44.4	55.5	0	9
Wash. Times	52.6	31.6	15.8	19
Totals	35.1	50.5	14.4	111

Table 6.3 Adjectives describing the Rather National Guard memo – news vs. editorial

	False (%)	Questionable (%)	True (%)	Total mentions
News stories	29.3	52.4	18.3	82
Editorials	51.7	44.8	3.4	29

related letters. The documents were mentioned along with modifiers indicating their credibility 111 times.

Table 6.2 shows that the most frequently invoked modifiers connoted that the documents' authenticity was in doubt. However, a large minority asserted outright that the documents were forgeries, even though this was never proved, and relatively few assertions characterized them as valid. The variation among the papers was more substantial here, with the *New York Times* the least skeptical of the memos' authenticity and the other three ranging from about 85 percent to 100 percent skeptical. *USA Today* and the *Post* are closer to the conservative *Washington Times* than to the *New York Times*.

Separating the items into news pages versus editorial pages reveals that the latter (table 6.3), as expected, were far more opinionated, and in the skeptical (pro-Bush) direction. In fact, the op-ed pages accounted for many of the unqualified "false" adjectives, with 9 such assertions from Charles Krauthammer and other conservative *Post* columnists. The 3 from conservative *New York Times* columnist William Safire constituted the entire total for that newspaper. The view that the memos were definitely fraudulent received 15 times more representation on the editorial pages of the country's 2 leading newspapers than the view that the memos were possibly authentic. Only 1 of the 29 editorial-page mentions of the memos defended their veracity. Since the evidence the memos were forged was no stronger than that they were genuine, this table provides evidence against the claim that liberal bias colored the mainstream media's coverage of Bush's National Guard record.

The third analysis focuses on stories covering a key event subsequent to the main controversy: Dan Rather's filing of a $70 million lawsuit against CBS arising from its termination of his position at the network (September 19, 2007 – December 1, 2007). In order to obtain a sufficiently large group of stories for analysis of this far less covered incident, the search on LexisNexis was expanded beyond the four newspapers to include the "All News" category, yielding 150 print and television news stories for the lawsuit.[12] Reporting was broken down into print, TV news or TV interviews (since some of the reports were interviews rather than standard news stories). Print stories were coded based on the headlines and first three paragraphs; for television stories (which are much shorter), the entire transcript was the unit of analysis.

Coverage of the Rather lawsuit stuck with the Memogate/Rathergate frame, giving the legal action largely negative treatment. He received two opportunities to state his position in interviews on CNN (Larry King), and just one TV news story favored his side. Much treatment of Rather was condescending, if not cruel (see table 6.4).

An example of the tone could be found in CNN's *Reliable Sources*, a media criticism and analysis program hosted by Howard Kurtz, then also the *Washington Post*'s media reporter (September 23, 2007):

> KURTZ: . . . Why on earth would he go to court now? Because, Rather told me, he wants to prove that the 3-year-old story is true and to punish CBS executives with a big financial judgment. Here's how he put it on Larry King.

Table 6.4 Coverage of the Rather lawsuit

	Positive	**Mixed**	**Negative**	**Total stories**
Print	15.7%	47.1%	37.3%	102
Television	2.4%	31.7%	65.9%	41
TV interviews	0%	100%	0%	2
Total *n*	17	63	65	145

DAN RATHER, FORMER CBS ANCHOR:	It wasn't a fraud. The facts of the story were true ... The ownership and management ... sacrificed support for independent journalism for corporate financial gain.
KURTZ:	Why is Rather drudging up the darkest hour of his long and controversial career? ... Rome Hartman, you once worked for Dan Rather on the *CBS EVENING NEWS*, more recently you worked alongside him at *60 MINUTES*. What was your reaction upon hearing that he had taken this extraordinary step of suing CBS?
ROME HARTMAN, FMR. EXEC. PROD., *CBS EVENING NEWS*:	Well, Howard, more than anything, it made me sad. I just – it made me sad for him and for CBS News. I don't understand why he would choose to dredge back into the spotlight what's undoubtedly going to be remembered as the darkest moment of his career and a very dark moment for CBS News.

This excerpt from a long discussion gives an accurate flavor not just of the frame dominating *Reliable Sources* but of the mainstream media's perspective on Rather's lawsuit. Within this discussion, no one defends Rather or even lays out the key points of his story. The treatment takes as given that the memos were fraudulent, and assumes this proves the *60 Minutes* story worthless. By disregarding the bulk of the evidence that Bush did indeed receive special treatment on his way into and out of the Guard and during his service as well, media depictions of the lawsuit performed the kind of sloppy journalism for which so many denounced Rather. Ultimately, Rather's lawsuit was dismissed – because the Court found CBS did not violate Rather's contract, not because of any finding regarding the veracity of the *60 Minutes* report.

Economic limits to scandal journalism

Dan Rather's report on George W. Bush's alleged malfeasance illustrates the many economic and institutional impediments to detecting scandalous misbehavior and activating a scandal cascade. Like this story, investigative reporting often takes months or years of digging. Passing time can render findings less relevant politically and less believable as documents disappear, memories fade or witnesses die. More importantly, investigative reporting is costly to the provider, even if beneficial to the society at large. News organizations cannot capture extra earnings based on the value of the enhanced government accountability that flows from good journalism. Say an investigative story and ensuing scandal cascade put an end to a government program wasting $100 million a year. People don't buy a paper or purchase ad space in order to secure less government waste; that societal effect is external to the economic exchange. The private exchange is about individuals' motivations to satisfy their curiosity or entertainment needs,[13] and news businesses' motivations to earn revenue. Saving taxpayers' money is a positive externality, a public benefit arising out of private market transactions between the newspaper and its subscribers and advertisers. The paper might get a prize for the story and might attract a few new readers, but any boost to its bottom line would be an infinitesimal fraction of that $100 million in social benefits.

News organizations' inability to capture a fair share of the value that accrues from accountability news leads to its chronic under-production (Hamilton 2004). That situation grew worse because newspapers ceased earning monopoly profits during the 2000s. Profits from classified ads (formerly about a third of a paper's revenues) plummeted due to Craigslist, and younger people lost the habit of reading a daily paper as they turned to Facebook, Twitter, Google News and the rest. Newspapers' high profits had long subsidized the costs of investigative and accountability journalism. Policy analysts have proposed new forms of organization to produce this socially valuable information, such as non-profit or foundation-supported outlets like ProPublica (see Hamilton 2009). Unless and until these begin to flourish, the political communication system will be biased toward scandals that are the cheapest to report, simplest to illustrate visually and understand, and most likely to titillate or emotionally gratify mass audiences. Those that are expensive and complicated to report and understand tend to spawn less or no attention. The implication is that skilled power-holders wielding sophisticated public relations techniques can often gin up a simple, stereotype-confirming scandal of media malpractice – "liberally biased Dan Rather used fake evidence" – to shunt aside potential scandals that threaten to expose their own transgressions.

Other obstacles to scandal journalism further raise the cost, including reluctant informants and problematic documents. Sources typically don't want to talk. They fear getting involved in controversy or having their names publicized, houses staked out or worse. It took years to convince former Lt. Governor Barnes to speak with CBS on camera, for instance. Talking can also mean implicating themselves in wrongdoing, or at least raise questions as to why they stood by while nefarious deeds were done. When Barnes told his tale to *60 Minutes II*, he was admitting his own unethical and indefensible actions. As was certainly true in the National Guard saga, furthermore, a paper or computer trail can be hard to find, often ambiguous as to meaning, authenticity and provenance. Lacking loquacious and credible human sources or irrefutable documents, any suspicions of scandal can remain just that.

Cultural incongruence of Bush as AWOL

Returning to the cascade model, *cultural congruence* is another variable that may explain the seeming reluctance of the mainstream media to frame as a scandal the strong evidence that Bush failed to fulfill the obligations of his position with the National Guard. The prior *ethos* and stereotype of Bush in the political culture's stock of presidential archetypes established this particular politician – whatever his rhetorical and managerial limitations – as a good guy, an honest man of high character and strong religious principles and a fiercely patriotic supporter of the military. The National Guard allegations conflicted with that well-established image of George W. Bush. Central to his story was a self-admitted "irresponsible" youth and religious rebirth at 40. His story of salvation resonates deeply with Americans, and not just religious ones – ideals of redemption, personal transformation and second chances are all central to America's self-identity and political culture. One might argue that dissonance with this dominant schema helped immunize him from scandals involving the personal character that Bush enacted in the years before entering politics. The no-doubt-unconscious motivations – among journalists and their audiences – to avoid dissonance were perhaps compounded by reluctance among many in the media, inside the beltway and among the public to admit they were fooled by Bush's likeable public persona. Many admired, voted for or voiced approval of this redeemed American. He might not have seemed so righteous under careful scrutiny, but such due diligence was rare.

Bias toward reducing pressure

Beyond these standing hurdles to scandal production, intimidation by powerful people and institutions comes into play; these actors can threaten to initiate lawsuits or government regulatory sanctions, or withdraw advertising. Publishers and editors not infrequently spike controversial stories and fire individual reporters who push too hard against the powers that be.[14] In this instance, conservative bloggers who were aligned with the Republican party, as well as GOP officials, immediately denounced the Guard story and pressured Rather and CBS to recant, which CBS did.

The network's experience stood as a powerful warning to other news organizations on the perils of investigative journalism, even when the core facts of a story stand. The bigger the prey, the more powerful and nationally networked are the forces attacking the media, and the greater the risks. To compound the disincentives to pursue serious scandals involving powerful officials, as the Guard story also shows, handling the sources for investigative journalism can be a major challenge. It is hard for reporters to know whom to trust, which leaks or leads to follow, who has what axes to grind, and who's responding to which pressures. Even if grinding axes, sources might be providing at least some truthful information. In this case, Colonel Bill Burkett was apparently motivated to supply the controversial memos by personal bitterness about his failure to get a disability pension. That doesn't prove the memos were forged, but it doesn't instill confidence in them either.

The example of retired Major General Bobby Hodges, who changed his original claim that Bush was derelict in the Guard (Mapes 2005, pp. 172–3), illustrates the complexity of source motivations and the difficulty of reading them. It's not clear whether Hodges altered his story after being pressured by Bush allies or whether pressure arose only internally, even unconsciously, from his own preference for Bush to win in 2004. Mapes suggests Republican operatives did coerce Hodges to change his story. In any case, there is often no obvious way for reporters to figure out which elements of a source's shifting testimony are true. In many cases, even the testifiers themselves can't be sure – memories play notorious tricks on people and it's easy for them to convince themselves they remember something that didn't happen (Loftus 1996). It is certainly reasonable for journalists to treat a vacillating source skeptically and that alone can undermine a scandal cascade even if the allegation happens to be true.

That Hodges did change his tune helped to activate and spread the "Rathergate" scandal frame to displace the potential "Bush special treatment / AWOL from Guard" scandal frame, boosting doubts among journalists, audiences and elites alike. Whatever the truth of a counter-frame, if it's skillfully orchestrated, journalists in these circumstances have little choice but to balance original scandal accusations with defenders' ripostes. Thus actors seeking to block scandals can exploit the decision-making bias toward *relieving pressure over conveying truth*. If they are willing and able to mobilize allies and persuade, bribe or coerce sources to recant or stay silent, this norm is a potent ally for those seeking to forestall or, as in this case, redirect scandal coverage.

Aside from the forces that generally operate to reduce the number, staying power and substantive importance of the scandals pursued by the mainstream media, sometimes seemingly neutral, even random, factors play a role in shaping scandal news. Timing, motivations and just plain happenstance affected the *60 Minutes* report. According to Mapes, the Bush – National Guard story went on sooner than originally planned because, in part, new producers had just taken charge of the show. Responding to competitive pressures of other media on the trail of the same story, they were rushing to prove their mettle right away. Adding to this motivation, relative underlings such as Mapes (a producer at the time) feared alienating the new bosses who insisted on accelerating the air date. Furthermore, Mary Murphy, the new supervising producer, was on vacation the day of the broadcast; apparently failing to appreciate the stakes of the story, she didn't go to the studio. More time might have allowed all concerned to better consider the wisdom of structuring their report so heavily around the memo. It's also true that enthusiasm for getting an investigative story on the air after months or years of work, as in this case, can blind journalists to the warning signs about certain sources' credibility and lead them to rely on shaky evidence (Mapes 2005, pp. 172–4), even when better data are right in front of them (like the *Boston Globe*'s account of Bush's no-show at the Massachusetts Air National Guard).

Given more time, *60 Minutes* also might have been able to figure out ways to enhance graphics clarifying the complicated interactions and timelines of Bush's duties, whereabouts and actions. Mapes notes that the show omitted such illustrations because the story ran too long with them and, in any case, the graphics they came up with seemed confusing. The media's strong bias toward the *simple over the complex* is often critical to scandal stories. The need to simplify can work both ways. Sometimes it can damage genuinely innocent persons accused of malfeasance when their defense is multifaceted. Other times, as here, it can undermine the credibility of complex scandal charges by making thorough explanation and documentation infeasible within the confines of typical news formats. In general, the more the media are driven by intense economic competition for audiences' attention and advertisers' dollars, the harder it is to justify reporting complicated scandal information. It might be possible to place documentation on websites but few skeptics are likely to avail themselves of this opportunity and most of the believers won't need to.

Conclusion

Although journalistic lore assumes that competition yields diversity in the news, this case suggests that nominally competing media can converge on the same frame rather than conveying or encouraging vigorous debate. Not only did the Rathergate frame make for a better, stereotype-confirming story about the colorful Rather, who happened to be a competitor with the rest of the mainstream media, but also it ingratiated the so-called "liberal" media with the Bush administration at election time, when they're under special pressure and scrutiny.[15] Mapes says her defense was unable to "break through the wall" of the mainstream journalistic pack, even with the simple fact that IBM Selectric typewriters did offer a font capable of producing a "th" superscript (as in "111th Fighter Squadron") in 1972 when the memo was written, meaning that its presence did not impeach the authenticity of the Killian memo. The Rathergate scandal shows how mainstream journalism is capable of ignoring evidence in plain view when manipulators of the scandal production process exercise skill. The well-documented tendencies of national journalists to operate like a pack, combined with the Washington journalistic culture's tendency to converge on a simple conventional wisdom, apparently can discourage even minimal follow-up to scandal allegations when authorities exert sufficiently high pressure and opposition elites fail to push back, as Democrats did here.

More generally, the relentless pursuit of truth appears less important to the professional culture of US journalism, and perhaps to the larger political culture, than widely assumed. Contrary to some writing on scandals, then, fact may not eventually dominate over falsehood, nor must the preponderance of evidence necessarily trump a clever defense strategy. This is another instance of the syndrome introduced in chapter 3, illustrating that US journalism follows no coherent system for validating the truth of scandal claims that it variously accepts, attacks or ignores.

This case also raises further questions about the democratizing force of the blogosphere (see Hindman 2008). Intentionally or not, bloggers helped the Bush campaign deflect a dangerous scandal by implanting decoy issues. The blogger credited with making the first public allegation regarding the "fake" memo was actually a professional Republican activist, Atlanta attorney Harry MacDougald

(Wallsten 2004). Manipulative or ideologically blinded online populism can fail to serve the goals of democratic accountability, as it appeared to in this instance and others, such as some bloggers' obsessive (but low-impact) concern with the provenance of Sarah Palin's infant son in 2008, and others' circulation of bogus rumors about Barack Obama's birthplace (Sullivan 2009; Weigel 2010). Although Rathergate is typically cited as a landmark demonstration of grass-roots Internet activism, then, the course of this scandal is hardly a feather in democracy's cap. Aligning with our larger themes, this chapter shows how the political communication system, comprising newer online media alongside traditional mainstream journalism, remains susceptible to skilled manipulation and distraction that allow cover-ups to succeed.

7

Harkening to Other Matters: What News Looks Like When a Scandal is Silenced

This chapter maps in detail a potential scandal that did not happen, showing exactly what "not happening" looks like – and why some socially costly misdeeds never stimulate a damaging cascade of negative publicity. The malfeasance here involved a series of ethically questionable, and in some respects probably illegal, activities by George W. Bush, and by Harken Energy Corporation with the approval of Bush and its other corporate directors. As such, Harken embodied a potential scandal arising from Bush's failure to meet important social (and legal) obligations, a failure that imposed substantial costs on society.

The key actions occurred while Bush's father was president or vice president. The most important evidence of transgression by Bush is a legal memo warning him against selling his Harken stock based on inside information. Not only did Bush disregard the lawyers' admonition, selling most of his stock in 1990 after receiving inside information, but he also failed to notify the Securities and Exchange Commission (SEC) of the memo's existence until after the agency concluded its investigation of his insider trading. Bush received $848,560 in the sale, and that sum became the basis for his personal fortune. The proceeds enabled him to repay a loan from other family friends, which he used to invest in the Texas Rangers baseball team. Investing the borrowed money, he received an ownership interest disproportionate to the amount put in, and ultimately made $16 million when the team was sold.

A brief flurry of attention enveloped Harken and Bush around the time the Enron corporate scandal peaked, during July 2002. But later that year, after the *Boston Globe* published a smoking-gun story establishing the above malfeasance (Kranish & Healy 2002), almost every major media outlet ignored it. Bush's financial dealings also received minimal attention during the 2000 and 2004 campaigns. The bulk of this chapter tracks the manifestations of this scandal that never made news, exploring the tactics that helped prevent the scandalous potential from being realized, and drawing out implications.

Elements of the Harken misconduct

As we have seen, accusations against high-level politicians sometimes generate a scandal cascade before being proved or disproved. Among others, Hamilton Jordan's alleged cocaine use while chief of staff to President Carter, Ronald Reagan's involvement in Iran–Contra, and Clinton's Whitewater investments each illustrate the difficulty of confirming veracity, the ability of scandals to effloresce without much evidence, or both. Bill Clinton's Whitewater investments and related financial activities – which, like Bush's, occurred years before he became president – generated a $45 million special prosecutor investigation and thousands of news stories without yielding any evidence of lawbreaking on the president's part. Particularly if one interprets the Whitewater scandal as the norm for media behavior when allegations of presidential financial misconduct arise, given the raw material Harken provided, one would have expected it to ignite a major scandal.

In this context, the ultimate truth of the charges against Bush – of which insider trading is but one – does not particularly matter for understanding the media treatment. Several potentially newsworthy elements mark Bush's history with Harken. The key issue for this book is why some accusations of misconduct receive high-magnitude attention whereas other charges of similar gravity do not. As it happens, in this case Bush never flatly denied the allegations. Rather, he and his spokespersons issued non-denial denials, or simply failed to discuss them. Here is a selection of the numerous components that created the potential for scandal:[1]

1. Withholding the evidence of illegal insider trading from the SEC. This involved, most importantly, failing to provide the SEC, in a timely fashion, the attorney's letter disproving Bush's central defense: that his stock sale was vetted and approved by counsel. As noted above, a letter from Harken's outside attorneys clearly warned against just the kind of sale that Bush made. Moreover, according to an SEC staff memo obtained by the *Globe*, Bush

was generally uncooperative with the agency, raising further suspicion of a cover-up.

2. The insider trading itself. Even if Bush and other board members had not been warned by an attorney, they still would have had no right to ignore the law. The board of Harken was in fact told of financial problems that would have an adverse effect on the stock price once the news was released (about two months later). This sets up the classic condition for illegal insider trading. The reasoning behind the law is that possessing privileged information gives an unfair advantage if insiders are allowed to buy or sell stock based on that knowledge, and unfairly disadvantages the shareholding public. If unchecked, insider trading would eliminate any positive economic and social functions the stock market might perform. Bush never denied that he knew inside information and then proceeded to sell the stock, which in fact lost about half its value a few weeks later, when the bad news came out. Bush's defense was that his sale was not insider trading but just a coincidence in timing. In addition, he argued he lost out on potential profits when the stock price actually rose several months after the dip. Losing money because one's inside trade turned out badly in the longer term is not a defense for breaking the law. In Bush's case, he needed the money to repay the loan from his father's associates, and apparently was unwilling or unable to gamble that Harken stock would rebound.

3. The SEC's failure to carry out its duties with respect to Bush. Although the target of an investigation, he was never interviewed by the SEC (Harmon & Muenchen 2009). He received no sanctions. The agency declined to reopen its case when it learned he had withheld the legal memo proving, contrary to his claims, that he did engage in insider training after receiving legal advice not to. And the agency refused to release full records of its proceedings in this matter, conducted while George H.W. Bush was president.

4. Harken's accounting maneuvers. The company hid losses by selling its directors an asset and booking a loan from the buyer as an IOU, a positive item on its balance sheet of $11 million, thereby boosting the company's stock price. This was an accounting maneuver that got Enron into great trouble in 2002, and it was illegal back when Harken did it too. The SEC forced Harken to restate its earnings but did not prosecute its officers and board members, including Bush, who was on the audit committee. Assuming he was doing his job, he would have known about this illegal action.

5. Bush's refusal to disclose the buyer of his stock. Bush said he never knew the identity of the person who procured his stock just before it plunged in value, but this seems unlikely given that it was privately sold to a Bush family friend. A *Boston Globe* investigation found that the purchaser was an investment firm called Quest, now out of business, run by Charles Royce. A major Republican contributor, he later founded Royce Mutual Funds. Beyond whether George W. Bush actually was in the dark about the purchaser's identity, which is possible, the transaction raises questions about potential corruption and character. Why wasn't the stock sold anonymously on the stock market – why a private trade? Why would Royce, a world-class investor, hand over money for securities Bush knew were soon to plummet in value? Was Royce told the bad insider news, which would suggest he purchased the stock essentially as a gift to George W. Bush, in return for political favors from President George H.W. Bush? Or did the Bush family or its representatives actually rip off a loyal supporter and friend, unloading a shaky stock on Royce despite knowing it was about to tank?

6. Filing the papers declaring Bush's major insider sale of stock to the SEC a full 34 weeks late. This tardiness had the effect of cooling the investigative trail. Bush once claimed this was an oversight, and another time that he did submit the papers but somebody at his law firm or at the SEC must have misplaced the filing. Again, it's possible that one of these claims was true, but journalists in scandal mode would likely have pressed to resolve the inconsistency.

7. Harken's unexpected turn of fortune. Several months before Bush learned of the coming bad news and sold most of his stock, Harken mysteriously landed a huge contract to drill for oil in Bahrain, despite being in competition with much larger companies that had far more foreign experience. Evidence suggests Bahrain made the decision because of Harken's connection to the Bush family.[2] The Bahrain contract raised the value of Harken stock significantly in the months leading up to Bush's sale.

8. Other Harken practices that, although not illegal, could have fueled scandal reporting. Harken set up offshore corporate shells in the Cayman Islands to avoid taxes, and its officers, including Bush, dissembled about the motives for this (common and generally legal) practice. Also, insider loans were provided to corporate officers to purchase Harken stock, at less than market rates. This was legal at the time but embarrassing and problematic for Bush,

especially once the scandal around the Enron Corporation came to light in 2002.[3]

Any one of these might have stimulated systematic investigation by a press corps that devoted so much energy to the Whitewater investments of Bill (and Hillary) Clinton. Although the Clintons gave evasive answers to some of the questions raised about these investments, exhaustive investigation revealed no credible evidence of illegal or even unethical behavior on the part of the former First Family in this matter (Ray 2001). True, shady characters like James MacDougal were centrally involved in that failed real estate venture, as were others in Arkansas politics, including Clinton's successor as governor, Jim Guy Tucker, and Clinton's close friend and advisor Webb Hubbell. That these people were convicted of crimes in connection with Whitewater certainly and perhaps legitimately sullied the Clintons' reputations and fed media interest.

Readers may judge the substantive seriousness of George W. Bush's alleged financial shenanigans for themselves. There appears to be strong evidence of insider trading to the tune of nearly $1 million, and furthermore of deliberately deceiving the SEC about it. The SEC's failure to bring charges in the insider trading matter or the dishonest earnings restatement, far from revealing that Bush (as he claims) was *cleared* of wrongdoing, actually deepens the appearance and likelihood of corruption. The son of the sitting president who appointed most of the SEC's key members and staffers[4] was never sanctioned, despite all the evidence summarized above. Still, whatever the factual details of Bush's malfeasance, the major issue here is how and why the media failed to produce a financial scandal as they had for Bill Clinton.

Insider trading and reporting

A count was made of media items mentioning Harken during 2000–2, when Bush ran for and served as president, and Enron and related corporate scandals broke. LexisNexis was used to search for *Harken* and *Bush* in full text, within the Major Papers section for newspapers, and in the transcripts for ABC, CBS, NBC and PBS evening news programs, along with *Time* and *Newsweek*. Just three stories appeared in all of 2001, so that year was excluded. The year of peak attention was 2002. On March 4, 2002, the *Wall Street Journal* ran the first story of the year mentioning Harken, and it went into some detail. Then the *New York Times* played catch-up in a March 6 article (buried on page C-1, the business section). No other newspaper mentioned Harken again (except two passing references in letters to the editor in regional papers) until July 2, 2002, when Paul Krugman, the *Times* economics columnist, raised it again, referring to the *Journal* piece. That discussion was followed by considerable attention in July, and another briefer and far smaller burst in November. Despite investigative stories published in two of the most influential newspapers in March, far from assigning their own crack reporters to dig further, or even running a version of the *Times* or *Journal* stories, no newspaper in the LexisNexis library even bothered to mention Harken in editorials, and no syndicated or local columnist in the Major Papers file mentioned it during March.

This is what it looks like when scandal mode is blocked and a potential scandal remains on Path I. A few stories may appear, even in normally influential media, then, after a few days, coverage simply stops. Full-blown scandal mode, in contrast, involves several steps, of which newspaper editorial commentary, coverage on the evening television news, and attention from the Sunday morning news and cable TV talk shows are probably most critical to activating a cascade. They trigger repeat coverage in the major elite newspapers and in the rest of the country's major media that continues for at least a week – this book's standard for a high-magnitude scandal. They also typically trigger survey questions, which indicate pollsters' belief that their news organization clients perceive potential political fallout. If polls then reveal negative movement in public sentiment, that propels the momentum of coverage, given the media's process or horserace decision bias. Such a scandal did not happen in 2002. It only even threatened to happen for a few days in mid-July. That threat arose not because new information was discovered, but because the old Harken information became suddenly newsworthy in the context of the Enron revelations.

The goal of those hoping to block a scandal is to prevent significant negative impacts on perceived public opinion. Poll results suggest that for, all intents and purposes, Harken was blocked. A Gallup Poll taken at the end of July 2002 asked: "From what you have heard or read about George W. Bush's activities at Harken Energy Corporation, which of the following statements best describes your view of his actions in this matter – he did something illegal, he did something unethical but nothing illegal, or he did not do anything seriously wrong?" Only 7% said "illegal," and 28% had no opinion at all; 32% said "unethical," and 33% said he hadn't done "anything seriously wrong." So, according to the Gallup Poll, a comfortable 61% (adding 28% and 33%) did not see Harken as a Bush scandal; furthermore, a Hart Poll taken just after the peak of media attention (July 19–21, 2002) found 53% saying they did not know enough about the scandal to have an opinion. No polls could be found that asked about Harken after July. Nor, tellingly, were there any polls about Harken *before* July 2002 either. The existence of numerous polls on a subject is itself a measure of a scandal's magnitude. This one barely registered and the paucity of survey data may have both reflected and reinforced the media's disinclination to keep the scandal going. Meanwhile, Bush's overall Gallup approval averaged 71.4% during 2002, and in January 2003 70% rated him "honest and trustworthy" (Jones 2003), suggesting publicity about Harken did little if any damage.

Attention to Harken sputtered out within a few days in July, as the media turned their attention to a newly urgent foreign policy problem: ridding Iraq of weapons of mass destruction that threatened the US as well as the Middle East – more on this in chapter 8. One of the most important tools in a president's arsenal for short-circuiting a scandal is to create or heighten a foreign policy crisis, and Bush did just this. Although it is unlikely that his only motive in ratcheting up the stakes on Iraq during the summer of 2002 was to distract from Harken, it is equally unlikely that the domestic payoffs from doing so would have eluded the president, Karl Rove or other political advisors. Lending some credence to this linkage is the fact that, just two days after the Krugman column appeared, on July 5, a top administration figure leaked what had been a "highly classified document" outlining General Tommy Franks's original plans for invasion to the *Times* (Schmitt 2002). This was the first time the public had been told that there was in fact detailed planning underway for an invasion, and, as another story in the *Times* that day said, reflecting the new tone and urgency: "The warpath: pressures build on Iraq" (Tyler 2002). A *Times* editorial the next day was entitled "Battle plans for Iraq" ("Battle plans for Iraq" 2002).

By late July the Harken story had faded almost entirely, never to rear up again in major media except for the very short burst around the "smoking-gun" story in the *Boston Globe* revealing that, despite his denials, Bush had indeed been warned by counsel against selling his Harken stock. As for television news, CBS and NBC evening news programs each mentioned Harken six times, and ABC, five times. All but two of these came during the peak week (July 8–14, 2002). Harken did also receive considerable attention on *Nightline* (ABC) and the morning news talk shows during July (32 items) but, as just shown, this attention had no significant political impacts.

Only one television outlet mentioned Harken after July, and it was the single network evening news response to the October 30 smoking-gun revelation. The following is the entire relevant portion of that one story, from *CBS Evening News* (November 1, 2002):

DAN RATHER, anchor:	President Bush now finds himself dealing with two potentially damaging problems in what he says is his fight to clean up the corporate corruption mess: There are the multiplying difficulties of the man he appointed to head the Securities and Exchange Commission, Harvey Pitt, and there are new questions about Mr. Bush's sale of stock before he became president. White House correspondent Bill Plante reports.
BILL PLANTE reporting:	With new details emerging about the president's personal financial history and his chief financial enforcer under mounting scrutiny, Mr. Bush today slammed corporate greed with renewed zeal.
President GEORGE W. BUSH:	There isn't any easy money in America. There's only jail time when we catch you fudging the books.

[The story then focuses on current problems at the SEC and concludes:]

PLANTE:	And with the election just four days away, the president's conduct as a businessman has also resurfaced. In 1990, when Mr. Bush was a director of Harken Energy, he received this memo from company lawyers warning directors not to sell stock if they had unfavorable information about the company. One week later, he sold $848,000 worth of Harken stock. Two months later, Harken announced losses of more than $23 million. But Mr. Bush's personal attorney didn't forward the warning memo to the SEC until they had finished their investigation. The White House says Mr. Bush did consult the lawyers before he made his stock sale and got their blessing. They also say that the SEC could have reopened the investigation at any time they wished, but never did so. Dan.

The concluding paragraph of Bill Plante's story provides a particularly vivid example of the way blocked scandals look in news texts. A television audience member, unlikely to remember much if anything about Harken from way back in July, would have great trouble interpreting this matter as scandalous. (Of course, given increasingly fragmented media audiences, most Americans were not tuned to CBS and therefore were not exposed to a Harken story that day at all.) Therefore, the report would not stimulate many people to alter the evaluative criteria and weights undergirding their attitudes toward Bush. CBS's story did not explain that Bush *had* in fact received unfavorable information before his stock sale – something the White House wasn't actually denying. Instead, the White House offered a textbook non-denial that Plante, operating under the objectivity/balance norm, simply passed along: "The White House says Mr. Bush did consult the lawyers before he made his stock sale and got their blessing. They also say that the SEC could have reopened the investigation at any time they wished, but never did so."

As Plante or any reader of the original *Globe* story would know, though some lawyers (Harken's internal counsel) suggested selling stock would be legal, the point relevant to understanding the potential scandal was that Bush could not deny that other attorneys, the external counsel, explicitly warned against selling. That means the first sentence is literally untrue, as Bush did not consult "the" lawyers and get their blessing. Some lawyers blessed, perhaps, but others cautioned, and certainly the prudent response would have been to obtain a third opinion or in some other way resolve the discrepancy. Furthermore, Bush withheld the proof of the one counsel's warning, forwarding only the exculpatory evidence of the other's blessing. Plante mentioned that Bush's personal attorney did not provide the warning memo until after the SEC closed its investigation, but failed to explicitly state that withholding the memo raises the appearance of cover-up if not obstruction of justice. Furthermore, this unforthcoming behavior fitted with the earlier decision to wait eight months to file the original required paperwork with the SEC. Plante treated the final point, that the SEC failed to reopen the investigation, as supporting the White House's assertion that Bush did nothing wrong. Yet a news organization in scandal mode might well have taken that omission as evidence of something fishy, arousing new questions, such as: how often does the SEC fail to reopen an investigation when it learns that its target has withheld crucial evidence of guilt on the central charge against him?

One might expect a scandal cascade to have arisen in 2000 or 2004, when the president's business record at Harken was relevant to the presidential campaign. After all, both campaigns featured a heavy emphasis on the opposing candidates' (Al Gore's and John Kerry's) personal character and honesty (see Jamieson & Waldman 2002). During all of 2000, only six news items or editorial columns mentioning the Harken insider trading matter appeared. Three consisted of one paragraph within larger, general stories about Bush's career or biography (in *USA TODAY*, the *Cleveland Plain Dealer*, and the

Atlanta Journal-Constitution). This matter-of-fact reference in *USA Today* is representative (J. Lawrence 2000):

> Bush had come up with his small Rangers stake by borrowing money. In mid-1990, he sold $848,560 worth of Harken stock to cover the loans. Days later, the company issued a poor quarterly earnings report and shares plunged from $4 to $2.38. At the time, Bush was a Harken director who had been assigned to study the firm's financial problems. The Securities and Exchange Commission investigated allegations of insider trading and late notification of the sale by Bush, but took no action.

The three stories that did provide more detail appeared in regional papers (*Cleveland Plain Dealer*, *St. Petersburg Times*, and *San Diego Union-Tribune*). None of the major national newspapers, the ones capable of sparking a scandal cascade, discussed Harken as a potential scandal in 2000. Several other papers, including the major national ones, did run stories mentioning Harken in the course of biographical features – without alluding to the insider trading or other questionable matters during Bush's tenure at the energy firm. Some of these stories were unflattering in that they suggested Bush's ability to profit from Harken arose from his family connections rather than his business acumen, but none indicated anything illegal might have occurred.

As for the period 2003–4, the run-up to and occurrence of the presidential campaign, a total of eight items that mentioned Harken ran in LexisNexis Major Papers outlets (US papers only; excludes three letters to the editor). These included, by a very generous count, 29 sentences referring to allegations of Bush's involvement in insider trading. Four of the items were book or movie reviews, one covered a speech by George Soros (the billionaire Democratic contributor), and another covered interviews of Bush's first Treasury secretary, Paul O'Neill. One was an op-ed column in the *St. Louis Post-Dispatch* and one a column in the *San Francisco Chronicle*'s business section. None involved investigative reporting, and only one (a book review) appeared in a major outlet (the *Washington Post*). None of the evening news shows on ABC, CBS, or NBC mentioned the Harken matter even once in 2003–4.

Blocked scandal

Let us turn to a more detailed exploration of exactly what a Path I blocked scandal looks like. Answering this requires a finer-grained look at news texts. We will focus on 2002, when the Enron Corporation's spectacular collapse and similar corporate scandals finally made Bush's Harken activities sufficiently newsworthy to generate some traction in the media, albeit for barely more than a week.

BLOCKED SCANDAL TRAIT #1: Failure to follow up smoking-gun findings

This point is not tautological. Blocked scandals are those for which credible evidence of grave misconduct *does* appear prominently in a mainstream media outlet but then fails to spread through the rest of the media system, remaining on Path I. This trait is exemplified in the media's indifference to the *Boston Globe*'s investigative report showing that a lawyer did warn Bush against insider trading (Kranish & Healy 2002). The *Globe* itself failed to follow up (an op-ed columnist, Derrick Jackson (2002), did devote one sentence to the matter). How did the other media, which had paid some attention to Harken back in July, before this October smoking-gun story, react? The first and only other response by any newspaper in the LexisNexis Major Papers database was the *Washington Post*'s story on page A4 two days later (Behr 2002). The *Post* did not comment on its edit page, or initiate its own investigation. Nor did the *New York Times*, which also owned the *Globe*. But the *Post*'s story did bring to the attention of Washington elites and journalists sufficient information to raise suspicion of serious malfeasance. That the *Post* editors failed to put it on page 1 and neglected also to follow it up both reflected and helped to shape the ho-hum reaction in Washington.

So that readers can judge for themselves the substance of this story and decide whether they believe the *Globe*'s smoking gun could have precipitated a scandal, here are excerpts from the November 1 *Post* story, which basically summarizes the original *Globe* report:

> A week before George W. Bush's 1990 sale of stock in Harken Energy Co., the firm's outside lawyers cautioned Bush and other directors against selling shares if they had significant negative information about the company's prospects.

> The sale came a few months before Harken reported significant losses, leading to an investigation by the Securities and Exchange Commission.

> The ... [outside counsel's] letter ... wasn't sent to the SEC by Bush's attorney until ... one day after SEC staff members ... concluded there was insufficient evidence to recommend an enforcement action ... for insider trading.

No doubt this story is complicated and confusing. Readers would have to keep straight which lawyers said what to whom and when. But the basic facts are not in doubt and could be conveyed in a simpler story. Bush attended a meeting where he was given negative inside information. He asked the company's own attorney if he could then sell shares, and apparently that lawyer said yes, but more detached outside counsel said no. And Bush's personal lawyer withheld from SEC investigators the evidence that Bush was indeed warned by outside attorneys against insider trading, in contradiction to what Larry E. Cummings, Harken's general counsel, testified to the SEC. Furthermore, Bush arguably did not even require a lawyer's advice. The facts seem unambiguous: as a company director, he obtained negative insider information, and that is precisely the circumstance covered by insider trading prohibitions, as even casual investors – not to mention holders of a Harvard MBA like Bush – realize. Yet Bush undeniably proceeded to dump most of his shares and gave deceptive accounts of the situation to the SEC as well as the press and public.

BLOCKED SCANDAL TRAIT #2: Claiming the accused was cleared of wrongdoing by an official investigation when he/she was not in fact "cleared"

BLOCKED SCANDAL TRAIT #3: Asserting the allegations had come up previously, making them old news that obviously could not be serious because no scandal arose before

Both of these traits are illustrated in the following story. This was the one US newspaper story during all of 2001 (in the LexisNexis Major Papers file) mentioning the Harken insider trading issue. Among its total of 540 words about Bush's nominee for ambassador to Saudi Arabia, this story offered 51 on Harken:

> In 1990, [Robert W.] Jordan represented Bush in a Securities and Exchange Commission probe of insider trading allegations stemming from Bush's sale of stock in the Harken Energy Corp.
>
> The SEC investigation cleared Bush of wrongdoing, although the insider trading allegations were an issue in both his run for governor and presidential bid. (Mason 2001, p. A16)

The second sentence is inaccurate on two counts. The SEC did not clear Bush, but rather decided there was "insufficient evidence" to support a finding that Bush had violated insider trading rules. As we have seen, the major reason for the insufficiency was that the attorney representing Bush to the SEC withheld the key evidence, the letter from Harken's outside counsel warning against insider trading. The attorney who withheld the evidence was none other than Robert W. Jordan, the ambassador-designee and main subject of the story just quoted. And as we have also seen, the allegations were *not* an issue during Bush's 2000 presidential bid.

Another example of a claim that the matter had already been thoroughly aired comes from the otherwise estimable *Globe* smoking-gun story itself, which mentioned Bush's "now famous" sale of Harken stock, as if it were in fact widely known. The same story claimed there had been "many years of scrutiny" as if this had been an ongoing major story – as we've seen, an inaccurate characterization. This point illustrates that the same story can occasionally both highlight a potential scandal and yet participate in blocking it.

Bush himself advanced the notion that he had been investigated and cleared, and that it was old news, on one of the rare occasions he was ever personally asked about the Harken issue at a press conference (July 2, 2002):

> Pres. BUSH: Everything I do is fully disclosed, it's been fully vetted. Any other question? (Ray 2001)

No further questions followed Bush's answer.

BLOCKED SCANDAL TRAIT #4: Failing to aggressively question the alleged wrongdoer in press conferences or interviews, based on documentary evidence – or to call for official investigation or other action

Presidents and candidates can and do help to block scandals by refusing to hold press conferences and appearing only in friendly, highly controlled settings. But the media do have the power to exert pressure for face-time with the president, or at least the White House press secretary – and then to ask tough questions. The latter are particularly potent when they are based on detailed independent research in documents rather than relying on formulaic recitation of general charges, to which the president or spokesperson will inevitably respond with mechanical denials and evasions, as in President Bush's response just quoted. But for a scandal cascade to commence, the media must go beyond White House press conferences or briefings, since question–answer sessions rarely yield new evidence on allegations of scandal. The *Globe* let the ball drop, despite its investigative work on the smoking-gun story. It did not keep pressure on Bush's press office to answer questions about the results of its research. It did not call editorially for government investigation. Yet the *Globe* did more than any other mainstream media outlet. When journalists are largely silent on the heels of a smoking-gun story, potential scandals tend to evaporate – unless the opposition party seizes on the revelations, which the Democrats did not do.

BLOCKED SCANDAL TRAIT #5: Failing to connect the dots

Most of the stories that mention Harken exhibit this trait. They fail to draw explicit connections among the specific facts cited, or between them and larger issues of financial corruption, morality, and legality. In neglecting to contextualize, in stating just a few of the bare facts of the case, they render the potential scandal less resonant, less memorable, less worthy of attention by audiences and journalists alike. In other words, they fail to construct a scandal *frame.*

Since unconnected dots have already been illustrated, here is a rare item that *does* connect the dots (Krugman 2002). Doing this makes the true dimensions of the scandal clearer and also more memorable, more likely to alter citizens' evaluative criteria and weights and to be stored schematically in long-term memory associated with the attitude object "George W. Bush."

> Wednesday's *Wall Street Journal* reported another piece of the Harken Energy story, one that provides even more evidence of how family connections smoothed Mr. Bush's business career. The key defense against charges that his sale of his Harken stock amounted to insider trading has always been the fact that while that stock's price plunged soon after he sold his shares, it then recovered, albeit temporarily.
>
> Now we know why it recovered. It wasn't just the mysterious invitation to drill for oil off Bahrain. Harken also pulled a trick that would be emulated on a larger scale by Enron: In effect it borrowed money to pay its bills, while using loopholes in accounting rules to conceal the resulting debt.
>
> What made the trick possible was Harken's guardian angel, a powerful institution controlled by an oil man, Robert Stone, who was a strong political supporter of Mr. Bush's father. This institution acquired a large stake in Harken as soon as Mr. Bush became a board member, and subsequently showed itself willing to do whatever it took to keep the hapless company afloat. This included taking much of the company's debt off its books in return for assets of doubtful value, and giving

Harken a share in their partnership almost twice as large as its contri-
bution to the partnership's capital.

In other words, Krugman reported, Bush and the company he helped
direct, and in which he still had stock holdings, engaged in deceptive
practices to boost its stock price. And these maneuvers were made
possible by a political crony of the first President Bush. That the
senior Bush was himself at least peripherally involved in Harken
could help explain why his appointees at the SEC did not investigate
the younger Bush's dealings aggressively.[5]

*BLOCKED SCANDAL TRAIT #6: Labeling questions and
allegations of malfeasance as partisan sniping or politics
as usual, or focusing on the malfeasance only in terms
of political effects and process rather than substantive
societal impact*

A primary norm governing all mainstream political journalism is the
decision-making bias toward political process. This leads reporters to
concentrate more on the political game than policy substance. In fact,
politics and process so dominate political journalism that a Pew study
of news coverage leading up to the 2008 presidential primaries found
that 63 percent of news items focused on the politics/horserace, while
just 15 percent of stories explored the candidates' ideas and policy
proposals (Pew Research Center 2007). For instance, in a peak of
television attention to Harken, Ted Koppel's *Nightline* devoted an
entire show (July 18, 2002) to Harken and Halliburton, the oil-related
conglomerate headed by Richard Cheney before he became vice
president. Koppel introduced the program by asking: "Is it politics?
You bet. But does that imply that the White House needn't worry?"
Following such a script for structuring the narrative makes it into a
game story, with the key problem defined not as substantive corruption but as Bush's political power and standing under attack. Koppel
framed Harken and Halliburton as a "public relations problem"
making it hard for the White House to "sell" its concern with Enron
and corporate scandals because of "past business dealings." This tack
avoids raising questions about the president's behavior and ethical/
moral character. Koppel engaged in a long conversation with former
presidential advisor (to Reagan, Bush senior, and Clinton) David
Gergen, raising questions not about what Bush or Cheney and their
companies actually did so much as about the White House's level of
political sensitivity and acumen, employing such terms as "getting it"
and being "tone deaf."

The implicit assumption of this discussion was that the administration had nothing to hide, they just needed to realize the importance of paying attention to the story and getting beyond it through improved public relations techniques. Gergen opined to the effect that the president was honest and did nothing wrong and just had to get out the full story:

> I would say that the president – that "Mr. President, obviously, you've been honest with us, obviously, you haven't done anything wrong, but a course correction is needed now. And one part of that course correction, and a very vital part of that is, turn everything over from the SEC investigations, disclose – to the extent anything is known, get it out there."

Bush never did order the SEC to release "everything," yet no scandal cascade ensued and Bush suffered no political consequences.

Yet another noteworthy aspect of the Bush financial scandals is that similar, or perhaps more serious, malfeasance was alleged on the part of Vice President Cheney during his reign as CEO of Halliburton – and even afterward, once he was elected. The vice president allegedly used his power over energy policy to benefit Halliburton and other firms in the oil industry (Corn 2003; Ivins & Dubose 2003).[6] Since this chapter focuses on Bush it does not explore the Halliburton affair, but the involvement of both the president and vice president in alleged corruption within the same industry might have been expected to yield *more* rather than less attention to the scandal potential of Harken.

BLOCKED SCANDAL TRAIT #7: Absence of the opposition party from the narrative

The Democrats in this case, as in others, failed to supply newsworthy comments or actions that might have promoted cascading attention to the story. Illustrating the importance of opposition party action, in that July 18, 2002 *Nightline*, the independent activist Larry Klayman took a firmer stance than did Democratic sources, who merely called for "explanations." Klayman demanded the president and vice president testify on the matters under oath, for instance.

When the opposition party is silent or tepid in its rhetoric and actions, it undermines the newsworthiness of the potential scandal. This circumstance denies the media raw material for new scandal stories. After all, once a media outlet has conveyed the basic scandal allegations, it has no basis for putting out more stories unless it can dig up something new. That is usually difficult, since the investigative story itself is normally the culmination of weeks or months of expensive probing and it includes the best material reporters found.

It is far easier for political leaders or government agencies to take new actions relevant to the matter than for journalists to keep a story alive on their own. The Democrats' handling of Harken contrasts vividly with Republican responses to potential scandals during the Clinton administration. The GOP vigorously promoted many potential scandals involving the president or First Lady, and several attained enough currency to be labeled with the "gate" suffix. Examples include the firing of a White House travel agent ("Travelgate") and accusations a low-level Clinton staffer snooped in the FBI files of former staff members in the Bush White House ("Filegate"). The GOP was abetted by scandal-promotion networks that have little to no equivalent on the Democratic side (see Conason 2003; Brock 2004; Dean 2007; Jamieson & Cappella 2008; Dreier & Martin 2010).

BLOCKED SCANDAL TRAIT #8: Vaguely describing or obscuring the precise nature of the alleged malfeasance, stripping it of resonance, typically by failing even to use the term "scandal," with its politically damaging, attention-grabbing reverberations

An example of dismissing scandal while offering only vague references to the malfeasance comes from the *Washington Post* (Allen 2002): "Both Bush and Cheney face continuing scrutiny for their own business practices: Bush sold stock at an advantageous time when he was a director of Harken Energy Corp. . . ." This description borders on misleading. The matter under contention went beyond merely selling stock at an "advantageous time," which is entirely legal under most circumstances. Another example of draining the resonance from misconduct also comes from the *Post* (Balz 2002): "To restore confidence, Gore challenged the administration to release the names of energy company lobbyists who advised Bush on energy policy and called for the release of all documents at the Securities and Exchange Commission relating to Bush's sale of stock in Harken Energy Corp. in 1990, when he was a member of the company's board of directors." Perhaps the *Post*'s editors and reporters assumed that most readers were familiar with Harken and did not need to be told explicitly the reason that there was any interest in documents relating to a "sale of stock." Still, that two stories in this critical outlet of the media hierarchy failed to mention the actual problems of insider trading or those other Harken issues listed earlier, let alone branded them as *Harkengate*, reflected and bolstered the blockage of a scandal cascade and helped to keep the matter on Path I.

It is instructive to recall where the only unsigned *Post* editorial that mentioned Harken during 2002 (July 12, 2002, p. A-20), entitled "The Harken energy distraction," focused its concern: "Congress shouldn't let the temptation to play politics with this issue distract it from corporate reform." In making this recommendation, the editors noted that "People who worked inside the SEC during the early 1990s reckon that the organization would have gone after the son of the president if it had had sufficient evidence." The editorial relies on the anonymous assurances of some people who worked at the SEC, while overlooking Bush's own possible role in withholding evidence. It goes on to beg the question (of SEC malfeasance) again by citing the lack of agency enforcement as evidence that Bush's late filings of mandatory reports couldn't have been "egregiously late." The editorial concludes:

> But the Harken story took place years ago. It has already been investigated and aired. It affected far fewer people than the billion-dollar scandals that have been in the news lately. Congress's focus must now be on preventing more corporate dishonesty, not on Harken. The real scandal involving President Bush is that he claims to be outraged by corporate misbehavior but refuses to support the bipartisan Senate bill that offers the best hope of progress.

Perhaps the editorial was correct in arguing that investigating an old insider trading deal and other financial malfeasance would distract from the substantive policy goal of financial regulatory reform. My point is merely that this judgment at one of America's most influential newspapers helped to squelch the potential scandal even as it cooperated with the Bush team's strategy for non-scandal.

Washington Post op-ed columnist Michael Kelly (Kelly 2002) wrote the most detailed of the eight signed columns that mentioned Harken in the *Post* that year. After describing some of Bush's dubious acts, Kelly explained why the Democrats were loath to promote a scandal over Harken:

> But the Democrats' ability to really exploit this opportunity is far from obvious. In a recent survey, CNN asked respondents whom they blamed more for today's business scandals [e.g., Enron]: Bush ("because of his close ties to business") or former president Bill Clinton ("because of

his moral failings and the climate he set while he was in office"). Thirty-three percent blamed Bush more – but 40 percent liked Clinton as the fall guy.

The voters figure it this way because they are not stupid. They look at Democrats now in the grim, dim light cast by the years of Our Bill – the years of the rental of the Lincoln Bedroom, of the White House coffees, of Ron Brown's $50,000-a-seat trade missions, of Johnny Chung and Charlie Trie, of midnight-hour presidential pardons to well-heeled fugitives and felons. It is sometimes hard for voters, in this light, to clearly see the party of the New Deal.

In this passage Kelly provides a clear example of how the conventional wisdom (i.e. schema or stereotype) for a politician works to promote or repel scandal. Everyone knew Clinton ran a scandal-plagued administration, says Kelly. Voters were "not stupid" to look back on the Clinton years in a "grim, dim" light – and to blame him rather than Bush for such business scandals as Enron, even though the latter took place mainly during the Bush administration. Stating that the failure of a scandal to grow around Bush's business dealings was traceable to the Democrats' inability to call the kettle black might be valid. But it does conveniently omit the actual parallel to any potential scandal over Harken, which was Clinton's own thoroughly investigated business investments in the Whitewater real estate venture. (In addition, entertaining contributors at the White House and other questionable fundraising and influence-peddling activities Kelly mentions were hardly unique to the Clinton administration; see, e.g., Kevin Phillips 2004.)

Another op-ed (Mallaby 2002) provides a further sense of the thinking among Washington insiders, who bent over backwards to give Bush the benefit of the doubt. Here is the one passage mentioning Harken: "You could say that, given Harken and Halliburton, the Bush team could never pose as exponents of free-market capitalism as opposed to the cronyist variety. That's not fair; politicians can live down their histories if they demonstrate by their policies that they want to do the right thing." In other words, the issue here isn't corruption but cronyism, and that's something the president and vice president can "live down" if they "do the right thing." The administration did not release the documents. Such stonewalling might have suggested to an earlier generation of reporters at the *Post* that those documents contained substantive evidence of malfeasance or, at the least, politically embarrassing facts. The *Post* never followed up its brief editorial mention with further discussion of Harken. After framing the incident as ancient history, something from the past that could and should be forgotten, like the rest of the mainstream media they allowed it to fade away.

Harken coverage by the numbers

A quantitative content analysis of a six-month sample from national news coverage allows us to gauge more precisely the respective roles of the opposition and the media in aborting a Harken scandal, along with the extent to which the eight traits of non-scandals did appear in the coverage. The time span for the quantitative comparison began in July 2002 when, spurred by a push for financial regulatory reform, Bush was questioned about allegations of insider trading. To ensure capture of all relevant discourse, the sample period ran past the primary spike in coverage, extending through December 31, 2002, long after the coverage had dwindled. The sample used the Lexis-Nexis and Proquest databases to retrieve news items from the leading broadcast and print news organizations, including ABC, CBS and NBC evening news, and the *New York Times*, the *Washington Post* and *USA Today*. The search terms were the name *Bush* within the same paragraph as *Harken*. A 50 percent sample of transcripts and articles was drawn. Using the paragraph as unit of analysis, this yielded a total of 1,430 paragraphs across 51 articles and 19 broadcast transcripts. All 1,430 paragraphs were evaluated for the presence or absence of specific claims or judgments related to Bush's actions or tenure at Harken.[7]

This analysis addressed three overarching concerns related to the blocked scandal traits detailed above: overall, how was the Bush–Harken controversy framed – how frequently did the media present judgments and claims that either critically examined Bush's actions, supported and excused them, or merely treated the matter as partisan maneuvering? Second, what were the partisan or ideological identities of sources quoted and cited in the coverage and, in particular, how much of a role did the opposition Democrats play – were they widely quoted or mainly absent from the discussion? And finally, when Democratic and other liberal leaders were heard from, did any call for formal investigation or other government action crucial to initiating and sustaining a scandal cascade?

To answer these questions, we[8] counted each separate mention of partisan and non-partisan sources quoted, paraphrased, or otherwise cited making specific judgments about Bush's Harken activities. We also catalogued the presence or absence of what we defined as Harken framing statements – claims and judgments characterizing Bush's involvement with the Harken stock sale, and supporting or opposing the substantive validity of treating the matter as a scandal. The analysis showed several distinct clusters of assertions and evaluations that reflected the patterns described earlier as typical of blocked scandal. These included claims that there was no wrongdoing and President Bush had been fully vetted or cleared; that any misconduct was minor or mitigated because it was old news, occupied a gray area of conduct, or did not rise to the level of a prosecutable offense; or that Harken should be seen simply as partisan maneuvering by Democrats. Another trait of non-scandal detected by the content analysis involved a paucity rather than a presence: relatively few calls for urgent investigation and remedial action. This was one cluster that did promote scandal framing via critical assessment or accusation that included a call to action or further investigation.

Apart from the sources and framing, one of the most telling statistics was just how little coverage there was (and therefore how limited in magnitude the scandal remained in 2002). Even within the relatively limited number of articles and transcripts that did mention Bush in the same paragraph as Harken, only 20 percent (281 of 1,430) actually focused in any way on Bush's involvement with Harken Energy. Instead, the majority of these articles mentioned Harken in passing within the context of the broader financial troubles of the day while happening to allude to the president or the Bush administration.

Here are the findings keyed to the blocked scandal trait list:

Trait #7

Even though Democratic voices weren't completely absent on Harken, they were outnumbered and outmaneuvered, as well as inconsistent and contradictory. President Bush was the most frequently cited source, appearing in 13.7 percent of paragraphs. As shown in Appendix table 7.1, Republican and other conservative sources exceeded Democratic and liberal ones by nearly 2 to 1 (27 to 15 percent).

Even these numbers, however, may underestimate the disparity between Democratic and Republican voices heard by the largest audiences. Within the broadcast network evening news, Appendix table 7.2 reveals the differences in partisan sourcing were more dramatic. The vast majority (81 percent) of the liberal sources appeared in newspaper articles rather than broadcast news – a disproportionate amount even accounting for the greater number of Harken stories in newspapers. Counting Republican officials and

President Bush together, the official Democratic point of view was outnumbered 3.5 to 1 on television. Conservative commentators and experts also outnumbered liberal ones 2 to 1. A less predictable finding was that, beyond these official voices, the most important category of speaker within the coverage was the individual columnist, reporter, or the editorial board of the newspaper itself; a substantial 46 percent of all judgments and assertions about Bush's involvement with Harken were not attributed to any outside source.

Looking more closely at who said what, Appendix table 7.3 shows the breakdown of frames according to the source of the claim or judgment. Republicans demonstrated clear message control. Every time a GOP official was quoted or cited, they invoked at least one of the three non-scandal frames. Republican officials were almost completely united in conveying a message that there was no or inconsequential wrongdoing in Bush's Harken stock sale, and that accusations to the contrary were driven by political gamesmanship (an exception to this pattern was when Orrin Hatch said Bush should release all his financial records). Democrats, on the other hand, who were infrequently quoted or cited to begin with, split their message between critical and exculpatory statements. With such a weak Democratic opposition on this issue, much of the substantive criticism of Bush came through questioning or analysis by journalists in news articles, with particular assistance from the editorial board and columnists of the *Times*.

Traits #3 and #6

Given the tendency to cite more conservative and Republican sources, it is unsurprising that exculpatory and scandal-blocking framing also dominated the Harken coverage. As shown in Appendix table 7.4, we found that the administration's defense took three tacks. Sometimes Bush and his spokespersons claimed there was simply no wrong done. At other times, they tacitly acknowledged minor or vague but unintentional wrongdoing and excused it as old news (in keeping with blocked scandal Trait #3), or transgression only of recent, stringent norms that weren't applicable when the misdeed occurred. And sometimes, President Bush and his defenders claimed that the Harken investigation was mostly a matter of partisan politics (as per Trait #6). Together, these scandal-blocking assists to Bush appeared in 60 percent of paragraphs mentioning Harken. The most frequently presented argument was that there was no wrongdoing whatever (32 percent), followed by dismissal as political gamesmanship or treatment in process/horserace terms (19 percent).

Trait #4

Those aggregate numbers, however, don't tell the full story. There were important variations within these broad patterns. As shown in Appendix table 7.5, the type of news outlet – whether broadcast or print – was again an important factor. In the television broadcasts negative assertions were far less prevalent, accounting for 30 percent, versus 58 percent in newspapers. Proportionally, the newspapers sampled devoted twice as much of their coverage to critical framing of Bush's Harken involvement as did television news. More importantly to the sustaining – or in this case, blocking – of a scandal cascade, calls for more investigation, or for Bush to release further documentation on the matter were rare in all outlets (appearing in only 4.5 percent of Harken-related broadcast paragraphs and 7 percent of print news). And, as we've seen (e.g. *Nightline*'s Harken report and the *Washington Post* editorial), some of these presumed Bush's innocence and good faith. Looking at the relationship between the news outlet and the framing another way: news broadcasts accounted for a disproportionate 55 percent of statements presenting Harken as mere political gamesmanship. Conversely, newspapers accounted for most Bush critiques: 81 percent of critical statements made without calling for further action and 77 percent of those demanding further disclosure or investigation.[9]

Some of these disparities were driven by the type of articles that the newspapers ran. As Appendix table 7.6 indicates, opinion and editorial pieces – those not tethered as closely to what elites say and fail to say – tended to be far more critical than hard news. Since the evening news shows lack editorials, that absence accounted for much of the variation between print and broadcast news. Within the editorial and opinion sections of the three major papers, more than 83 percent of the claims and judgments were critical of Bush. Given the paucity of coverage, certain writers had an outsized impact on these numbers as well. Columnists Frank Rich, Maureen Dowd, and – especially – Paul Krugman stood out as large-scale producers of critical Harken paragraphs on the *New York Times* op-ed page.

Explanations

The Bush–Harken affair exemplifies the blocked scandal, the potential scandal that never was. Considering the media's intense interest in Clinton's Whitewater financial scandal, which kept his presidency on Path II for most of his two terms, what explains the political silence for Bush – the Path I treatment of Harken? Two obvious explanations offer only weak purchase on the matter: the complex nature of the misconduct and its datedness. Insider trading is not always too arcane for high-intensity media treatment. One insider trading story attained sizeable attention in the key year of 2002: a $45,000 stock sale by television celebrity / magazine publisher Martha Stewart. The contention that Stewart traded on inside information about ImClone Corporation stock surfaced on June 7, 2002. During that month alone it was mentioned in over 200 newspaper stories (in the 27 US papers of the LexisNexis Major Papers file). For the entire year, over 600 stories mentioned Stewart's woes, many of them focusing exclusively on the details of her transactions. Television news and celebrity gossip shows crawled all over the story as well. The media turned a second-tier celebrity's possible malfeasance with what was (to her) essentially pocket change into a major scandal, while largely ignoring insider trading by the president, a sale netting 19 times as much money and constituting the bulk of his assets at the time.

That said, financial scandals *are* more difficult and boring to cover as such – and to read about – than sex and power-abuse scandals. Although this didn't prevent attention to Whitewater or Martha Stewart, it no doubt contributed to the media's lack of interest in Harken. At Level 3 of the cascade system (see again figure 2.3), the media had commercial motivations for keeping the Stewart scandal going. At Level 5, audiences likely obtained gratifications of various sorts from watching the all-too-perfect businesswoman cut down to size. This meant the matter didn't need energetic sponsorship by political elites on Level 2, though it did require continued action by government (the prosecuting attorneys and court). Compounding the financial and psychic rewards of scandalized attention, Stewart appeared to be widely disliked, for reasons ranging from envy of her success, to her purportedly tough treatment of subordinates, to sexism (Carr 2002; Grossman 2002; Fournier 2004, January 26; Price 2007). The stories allowed audiences to pierce the veil of perfection, to penetrate beyond the sunny performances to the dark backstage maneuvers of a celebrity (see Meyrowitz 1985 on the distinctions between public and backstage spaces in the media). Still, Stewart's case did involve complicated financial maneuvers, multiple players, and confusing timelines, as did Whitewater, so it would be wrong to conclude that business investments are too esoteric to catalyze a scandal cascade. On the contrary, even mass-oriented general-interest publications like *People* magazine covered the Stewart story extensively and in some financial detail.

A second weak explanation would be lack of timeliness. Bush's potential scandals occurred 9–10 years before he ran for president and this made the news both harder to dig up and perhaps less interesting to reporters and readers. However, if mere temporal distance were the determining factor, Whitewater would never have excited media interest, as it occurred nearly 14 years before Bill Clinton sought the presidency. The contrast to treatment of Clinton and Whitewater in 1992 is thus instructive. Whitewater did not reach scandal status in Clinton's election year. Only eight newspaper stories were published in 1992 (by the 27 papers of the LexisNexis Major Papers file).

But there were two critical differences in election-year treatment of Whitewater. All eight stories went into detail on the allegations of wrongdoing and the nature of the Clintons' transactions, and five appeared in the *New York Times*, two in the *Washington Post* – papers near the apex of the scandal system hierarchy (one ran in the *Boston Globe*). The *Times* published 4,878 words on Whitewater in 1992, the year Clinton first ran, and the *Post* 1,011. In 2000, neither paper ran any words on allegations of wrongdoing by Bush at Harken. ABC, CBS and NBC evening news shows ran nothing on either Whitewater or Harken during the respective election years, and the same was true of *Time* and *Newsweek*. But the *Times* and *Post* had planted the seeds among the politically attentive for what became an explosion of Whitewater coverage from 1993 on. Whereas only one story in the LexisNexis Major Papers file even mentioned the Harken insider trading issue during Bush's first year in office (2001), hundreds of stories mentioned Whitewater in 1993, Clinton's first year, many of them focused exclusively on his alleged scandalous malfeasance. In fact, during 2001, Bush's first year, *with Clinton no longer in office*, hundreds of newspaper stories mentioned Whitewater. The only mention of Harken insider trading in 2001 came in the *Houston Chronicle*'s 540-word story on Bush's nominee for ambassador to Saudi Arabia, quoted earlier.

Given the contrasting treatments of Harken and Whitewater, better explanations for this blocked scandal seem to hinge on the shortcomings of the Democratic Party. They did not possess as thoroughly developed a scandal promotion apparatus as the Republicans – the GOP could rely on a deeper bench of loyal think-tank experts, wealthy supporters funding private investigations, and patrons for the writing of books unbound by journalistic norms, books that could make scurrilous charges to generate publicity on a large network of radio and TV talk shows and ideologically aligned blogs.[10] Nor did Democrats – at least after their failure with Iran–Contra (Fried 1997) – have the discipline or ideological inclination to mount a unified campaign for scandal (see Entman 2005; Jarvis 2005; Westen 2007; Lakoff 2008).

Even though they controlled the Senate in 2002, the Democrats did not seize the opportunity afforded by the spectacular implosion of Enron, and Bush's connection with that Houston-based company, to open investigations that might have fed a series of fresh, newsworthy revelations on Harken. Enron's CEO, Kenneth Lay, was a top fundraiser in Bush's gubernatorial campaign of 1994. He also served as local host chair of the GOP convention that nominated George H.W. Bush in 1988, and national campaign co-chairman in 1992.[11] Indeed, an alert, aggressive Democratic Party might have exploited the Harken opening in 1991, when it controlled Congress, George H.W. Bush was president, and his son was a well-connected investor suspected of unsavory business practices. If President Clinton had an adult son accused of (and ultimately admitting) insider trading, and his SEC gave the appearance of whitewashing the matter, it seems reasonable to suggest that a Republican-controlled Congress might have feasted on the potential scandal. That's what they did with Whitewater and much other purported malfeasance by Clinton.

In light of his party's record of passivity, perhaps it's no surprise that the Gore presidential campaign neglected to use Harken against Bush in 2000, when it was relatively fresh, newsworthy and relevant to voters. Beyond party tradition, another reason for Gore's timorousness might have been his own vulnerability to a finance-related scandal involving his participation in possibly illegal Democratic campaign fundraising (Cooper & Isikoff 1997; Fineman 1997; "Gore discusses fundraising, his role in the campaign" 1997; Klaidman & Breslau 1997; Isikoff 2000). The press let Gore get away with evasive answers on his fundraising activities, and although the Republicans mentioned them many times, they did not go for the jugular on the matter. Republicans appeared content to emphasize Gore's alleged propensity to lie and exaggerate about his accomplishments (e.g. his putative claim to have invented the Internet). This became a major theme of campaign coverage (Jamieson & Waldman 2002). Ironically, absent a scandal over Bush's questionable financial dealings, the negative character framing damaged Gore's standing (Bishin, Stevens & Wilson 2005, 2006), with poll data showing Bush more widely perceived as honest and moral than Gore (see also R. Johnson et al. 2004).

Political and economic pressures also worked against pursuing Bush scandals. Most national news organizations live in constant fear of charges that an ostensible liberal bias against Republicans inclines them to go after GOP politicians more aggressively than after Democrats. Although unsupported by systematic evidence (see Entman 2010c), the accusation appears to exert a powerful chilling effect on news organizations (see Watts et al. 1999; Alterman 2003). Ideology aside, both Presidents Bush were known among journalists for skillfully balancing personal charm with professional intimidation (Conason 2003; see also Corn 2003; Ivins & Dubose 2003; Fritz et al. 2004). News organizations, and individual reporters and editors who wanted to maintain access to interviews and good relations not just with Bush but with the entire administration, had compelling incentives to avoid digging into Harken. In contrast, Martha Stewart didn't pose much of a threat to news organizations. As suggested in chapter 2, nobody can match the public relations resources available to the president. Those below that level, even powerful senators and wealthy CEOs, enjoy much less leverage with the media.

One standing media decision-making bias or heuristic also likely came into play. The *stereotyped novelty* norm would have discouraged pursuit of the scandal after the *Globe* unveiled its smoking gun in late October. It was easy (though fallacious) for news organizations to dismiss the new evidence as an old story that they'd covered thoroughly during the summer. If the *Globe* story had run in July it might have unleashed a cascade. But, in yet another illustration of the limitations on media's ability to pursue scandals autonomously, it no doubt took a long time for *Globe* reporters to put together a credible follow-up on the July allegations – long enough to render the scoop, however substantively relevant, stale. Nonetheless, had Democrats exploited the revelations, the story might have evolved differently. New actions that could stir up a partisan spat, such as announcing a Congressional hearing to investigate, or demanding appointment of a special prosecutor, could have generated more media attention. Though much time had passed since his Harken days, the scandal wasn't old news from the outset. After all, during the 2004 campaign, both candidates' 35-year-old military records received scrutiny, especially the Democrat's.

Conclusion

Contrary to the emphasis in much criticism of scandal journalism, and in accordance with this book's themes, the news can pay too *little* attention to misconduct. Even though the events took place a decade before Bush ran for president, his insider trading and other Harken-related activities should have raised as many questions about his fitness for office as Clinton's 1978 Whitewater investments did when he ran for the White House 14 years later. Bush's actions probably violated the law and raised reasonable suspicions of a cover-up (what Thompson 2000 terms a "second-order" scandal) and abuse of power by the White House and a putatively independent regulatory agency, the SEC.

Here, as in previous cases, readily discernible facts appeared to have surprisingly little role in determining whether a scandal cascaded into political importance. Even without the painstaking research that produced the *Boston Globe*'s smoking-gun story, evidence of scandalous malfeasance was out in the open. From the insider trading that Bush admitted but fallaciously excused, to the impropriety of the SEC commissioners' desultory inquiry, there was no dearth of easily confirmed, seemingly incriminating facts. Harken also offers another illustration of the media's apparent inability to calibrate the magnitude of their investigative efforts and coverage either to the ease of confirming allegations or, if true, to the misdeeds' social costs.

This chapter also supports the theme that media do not eagerly shift themselves into high-scandal gear. Not one major news organization went after the Harken story energetically, let alone threw itself into a frenzy. That point in turn illuminates an important theoretical implication: although some scholarly and journalistic critics have implied that journalists fully determine their own outputs, the Harken case reveals how politically significant scandals are not only produced but also often blocked by a larger system of which journalists are only a part.

Beyond this, the Harken case and other political scandals that never were suggest another theoretical proposition: that the scandal system changes its capacity and outputs with alterations in partisan control. (For examples of potential scandals in which Bush might have been cast, fairly or not, as the chief villain, see Ivins 2000; Corn 2003; Ivins & Dubose 2003; Kevin Phillips 2004; I. Williams 2004; J. C. Wilson 2004; Isikoff & Corn 2006; Suskind 2006; Woodward 2006; J. Mayer 2008; McClellan 2008). Republicans during 1988–2008 seemed to possess greater ability to initiate, sustain, or block media scandals than did Democrats. Even when in the Congressional minority and out of the White House, the Republicans successfully promoted a wide variety of scandals involving the Clinton administration (as they did during Jimmy Carter's administration – see Entman 1989). Yet whether Democrats composed a majority or minority in Congress, they seemed unable or unwilling to seek partisan leverage using such potential scandals as Harken, the National Guard and draft issues (chapters 5 and 6), or the infidelity allegations about

George H.W. Bush (chapter 3). Regardless of what one thinks of either Bush or Clinton, the point here is a larger one. The media's watchdog function is in some ways hostage to the partisan balance of power. It becomes difficult for America's passive, but occasionally attentive, "monitorial" citizenry (Schudson 1998; Zaller 2003) to hold different presidents accountable to the same standards when the watchdog only barks for some. And this holds true even for allegations of the gravest, most costly misconduct, as chapter 8 discusses.

Appendix to chapter 7: Harken data tables

Appendix table 7.1 Prevalence of partisan and non-partisan sources

Source of frame	Responses	
	N	**Percent**
Democratic official	36	14.5
Republican officials including President Bush	63	25.3
Conservative expert or commentator	6	2.4
Liberal expert or commentator	3	1.2
Non-partisan expert	21	8.4
Polling results	7	2.8
Man on the street	2	0.8
Columnist / author of article	111	44.6
Total	249	

Appendix table 7.2 Relative prevalence of partisan and non-partisan actors as Harken sources (TV only)

Sources	Responses	
	N	**Percent**
Democratic official / liberal	8	<9.5%
Republican official / Bush / conservative	28	<33.3%
Non-partisan expert	7	<8.3%
Polling results	1	<1.2%
Columnist / author of article	40	<47.6%
Total	84	

Appendix table 7.3 Sources of framing judgments on Bush–Harken

Source of frame	No wrongdoing	Excused / mitigated / minor wrongdoing	Harken as political game	Critical w/o call for action	Critical w/call for action	Total
Democrat/liberal	5	1	4	21	9	40
Bush / Rep. / Conservative	43	10	13	4	1	71
Other	9	3	5	13	0	30
Columnist / author of article	13	7	19	54	3	96
Total	70	21	41	92	13	237*

* In 9 instances, multiple framing judgments were attributed to a source category (e.g., some Democrats described as thinking Bush did wrong, others that he didn't), or two different sources were described as taking the same position.

Appendix table 7.4 Prevalence of different framing/judgments

Harken frame	Responses		Percent of all cases*
	N	Percent	
No wrongdoing	66	28.9	31.7
Tacit acknowledgment of excused or mitigated / minor wrongdoing	19	8.3	9.1
Harken as a political contest / game / Democrats trying to get a political advantage	40	17.5	19.2
Critical assessment/accusation of wrongdoing without call for action	90	39.5	43.3
Critical assessment or accusation with call to action/investigation	13	5.7	6.3
Total	228	100.0	109.6

*Percentages add to more than 100 because paragraphs could contain more than one frame.

Appendix table 7.5 Framing in broadcast vs. print news

Type of news outlet	Harken frame					Total
	No wrongdoing	Acknowledgment of excused or mitigated minor wrongdoing	Harken as a political contest/ game	Critical assessment or accusation without call for action	Critical assessment or accusation with call for further action	
Broadcast	25 37.9%	0 0.0%	22 33.3%	17 25.8%	3 4.5%	67
Newspaper	41 28.9%	19 13.4%	18 12.7%	73 51.4%	10 7.0%	161
Total	66	19	40	90	13	228

Appendix table 7.6 Prevalence of frames within different categories of news

Publication type/ section	Harken frame					Total
	No wrongdoing	Acknowledgment of excused or mitigated minor wrongdoing	Harken as a political contest/game	Critical assessment or accusation without call for action	Critical assessment or accusation with call for further action	
Any TV news	25 37.9%	0 0.0%	22 33.3%	17 25.8%	3 4.5%	67
Section A / top news	31 28.4%	16 14.7%	14 12.8%	53 48.6%	8 7.3%	122
Financial news	8 53.3%	1 6.7%	3 20.0%	5 33.3%	0 0.0%	17
Op-ed	2 11.1%	2 11.1%	1 5.6%	15 83.3%	2 11.1%	22
Total	66	19	40	90	13	228

8

Silenced Scandals of Grave Misconduct

Having moved through scandals or non-scandals involving minimal impacts on public welfare (infidelity), to those imposing some costs (evading the military draft or duties), to one of more substantial social damage (George W. Bush's insider trading and the SEC's passivity), we now focus on two potential scandals that might have arisen over high-cost presidential misconduct. The first concerned the Bush administration's campaign to justify the Iraq war by claiming Saddam Hussein could deploy weapons of mass destruction (WMD) against the US or its European friends. Iraq possessed no such weapons. Despite leading the US into a costly war against Iraq based on a non-existent WMD threat, George W. Bush was not framed as scandalously incompetent or dishonest. How this potential presidential scandal was silenced, despite the war's yielding few benefits to the US in exchange for death, destruction, and immense financial cost – over $3 trillion (Stiglitz & Bilmes 2010) – recapitulates and extends our model of scandal politics.

A closely related potential scandal centered on the revelation of Valerie Plame Wilson's identity as an undercover agent for the CIA. President Bush, Vice President Cheney, and their chiefs of staff (Karl Rove and I. Lewis "Scooter" Libby) were responsible for leaking her name to conservative columnist Robert Novak, who publicized her CIA affiliation, and to other reporters ("Key players in the CIA leak investigation" 2007). Beyond destroying Valerie Plame's career at the agency, this act damaged the covert endeavors she ran as operations chief of the Joint Task Force on Iraq (Isikoff & Corn 2006; V. P. Wilson 2008). Those activities were ironically intended to discover and help eliminate Iraq's WMD. In this case, there was a major scandal but accusations centered on the two underlings, Rove and Libby. Only Libby had to face indictment and conviction, and only for perjury. Bush later commuted his prison sentence.

Plame's name was leaked to retaliate against her husband, Joseph Wilson, who had publicly criticized the Bush administration's WMD claims (Fitzgerald 2006; cf. Sanger & Johnston 2006; see also *United States of America* vs. *I. Lewis Libby* 2005). Explaining the course of this scandal will complete exposition of the scandal process and serve as prelude to the concluding chapter's discussion of normative matters: how *should* media handle presidential misconduct and potential scandals across the different realms of behavior and levels of social cost?

The administration certainly received an enormous amount of criticism for its policies toward Iraq, particularly after 2005 (Entman, Livingston, Aday & Kim 2010). Illustrating the crucial difference between politically *damaging* attacks on an administration and presidential *scandal*, however, the data reveal that Bush minimized his personal accountability through a variety of diversionary techniques. The case studies also provide more granular insight into the scandal operations of the political communication system, especially the gap between elite newspapers' editorial pages on the one hand, and the television and cable news outlets that more powerfully shape perceived and actual public opinion on the other.

Missing weapons of mass destruction

The WMD matter follows Scandal Path I. After the US, with some allies, invaded Iraq (March 2003), early reports suggested that no WMD could be found. From that point through the release of George W. Bush's memoir, *Decision Points*, in late 2010, the breakdown of the primary justification for the war was generally treated in non-judgmental terms: little causal responsibility or moral condemnation attached to the president as knowingly acting against the law or the public good. Instead, Americans heard a tale much like Ronald Reagan's during Iran–Contra, in which the president admitted incompetence and thereby diverted attention from the more volatile and threatening possibility of presidential law-breaking or violating more serious positional norms. Even better from the Bush administration's vantage-point, the incompetence was not even located in the White House, but somewhere out in the impenetrable bowels of the intelligence bureaucracy.

Tracing the path of non-scandal

At Level 2 of the political communication network hierarchy (figure 2.3), neither the media nor opposition party elites promoted a scandal investigating whether President George W. Bush and Vice President Richard Cheney knowingly manipulated, selectively chose and discarded, or exaggerated intelligence data – whether they inflated a threat they had good reason to believe didn't exist. Perhaps Bush and Cheney sincerely believed Iraq posed a direct threat to the US with or without WMD, so felt it acceptable to claim more certainty about WMD than they possessed. Their avoidance of looking for weaknesses in intelligence reports indicating the presence of WMD and their pressure on intelligence agencies to find evidence for WMD rather than against might then have seemed justifiable to them (see, e.g., Pincus & Priest 2003; Isikoff & Corn 2006; Pillar 2006; Suskind 2006). Putting aside assessments of truth and culpability, this chapter aims to illustrate the book's model by showing: (1) how facts with great potential to be framed as grave presidential scandals often escape such framing; and (2) how this treatment renders openly available facts less potent politically – even when the costs to society are massive. Not only was there considerable evidence that Bush and Cheney intentionally misled the US (and UK) to war in Iraq; their shifting focus to Iraq also arguably contributed to prolonging America's costly war in Afghanistan. By tracing responsibility mainly to unnamed underlings in the defense and intelligence bureaucracies, reporting contained a potential scandal.

A Bush–WMD scandal might have altered enough evaluations of Bush's competence and morality to cost Republicans the White House in 2004. Instead, Election Day exit polls showed the Republicans with an 18 percent lead over Democrats as the party voters trusted to protect the US against terrorism ("Ronald Reagan from the people's perspective: a Gallup Poll review" 2004). Majority opinion on Iraq did not decisively turn against Bush and the Republicans until the summer of 2006, more than three years after the WMD failure should have been plain to all (Entman et al. 2010). In fact, as further evidence for the absence of high-magnitude scandal framing, polls show 69 percent believed in June, 2003, that WMD *had* been found. And 51 percent still believed that in 2004, 50 percent in 2006, and 37 percent even in 2008 (Harris Polls in 2003, 2004, 2006, 2008;[1] see also Kull 2004).

Now, it is true that mainstream media show particular deference to government officials when it comes to national security. This treatment establishes a higher bar for scandal framing than exists in domestic affairs. Nonetheless, the Iran–Contra scandal offers a precedent for a presidential scandal over foreign policymaking. The societal cost of the WMD miscue and ensuing Iraq war was far greater than Iran–Contra. Irrespective of whether Bush was motivated by conviction that some greater good would be served by marketing the war via the WMD threat, this blunder had the potential to turn into a scandal of high magnitude. That it did not therefore merits further explanation, particularly in light of conventional faith in the vigilance of watchdog journalism.

How the news deflected a presidential scandal

To obtain a concrete sense of how the national media framed the blame for the faulty case favoring war in Iraq, we[2] conducted a quantitative content analysis of news coverage related to the White House and weapons of mass destruction after the Iraq Survey Group reported that they had found no such weaponry in Iraq. We used the LexisNexis news database to identify relevant articles and transcripts published or aired between January 1, 2004 and December 31, 2005, by any one of six national media outlets: the *Washington Post*, *USA Today*, the *New York Times* and ABC, CBS and NBC evening news programs. The search terms were *weapons of mass destruction* or *WMD* along with at least one of the following key terms representing the Bush administration: *Bush* or *President* or *White House* or *Cheney*. This search yielded a universe of 1,068 articles and transcripts. In addition, with the paragraph as our unit of analysis, within this overall universe of over 1,000 media texts, we used the data analysis program MAXQDA to create a subset of passages consisting exclusively of paragraphs relevant to our research question – those containing the terms *WMD* or *Weapons of Mass Destruction* within 100 words of commonly occurring terms identified as exculpatory or indicative of guilt: *wrong*, *fail*, *mistake*, *flaw* (innocent) or *misled*, *spin*, *deliberate*, *lie*, *fix* (guilt). This subset of exculpatory and guilt-related passages included 560 unique paragraphs.

We then evaluated a random sample of 25 percent of these passages (n = 142 paragraphs) against three criteria to determine the degree to which these outlets' coverage tended to reflect the White House line that the problem was bad intelligence or, alternatively, that the Bush White House knew that intelligence claiming Iraq possessed WMD was tenuous and either exaggerated it or ignored contradictions.

Of the 142 articles in the sample, 12 were excluded for irrelevance or because they were duplicative, yielding the final sample *n* of 130. Specifically, the three questions the content analysis sought to answer were: (1) what percentage of paragraphs in the selected text actually provided any attribution of responsibility or explanation of the faulty case for war; (2) when the paragraph did provide an explanation, did it characterize the problem as unintentional error – a case of flawed intelligence (making the CIA and other agencies rather than Bush ultimately responsible) – or did it suggest presidential wrongdoing?; and (3) if the text indicated malfeasance in making the case for war, was it presented as a serious breach or merely a case of exaggeration and hype?

Despite the seriousness and grave societal costs precipitated by making a false case for war in Iraq, only 61 percent of the 130 paragraphs (*n* = 80) containing mentions of the Bush White House along with WMD actually referred in any way to an explanation of the enormous error. The other 39 percent of passages mentioning WMD in the required proximity to mentions of Bush, Cheney or the White House offered no explanation of the miscue. As shown in table 8.1, adding the paragraphs not mentioning any cause (50) to those deflecting the blame from the White House (47), we get 97 of the 130, or 75 percent explicitly or by omission excusing Bush from anything worse than poor management. Many of the explicit mentions actually cast Bush as the unwitting victim of subordinates' mistakes rather than indicating he shared any responsibility for them.

In determining whether the text indicated that there was intentional wrongdoing, we cast a wide net, considering a wide variety of malfeasance. Even using a broad definition, however, only 33 (25

Table 8.1 Intentionality and type of fault or malfeasance

Explanation or judgment	Frequency	Percent of paragraphs	Cumulative percentage
None provided	50	38.5	38.5
Unintentional error / no malfeasance / faulty intelligence	47	36.2	74.6
Hype or exaggeration	10	7.7	82.3
Other serious wrongdoing	16	12.3	94.6
Lying or deliberate deception	7	5.4	100.0
Total	130	100.0	

percent) of the 130 WMD-related passages indicated that any sort of presidential malfeasance had occurred.

Arraying these 33 allegations along a continuum, the least serious would be charges of hyping or knowingly exaggerating the existing evidence, and the gravest would be unambiguous accusations that Bush (or Cheney) lied to the American people. Hyping the evidence was indicated in 10 paragraphs. In the other 23 instances, Bush was charged with a variety of willful violations of the public trust, including deceiving or intentionally misleading the public about the quality of evidence, ignoring important data, and failing to investigate WMD information thoroughly enough. Explicit allegations of lying, the most serious type of misconduct, were the least common and rarely leveled at Bush directly, occurring in only two instances in the random sample. One of these merely quoted the wording of a survey that asked respondents whether they thought that the administration had "lied." The same pattern held true in a separate, broader search of the entire sample of 560 paragraphs. Although the blogosphere was replete with accusations that Bush himself engaged in deliberate distortion or lying, such direct claims were all but absent from the mainstream media.

Discussion

Even after gaining the majority in Congress with the 2006 elections, Democrats demanded no special prosecutor, held no hearings designed to spotlight Bush and Cheney's role. Prior to Democrats' assumption of the control in Congress, Senator Pat Roberts (R-KS), chairman of the Senate Intelligence Committee, promised but failed to hold public hearings and produce an unclassified investigative report on exactly what went wrong. Such a document was issued only after the Democrats regained control of the White House (Rockefeller 2009), and Democrats did not use the Intelligence Committee's findings to launch a scandal inquiry directed at Bush. One explanation for the Democrats' passivity might be their own culpability. The Democrats' leading lights mostly cooperated with the Bush administration's selling of the Iraq war. Senators Hillary Clinton, Chuck Schumer, John Edwards and John Kerry – all with party leadership or presidential ambitions – declared their own forceful warnings about Iraq's nuclear program in 2002 without verifying the intelligence reports or exerting much effort to slow the march to war (Sarat & Hussain 2010). Even though Democrats in 2009 controlled the presidency as well as Congress, it would have been difficult for them

to look backwards and investigate the pre-war period without implicating themselves.

Arguably the media played a role in establishing disincentives
for members of either party to vigorously challenge the Bush
administration's military solutions to the perceived problems created
by the September 11, 2001 terrorist attacks (see Entman 2004; Mueller
2006; Entman et al. 2010). The fear of seeming "soft on defense" is
an especially powerful deterrent to Democratic members of Congress
who seek party leadership or national office, or who represent swing
states or districts. Democrats anticipate – accurately – that they will
be unable to penetrate the media's decision biases favoring simplicity
and stereotyped novelty to make a complex, nuanced argument in
response to attacks for weakness on defense. Republicans "own" the
traits of strength and expertise on defense issues, and the Bush
administration mounted an intensive communication campaign,
including intimidation of news organizations (Bennett et al. 2007), to
frame any dissent from its war on terrorism as unpatriotic. Such
conditions made it relatively easy for Republicans to stereotype any
dissenting Democrats for insufficient devotion to national security
(see, on issue ownership and journalistic expectations, Hayes 2008).
Explaining that strength and patriotism might lead thoughtful leaders
to oppose a military intervention of little use in containing al Qaeda
or fundamentalist Muslim terrorism was difficult for Democrats,
especially in the aftermath of 9/11.[3] Thus Democratic voices were
quite sparse, at least in the network evening news. Saddam Hussein
himself was quoted nearly as frequently as all Democratic sources on
ABC, CBS and NBC during the pre-war debate: 3 percent of quotes
came from Saddam, 4 percent from Democrats. Fewer than three-
fifths of these statements opposed the president's policy, and most of
the Democrats' quotations were aired in August and September,
drying up as the 2002 elections approached (Hayes & Guardino 2010,
pp. 74–8).

Functionally, the Democrats' diffidence meant that there was little
differentiation between Levels 2 and 3 of the political communication
network hierarchy, causing inputs into production of the news text
at Level 4 to be largely homogeneous. These are the key traits of
Path I, the route taken by silenced scandals. The narrative that dominated WMD coverage was essentially a never-explained failure of
unidentified intelligence bureaucrats (for a detailed study of the early
WMD coverage, see Moeller 2004). A nearly identical story could be
told about the Bush administration's other major justification for the
Iraq policy: that Saddam Hussein was involved in the September 11
attacks (see Pillar 2006). Looking at every ABC, CBS and NBC

network evening news story mentioning Iraq before the war (August 2002 – March 2003), Hayes and Guardino (2010, p. 69) found WMD to be the single most frequent focus of news coverage, at 22 percent of all stories. The second most common problem definition in pre-war coverage was Iraq's link to terrorism (the focus in 4 percent of stories). These data demonstrate for our purposes how Bush's problem framing dominated the news.

One important consequence of the failure to frame either of these unfounded justifications for war as scandalous misrepresentation was Bush's victory in the 2004 election. The election came a year and a half after it became clear there were no WMD or Iraqi connections to 9/11. In truth, however, this was mainly clear to Democrats, as responses to the news of the Iraq war were highly polarized. Surveys indicate substantial majorities of Bush supporters before the 2004 election believed WMD had been found and that Saddam Hussein was either directly involved with 9/11 or provided support to al Qaeda. Most Democrats rejected these views. More significantly, majorities of undecided voters swallowed the key rationales for war (Kull 2004). The same poll showed 49 percent of respondents believing Bush acted in good faith (that he thought his assumptions about Iraq were correct) and 24 percent assuming he did not (i.e. knew the assumptions were false). Most other respondents (23 percent) continued to believe that Bush's "assumptions about Iraq" were correct (and 4 percent didn't answer).

By 2006, more Americans expressed doubts about the administration's good faith, though it's unclear how many blamed Bush personally.[4] In a Gallup Poll taken during January, 53 percent of respondents said they thought the "Bush administration deliberately misled" Americans about Iraq's WMD. Yet 57 percent in a March 2006 Gallup Poll said they were either certain that Iraq had WMD, or thought it likely. And 50 percent in a July Harris Poll said they believed WMD had been found (Hanley 2006). Since half or more seemed to believe the WMD claims were true, these three polls together imply that many people felt the Bush administration had misled Americans but not specifically on the WMD issue. As is often true, polls yield conflicting results. Most surveys cannot yield definitive conclusions on the full range of opinions, values, emotions, and contradictions any individual citizen actually exhibits. In prior work (Entman 2004: ch. 4), I suggested that, given the difficulties in ascertaining actual public opinion, elites contemplating their best political moves must use what they *perceive* to be majority opinion and where they anticipate it's heading. Elites appear to rely heavily on media coverage in making those determinations.

This book's model of political scandal assumes the media influence *indicators* of public opinion (figure 2.3), which feed back to affect elites' political words and deeds. The model doesn't assume the media influence the public's actual (and maddeningly difficult-to-determine) opinions. In the face of clashing indicators on the public's WMD sentiments in 2006, nearly four years after the invasion found no such weapons, elites had little incentive to stick their necks out by fomenting a presidential scandal. One conclusion from this case is that scholars ought to delve further into the phenomena of perceived and anticipated public opinion as forces shaping elites' political incentives and rhetorical options – and into the reciprocal relationships between those elite activities and media frames.

Although framing in the mainstream media – and in survey questions – failed to emphasize Bush's personal culpability, evidence for the proposition that Bush knowingly ignored contrary evidence in order to pursue a pre-determined course of war did circulate along certain networks of association, particularly among Democratic bloggers, intellectuals, policy experts, book writers and attentive citizens (Corn 2003; Pincus & Priest 2003; Suskind 2006; Pfiffner 2007).[5] But in essence these ideas looped around endlessly at Levels 3, 4 or 5 (journalists, texts, and limited segments of the public) without altering behavior at Level 2, where the power resides. Another characterization for this situation might be "preaching to the choir." Unless elites create news by taking governmental actions that uncover new evidence, force the misbehaving official to answer questions, or in other ways potentially threaten the politician's standing and position, a scandal cascade cannot generate sufficient energy to become self-reinforcing – to embark on Path II.

Democrats were loath to take that route, as evidenced by party leaders' response to Rep. Dennis Kucinich's (D-OH) efforts to launch impeachment proceedings. In the words of a *Washington Post* report (Pershing 2008):

> As they have previously, Democratic leaders staunchly oppose Kucinich's impeachment effort. They expect to table the resolution by referring it to the Judiciary Committee, where they expect it to die.

> House Majority Leader Steny H. Hoyer (D-MD) suggested yesterday that engaging in a lengthy debate over impeaching Bush in the waning days of his administration is not a productive use of the House's time.

As noted earlier, this reticence can be traced at least in part to Democrats' own active support for or acquiescence to war, as well as to their fear that media messages and public opinion would punish them for overly assertive opposition.

The Downing Street memo scandal and the contrast with America

Along these lines, it's revealing to compare the official actions and media responses that occurred in the United Kingdom on publication of the "Downing Street memo." The memo's key passage, published in the UK on May 1, 2005, was this: "Bush wanted to remove Saddam, through military action, justified by the conjunction of terrorism and WMD. But the intelligence and facts were being fixed around the policy." These words, paraphrasing a report from "C," the chief of the famed MI6 (British Intelligence), appeared in the memo, which summarized a meeting of senior ministers on July 23, 2002, in the Prime Minister's office at 10 Downing Street (London). The memo went on to describe the two options the US was considering, both involving war, and mentioned that Bush's National Security Council had "no patience with the UN route" (see Manning 2005). Within a few weeks, six more memos were revealed in the British media (Bicket & Wall 2007). British treatment of the memo – and, more generally, the WMD controversy – differs markedly from that accorded the matter in the US. Although one might expect British media to pay more attention than the American since the memo originated in Britain, its content actually focused on the behavior of the Bush administration, making it directly relevant to the US. Yet American media treated publication of the memo as old and therefore unimportant news (see Schiffer 2006; Bicket & Wall 2007). American political leaders responded similarly. In the UK, on the other hand, the revelations blew up into a major scandal that arguably helped destroy the political career of British Prime Minister Tony Blair, along with the Labour Party government.

America's two leading newspapers, the *New York Times* and *Washington Post*, gave the matter scant attention. The *Post*, for example, ran its first story about the memo and ensuing political storm in Britain on May 10, well over a week after its initial publication in the UK, placing it on page A-18. This came after the *Post*'s Ombudsman reported a deluge of blogs and emails assailing the *Post*'s neglect of the story (see McLeary 2005; Rieder 2005). The *Times* didn't publish a full story on the issue until May 20 (page A10). Meanwhile, the three traditional networks' nightly news programs together produced only one story focusing on the Downing

Street controversy during the 13 weeks following the initial news (Schiffer 2006, pp. 498, 501–3). White House correspondents didn't ask presidential press secretary Scott McClellan any questions about the matter until May 23, more than three weeks after the news broke.

A *Washington Post* editorial (June 15, 2005) explains its own treatment of the story and summarizes what was perhaps the conventional wisdom in the mainstream media at the time: "The memos add not a single fact to what was previously known about the administration's prewar deliberations. Not only that: They add nothing to what was publicly known in July 2002." Reflecting this view, Andrea Mitchell said on NBC (June 14, 2005) that people would have to be "brain dead not to know" that the administration was committed to war early on. James Fallows (*Atlantic Monthly*), Chris Matthews (MSNBC), David Broder (*Washington Post*), John Harwood (*Wall Street Journal*), Michael Kinsley (*Los Angeles Times*) and Susan Page (*USA Today*), among other elite journalists, treated the Downing Street news in similarly dismissive terms as old news (Bicket & Wall 2007, pp. 212–15). As often happens in the realm of scandals (recall the sex scandals of chapters 3 and 4), the elite Washington press corps perhaps mistook its own inside knowledge for that possessed by most Americans. Otherwise it would be difficult to explain the mainstream media's taking at face value and passing along without contradiction during 2002 and 2003 the administration's many assurances and diplomatic activities designed to signal that the US sought a peaceful solution. Bicket & Wall (2007) are somewhat less charitable. They see the low level of mainstream media attention as a "de facto containment strategy" (p. 213) that functioned to prevent damage to major news outlets' own credibility.

The liberal media watchdog organization Fairness and Accuracy in Reporting (FAIR) pointed out that such ho-hum reactions to the Downing Street revelations are difficult to square with media coverage of the run-up to the Iraq war (FAIR 2005). Between July 2002 and March 2003, when the war began, the Bush administration repeatedly claimed that (in President Bush's words of March 6, 2003) "I have not made up our mind [*sic*] about military action." The only time he personally answered reporters' questions on the Downing Street memo, Bush said:

Nobody wants to commit military into combat. It's the last option. . . . And so we worked hard to see if we could figure out how to do this peacefully, take a – put a united front up to Saddam Hussein, and say, "The world speaks," and he ignored the world. Remember,

[UN Resolution] 1441 passed the Security Council unanimously. He
made the decision. And the world is better off without Saddam Hussein
in power. (Joint press conference of George W. Bush and Tony Blair,
June 7, 2005)

These words are belied by the evidence of the memo and by other
sources as well. Books published since, including Bush's own memoir
(2010, p. 189), have confirmed that top members of the administration
were strongly inclined to launch war against Iraq immediately after
9/11. By some accounts, the administration was intent on eliminating
Saddam Hussein even before that (see Clarke 2004; Suskind 2004,
2006). Aside from the WMD debacle itself, some might argue that
leading the United Nations in a charade that, contrary to Bush's
implication, did *not* end in a UN resolution supporting the US invasion, itself constituted a scandalous abuse of the presidency.[6]

The mainstream media's accommodating coverage of the administration's WMD claims was almost universally acknowledged as
deficient by journalists and observers, including editors at the *New
York Times* and *Washington Post* (Entman 2004; Moeller 2004; W. L.
Bennett et al. 2007; Entman et al. 2010). Bush's own press secretary,
Scott McClellan (2008, p. 125), wrote that, throughout the run-up to
the war, the media served "as complicit enablers" and "neglect[ed]
their watchdog role" to focus on domestic and international political
maneuvering as war approached.

The two papers' self-critiques appeared in 2004, whereas their lack
of interest in the Downing Street memo came the following year.
Even within the papers' own pages, then, the dots remained
unconnected. If they admitted in 2004 doing a poor job at covering
the pre-war WMD claims, then the new evidence of 2005 that the
Bush administration "fixed" the data – or in the more resonant phrase
from a BBC report,[7] "sexed up" the intelligence (see Morris 2009;
Ames & Doward 2010) – the Downing Street document would seem
revelatory, not familiar, irrelevant old news. That is, their admissions
of journalistic failure imply that the average reader would not (despite
Andrea Mitchell's claim) have realized how tenuous the evidence for
WMD was in 2002–3 – or later, how substantial the evidence was for
Bush's negligence or deception.[8]

Why the media slept

Reflecting American elites' comparative lack of interest in sponsoring a scandal in 2005, no formal US inquiry focused on uncovering

the ultimate responsibility for the WMD failure. In the US, elites' passivity reinforced what might have been a natural inclination of media to avoid stirring up memories of their past shortcomings. After all, looking too closely at what the president knew about WMD and when he knew it could lead to similar questions about what the media knew and why they botched their watchdog duties (see Bicket & Wall 2007 on the media's self-interested cooperation in minimizing the Downing Street story). And the Democrats' reluctance to look backwards could be explained similarly. This shared disinclination illustrates the reciprocal influence of the opposition party and the media. When Rep. John Conyers (D-MI) held an informal hearing on the WMD debacle, outside the normal committee process in the House of Representatives, Dana Milbank wrote a news analysis in the *Post* that led with this disparaging sentence: "In the Capitol basement yesterday, long-suffering House Democrats took a trip to the land of make-believe."

It wasn't only the failure of the Democrats to exploit the potential that short-circuited a Bush–WMD scandal in the wake of the Downing Street memo or earlier. It was also the Bush administration's clever diversionary tactics. These included the claim that intelligence agencies around the world all agreed that Saddam Hussein had WMD; vociferous denials that there was any basis for doubt in the reports received by the president from the CIA and other intelligence sources; careful rhetoric that always placed responsibility on the intelligence agencies; and establishment of an "independent" commission of inquiry whose mandate was to investigate the reasons for the intelligence failure – i.e., it was set up to reinforce the Bush-exculpating assumption that the failure was in the bureaucracy, not in the White House.[9] The support of a disciplined Republican majority in the Congress during the period also helped by ensuring there would be no investigation on Capitol Hill.

Since the minority Democrats did not determinedly pursue an investigation either, and continued their forbearance even after assuming the Congressional majority in 2007, there was no government action to serve as the political stimulus (analogous to an economic stimulus) that might jump-start the process. The market in scandal, at least the segment relating to Iraq, remained in deep recession. Indeed, after Democrats took control of the White House too, in 2009, President Obama was at pains to specifically reject investigations of the Bush administration's actions before and during the Iraq war, keeping the market moribund. He proclaimed "a belief that we need to look forward as opposed to looking backwards" and said, for example, that he didn't want CIA staffers "to suddenly feel like they've got to spend all their time looking over their shoulders" (Johnston & Savage 2009; cf. Holmes 2010).

The Democrats failed to establish a scandal narrative around any of the problematic aspects of the Bush administration's war on terror. As documented in many books, these included its authorizing torture in contravention of the Geneva Convention; incompetent governance of post-Saddam Iraq; ineffective response to Iraqi insurgency and ethnic civil war; lax oversight of the reconstruction and aid efforts in Iraq and Afghanistan, leading to multi-billion-dollar corruption; shifting of military responsibilities onto politically well-connected private security contractors without requiring accountability – and the list goes on (see, among other sources, Packer 2005; J. A. Baker et al. 2006; Chandrasekaran 2006; Ricks 2006; Hayes & Guardino 2010).

Despite this lengthy catalog of costly shortcomings, the potential for scandals of presidential incompetence or dishonesty receded and accountability was left largely to the editorial and op-ed pages of a few newspapers, to some poorly publicized Congressional and think-tank reports, to books such as those just cited, and to some liberal magazines. On their own, even if their total volume is substantial, these outlets cannot create a major scandal as defined here.

The WMD case thus provides a fitting summary of how the cascade system works. It suggests that an administration allied with a determined, disciplined and unified presidential party can short-circuit a scandal – especially where the opposition party shows little proclivity to ignite or sustain one. Bush himself was only rarely questioned about the WMD failures. Unsurprisingly, he avoided press conferences around the time that his own Iraq Survey Group concluded the Saddam Hussein regime held no WMD stockpiles (October 2004) and when the search for WMD was finally called off (January 2005). When he was asked about WMD, his answers were not forthcoming (see Benoit 2006). Reporters failed to press him or correct such artfully obfuscating statements as the one quoted above.[10] Revealing excerpts from Bush's press conference responses to WMD questions are posted at www.robertmentman.com.

Absent investigation by Congress or legal agencies, there was of course no way for news organizations to confirm as fact that Bush led an effort to deliberately distort or "sex up" the evidence and thereby justify a foreordained decision to wage unnecessary war on Iraq. Even with a thorough inquiry, this is the sort of conclusion about what the president knew and when he knew it that defies conclusive confirmation in most cases, including many covered in prior chapters. George W. Bush's decision to initiate war could have been caused by many forces. Among them: willful self-delusion; Oedipal impulses to surpass his father, who left Saddam Hussein in power after putative victory in the Gulf war (1991); passivity in the face of a determined effort to make war by his far more experienced and only nominally subordinate advisors Cheney and Rumsfeld; genuine conviction combined with the lack of intellectual curiosity that initially kept him from understanding the differences between Sunni and Shiite Muslims; political calculations on the benefits of being a successful war president; and the fear these dividends would fade after the US's apparent quick victory in Afghanistan well before 2004.[11]

Only a systematic investigation of the sort conducted in the UK could yield much insight into the reasons that, for example, top officials relied heavily on the word of a single low-credibility source nicknamed "Curveball" – a man who later admitted he wholly invented his reports of Iraqi WMD capacity in order to encourage a US war on Saddam (Chulov & Pidd 2011). Rumsfeld himself released a memorandum he received from the head of military intelligence reporting his group's confidence level in estimating various Iraqi threats as ranging between 0 and 75 percent – very far from a slam dunk (Dowd 2011). Careful investigation would be needed to determine why Rumsfeld, frustrated at the insufficiently robust confirmation of suspicions about Iraq's capabilities and intentions, established a special new intelligence unit reporting to the pro-war, neoconservative political appointee Douglas Feith. Yet all this evidence and more, however thoroughly probed, could not establish President Bush's culpability with absolute certainty. In fact – and this is a key point – aside from the instances in which indisputable evidence forced presidents or candidates to confess or resign (e.g., Nixon–Watergate, Clinton–Lewinsky, Edwards–Hunter), few allegations of scandal against high-level politicians are ever definitively proven. That doesn't prevent some of them from becoming high-magnitude scandals. Understanding why some do and others don't has been the focus of this book.

The WMD case also suggests again the limited ability of the blogosphere, social media or other newer communication technologies to guarantee government transparency or to initiate a scandal from below. Aside from the liberal activists' success at pressuring the *Post*'s and *Times*' editors over their neglect of the Downing Street Memo, to which the papers did respond, albeit grudgingly, belatedly and sketchily, research suggests liberal blogs *were* able to promote greater discussion on major newspapers' op-ed pages (Schiffer 2006, p. 504). This effect is noteworthy in the sense that influencing the op-eds could in theory have stimulated additional and more prominent digging by reporters into the WMD story. However, this was not to be. Furthermore, plain old letters to the editor and phone calls might well have yielded the same limited impact on the *Post* and *Times* as the messages conveyed via online conduits. The Valerie Plame case also shows that leading newspapers' op-ed pages enjoy the autonomy to convey more diversified views than other media venues, without being able to ignite a full-scale scandal. In the WMD matter, then, where evidence of presidential misconduct – as catastrophic managerial failure, conscious deception or both – was abundant, newer media outlets could not displace or even substantially move the traditional hierarchy of scandal news production.

Finally, the Iraq war indicates more generally a somewhat stronger interest in contemporary and retrospective accountability among elites and media in the UK than in the US (see Moeller 2004, p. 19; W. L. Bennett et al. 2007; P. Robinson, Goddard, Parry, Murray & Taylor 2010). After Blair's resignation in considerable disgrace, the new Labour prime minister, Gordon Brown, set up the Iraq Inquiry (also known as the Chilcot Inquiry after its chairperson) to investigate the UK's role in the Iraq war. Sitting for about two years (2009–11), it took detailed and self-incriminating testimony from those men and many other participants in the war decision, such as the head of British Intelligence (see, e.g., Ames 2011). Blair testified over the course of two days; video and transcripts are available on the Inquiry's comprehensive website (www.iraqinquiry.org.uk). American leaders were held to no such account.

Bush–Cheney vs. Plame–Wilson

It is difficult to say exactly what Valerie Plame did for the CIA and, therefore, exactly how much damage was caused to US national security when she lost her cover. The CIA was never particularly forthcoming with details, nor was Plame or her husband, Joseph Wilson. We do know that her assignment was to monitor and derail proliferation of WMD with particular respect to Iraq (see, e.g., her testimony to Congress, "Plame hearing transcript" 2007; also J. C. Wilson 2004; Isikoff & Corn 2006; V. P. Wilson 2008). She was chief of operations for the CIA's Joint Task Force on Iraq, a component of the agency's clandestine Counter-Proliferation Division within its Directorate of Operations. She worked at the headquarters building but also frequently conducted covert missions overseas. Both domestically and internationally, she assumed the identity of an executive for a (CIA front) venture capital company called Brewster, Jennings and Associates. She worked under "non-official cover," which is a deeper level of secrecy than that possessed by many CIA operatives who are given an official cover (e.g. cultural attaché at an American embassy).

In this light, the destruction of her career and the resulting threat to her network of foreign informants becomes especially noteworthy. Bush, Cheney, Rove and Libby[12] cooperated in divulging Plame's identity as a covert employee of the CIA in order to punish her husband for dissenting from the administration's story-line on Iraq – and warn other potential dissenters. The special prosecutor, US Attorney Patrick Fitzgerald, said that: "It is hard to conceive of what evidence there could be that would disprove the existence of White House efforts to 'punish Wilson'" (Fitzgerald 2006, p. 30). In other words, Bush and Cheney[13] compromised an important CIA operation, the goal of which was to keep WMD out of Saddam Hussein's hands, purportedly to protect the mission of invading Iraq for the stated purpose of keeping WMD out of Saddam's hands.

In a further irony, since there were no Iraqi WMD and no nuclear weapons program, the destruction of Plame's career and damage to the operations of the CIA's Joint Task Force on Iraq didn't hold catastrophic implications for the security of the US. It did, however, have implications for the personal security of Plame and her family, as well as some of the foreign CIA informants with whom she worked; this meant some unknown amount of disruption to the CIA's effectiveness in tracking nuclear, chemical and biological weapon proliferation. Various CIA insiders have leaked to the press information both confirming and denying the existence of an official damage assessment, and claims about whether one exists seem to depend on the partisan predilection of the sources. One CIA insider anonymously told the *Washington Post*, "You'll never get a straight answer about how valuable she was or how valuable her sources were" (Linzer 2005). A press release issued by the office of Patrick Fitzgerald (a Bush appointee) on October 28, 2005 alluded to the harm caused by the Plame outing: "Disclosure of classified information about an individual's employment by the CIA has the potential to damage the national security in ways that range from preventing that individual's future use in a covert capacity, to compromising intelligence-gathering methods and operations, and endangering the safety of CIA employees and those who deal with them" (Office of Special Counsel 2005, p. 2). If nothing else, naming Plame and disrupting the CIA's counter-WMD operations just as the US was preparing to go to war on the basis of the purported WMD threat would constitute an indictment of Bush's management style at least as serious as that of President Reagan during Iran–Contra. Yet

Reagan had to face hearings in Congress and massive publicity focusing on exactly what the president knew and when he knew it. Why didn't this fate befall Bush? After all, by publicizing Valerie Plame's identity, Bush and Cheney undermined achievement of the president's stated goals for the Iraq war. Therefore, the act raised logical questions as to whether they truly believed the rationale for the policy. If the Bush administration's goal was to separate Iraq from WMD, it would hardly have made sense for the president to damage covert operations designed to do exactly that. On the other hand, if Bush and Cheney were fairly confident that Iraq did not possess WMD, imperiling the CIA's counter-proliferation efforts wouldn't much matter. It might reasonably be argued that Bush and Cheney could rationalize any harm to the CIA operation as a short-term inconvenience, since they were confident the US war would soon topple Saddam Hussein and put an end to his WMD. The point here, again, is not to establish a definitive account of the president and vice president's true motivations, but to suggest that their actions could have spawned a high-magnitude presidential scandal.

In Fitzgerald's interview of Bush, the president denied specific knowledge that Cheney would have Valerie Plame's name leaked. It would be unlikely for a president whose leadership style emphasized delegation rather than micromanagement to get into that kind of detail. According to a *National Journal* report of the interview, what Bush admitted was that "he directed Vice President Dick Cheney to personally lead an effort to counter allegations made by former Ambassador Joseph C. Wilson IV that his administration had misrepresented intelligence information to make the case to go to war with Iraq" and "had directed Cheney, as part of that broader effort, to disclose highly classified intelligence information that would not only defend his administration but also discredit Wilson" (Waas 2006; cf. Leopold 2007; McClellan 2008). In his own interview with Fitzgerald, Cheney responded 72 times with variations on "I don't recall." This and other evidence led Fitzgerald himself to observe at the end of the Libby trial that "there is a cloud over the vice president" (Perel 2011).

Framing Scooter Libby

We now consider the evidence that the scandal arising from the outing of Valerie Plame was limited in ways difficult to square with most understandings of scandal politics – but predictable in accordance with the approach developed in this book. With respect to the White House, the Plame scandal traveled on Path I. That is, the potential for a major presidential scandal remained dormant. Despite the evidence that Bush and Cheney acted to allow Plame's identity to be publicized, analysis shows that the spotlight focused on their chiefs of staff, Libby and Rove. Libby became the central villain of a sub-presidential scandal; Rove was called to testify before a grand jury several times and there was considerable speculation in the press that he might be indicted, but he was not, and that limited the scandalous publicity linking him with the Plame affair. Bush's political goal would have been to channel blame away from himself, Cheney and his own chief of staff, Rove. A content analysis[14] using MAXQDA software sampled the voluminous coverage of this case to determine the degree to which national media focused on the actions of Scooter Libby and others subordinate to President Bush, rather than on the president himself. The method chosen was a proximity search for the principals' names in the texts.

To construct a representative sample of news in the leading outlets, we used the LexisNexis news database to identify articles and transcripts published or aired between January 1, 2004 and December 31, 2007. The search included ten national outlets: the *Washington Post*, the *New York Times*, *USA Today*, *Newsweek* and AP Wire, and the CBS, ABC and NBC evening news programs, CNN and Fox. Search parameters identified articles and transcripts that included *Plame* or *Mrs. Wilson* or *Ms. Wilson* within the same paragraph as *Bush*, *Cheney* or *Libby*. This search yielded 1,990 articles and transcripts. Using the WordStat content analysis module of MAXQDA, a dictionary of the principals' names and the terms *White House*, *Administration* and *Chief of Staff* was developed. The dictionary provided the ability to isolate the names and titles from their relationship to other actors in the study. Key examples are making the distinction between sentences in which Vice President Cheney was described as doing or saying something, and those in which the term *Cheney* is invoked only to identify Libby as "Cheney's former chief of staff" or "former top aide to Vice President Cheney." WordStat allows for the creation of rules to eliminate these passing mentions from the analysis. By isolating the actions of the individual actors, we can clarify the degree to which they were directly implicated via naming in the scandal coverage. Once the dictionary was created, cross-tabulation determined co-occurrences of the terms (using the dictionary exclusions)[15] within the same paragraph. This method does not account for subtle ways in which even the use of Bush and Cheney's names as modifiers, rather than in referring to the president or vice president themselves, could have imposed political damage on them. The trade-off was the ability to employ computer-assisted content analysis on a very large sample of coverage.[16]

The data show an inverse relationship between the co-appearance of *Plame* and the actor's closeness to President Bush. The closer the official to Bush, the more distant was his name from that of Plame. *Bush* and *Plame* only appeared 287 times in the same paragraph, *Cheney* and *Plame* 684 times, *Rove* and *Plame* 1,011 times, and *Libby* and *Plame* 2,916 times – more than 10 times the Bush–Plame level.

A semantic proximity chart using Jaccard coefficients allows the visualization of the relationships.[17] It shows a much closer relationship (a higher Jaccard coefficient) between *Plame* and *Libby*, and *Plame* and *Rove*, than *Plame* and *Cheney* or *Plame* and *Bush*. For this analysis we included two other terms, *administration* and *chief of staff*, to reveal how often they occurred as compared to the names of the key actors. These data show that Libby was far and away the main actor named in coverage of the Plame scandal. Figure 8.1 suggests

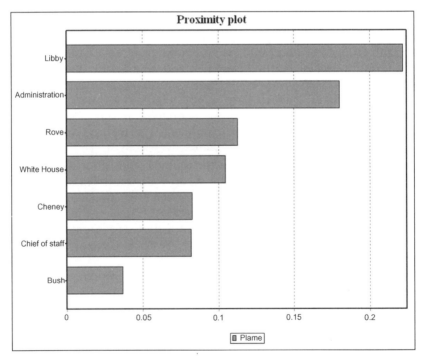

Figure 8.1 Proximity of *Plame* to officials' names

that the media coverage diverted most responsibility for outing Plame onto lower-level administration members. The Jaccard coefficient for *Libby* and *Plame* is far higher than that for *Bush* and *Plame*. The chart supports the argument of administration critics that Libby was a scapegoat or fall guy (see below).

Bush's success at distancing himself from this scandal is also revealed by the infrequency with which he was questioned directly by the press about his role, let alone aggressively asked to justify it. Recall that one criterion for high-magnitude scandal is direct interrogation of the accused by journalists. Using the American Presidency Project (APP) website, a comprehensive online collection of resources pertaining to the president of the United States, multiple searches of White House news conferences were conducted. We searched the archive for each of the following terms occurring with *news conference*: *Plame, Wilson, Libby, Cheney, CIA, CIA Employee Identity Disclosure Investigation* and *Disclosure of CIA Employee's Identity* (the latter two were APP's own classification). The search found 11 instances in which President Bush was directly questioned about the Plame matter and the resulting investigation. In only 2 of the 11 instances did reporters attempt follow-up questions.

Bush focused journalists' attention away from himself and onto the Justice Department and the US Attorney's office in several ways. Sometimes the president said he would not comment on an "ongoing investigation" (n = 5), other times he recommended reporters pose questions to representatives of the investigating agencies. This technique helped foster the impression that the issue was out of the president's hands and was being handled by others. Reporters' questions chiefly sought the president's predictions of potential consequences for the leaker should he/she be exposed; the implicit premise of such queries is that the leaker was not Bush or Cheney.

Explaining the Plame–Libby connection

Our explanation for the Bush administration's success in containing the Plame scandal starts with an analysis of 125 editorial-page items (73 unsigned newspaper editorials and 52 signed opinion columns) – all those in the "US Newspaper and Wire" library of LexisNexis that contained the terms *Libby* and *CIA* or *Plame* from the period Jan. 1, 2007 through June 20, 2007. The period analyzed encompasses 15 days before Libby was indicted until 15 days after he was convicted and sentenced for perjury. In the case of WMD, as noted in the prior section, editorials evinced more autonomy – their content was less tethered to the (minimal) degree of scandalized opposition by opponents of the Bush administration. The same is true here in that criticism of Bush or allusions to his possible responsibility for naming Plame were more common on the editorial pages. But, as for the WMD matter, truly scandalized attention to the president was limited.

Of the 125 items, only 4 treated Plame's outing as an offense demanding that Bush himself be held accountable through a determination of his own culpability. About 46 (36 percent) did trace causal responsibility to Bush or Cheney, and 14 of these (11 percent of the total sample) actually called Libby a scapegoat.[18] Nonetheless, it is striking that hardly any of the editorial discourse about the Plame outing and the Libby trial – which was its chief accountability mechanism – focused on the need to hold Bush (or Cheney) personally accountable.

Even when an item noted Bush's personal responsibility in the incident – with just the four exceptions – it stopped short of demanding that his role be thoroughly investigated or that he face sanctions if found culpable. Absent that moral demand for thorough assessment of causal responsibility and punishment of the chief executive if merited, there can be by our definition no major presidential scandal. Hardly any of the commentary took the critical steps needed for a presidential scandal cascade: targeting the president, and in this case perhaps the vice president, as primary causal agents, the identified villains who created a problem for the entire society demanding urgent resolution through official procedures of accountability. Neither Bush nor Cheney became a primary object of legal or criminal inquiry by any government entity. Although the two men were interviewed by prosecutor Patrick Fitzgerald, neither was deposed or required to testify under oath.

One illustration of how the president's distance from the Libby–Plame affair was maintained can be found in the way a threatening moment during Libby's trial played out. In his opening statement, Libby's lawyer identified Libby as the "fall guy" for Karl Rove. The lawyer sharply attacked Rove and announced he would call him and Vice President Cheney to testify (N. A. Lewis 2007). Concentrating the defense on Rove potentially put not only Cheney but also Bush in the crosshairs of the investigation. Yet ultimately, for reasons never explained, the defense did not carry out its announced plan and failed to require testimony from Rove, Cheney or even Libby (see, e.g., Blumenthal 2007).

Analysis of the 44 news items[19] in our sample containing *fall guy* offers no hint that Libby was taking the rap specifically for President

Bush. Three stories suggested Cheney as Libby's beneficiary (a *Times* story reported that "some say the Vice President bears responsibility for the fate of his former aide," CNN had a man on the street saying he thought Libby was protecting Cheney, and ABC showed a juror echoing that sentiment). As the proximity analysis showed, Cheney's name was more closely aligned with Plame's than was Bush's, while remaining at far greater remove than Libby's and Rove's. Cheney came up in part because a defense lawyer's statement mentioned a memo from Cheney onto which the vice president scribbled: "Not going to protect one staffer + sacrifice the GUY that was asked to stick his neck in the meat grinder because of incompetence of others." With these words, the vice president deftly deflected guilt from himself onto lower-level staffers, just as did his own superior, President Bush. Cheney also projected determination to do right by Libby, his loyal aide. Aside from this quote, media depicted the beneficiary of Libby's sacrifice as a vague entity such as "the Bush administration," rather than Bush or Cheney (though two stories identified Rove as the one who benefitted, that claim also implicitly cleared the president and vice president).

The demotion of the scandal to focus on a lower-level figure like Libby contained the political damage for Bush.[20] As evidence for the limited effects on Bush's moral standing from the Plame affair, it's useful to compare poll ratings of Bush's and Clinton's morality at the end of their second terms in office. In 2008, Bush was rated as moral by 51 percent of respondents (The American National Election Studies 2008). In 2000, Clinton's rating for morality was 16.3 percent (combining the codes "quite well" and "extremely well" when people were asked if the phrase "he is MORAL" describes the person). In fact, the percentage of Americans who considered Bush to be moral may be even higher; using the five-point response scale piloted by the National Election Studies in 2008, a total of 63.2 percent of respondents indicated that "moral" described Bush either "extremely", "very" or "moderately" well. The resilience of Bush's standing makes a prima facie case that neither Plame nor the rest of the potential scandals the president evaded inflicted much damage on his moral reputation, even if his image of competence deteriorated substantially as his administration wore on.

Conclusion

What both motivates and guides the media when Path II presidential scandal occurs is, in major part, the inherent drama: villains and heroes (e.g. Richard Nixon vs. Senator Sam Ervin, chair of the Senate's Watergate inquiry), accusations and defenses, maneuvering for political advantage, and, perhaps above all, the suspenseful uncertainty inherent in the ultimate threat of impeachment. When the opposition (and perhaps a few breakaway members of the majority party) fail to seize the initiative, the media are left to their own devices, which limits the scope and scale of scandal.

A vicious circle helps explain the larger pattern of presidential scandal during 1988–2008: one Democratic president constantly fending off scandals and actually impeached for an act of scant public relevance (see again figure 2.2) and two Republicans who never faced a threat of impeachment despite alleged misconduct inflicting significant costs on society: Iran–Contra, the Plame outing and the baseless WMD rationale for war. No doubt Democrats hesitated to vigorously pursue presidential scandal for a variety of reasons, but one might well be the sense that they would not get much help from the mainstream national media, pressured as news organizations would be from Republican defenders. That certainly is the tale told by the stillborn scandals discussed in this book. And perhaps the media failed to sound a vigorous alarm for Republican presidential scandal because, in some unknowable measure, they feared they would find themselves out on a limb alone without support from powerful Democrats.

Thus the paucity of scandalized editorializing or news coverage focusing on the president himself may be traceable in part to the meekness of the Democrats. Editorialists and Washington reporters were savvy enough to gauge the political environment and recognize the slim chances that any journalistic calls for further investigation and accountability would be followed by Democratic action. Meanwhile, critical editorials and vigorous reportorial investigation would likely engender pressure from Republicans, always ready to denounce the "liberal media." When the situation is reversed, when media begin digging into a potential scandal involving Democratic leaders, research indirectly indicates that party's elites rarely if ever unify around a campaign of outraged protest against the "conservative media" (see Entman 2010a for evidence that the term *conservative media* is rarely used as a synonym for the mainstream national news media whereas *liberal media* is used constantly as a synonym for them – even by journalists themselves; see also Watts et al. 1999). And that very dynamic undermines the Democrats' incentives to sponsor presidential scandals.

Furthermore, it's not just a matter of journalistic or Democratic timidity. Lacking a constant flow of colorful accusations and denunciations, the media's reporting of presidential misconduct cannot help but take the form of sporadic and scattered reports rather than a dramatic narrative of burgeoning presidential jeopardy. That in turn discourages scandalized editorializing – which still further depresses the news interest as assignment editors see little potential for politically decisive future developments or positive reactions from audiences to granting the malfeasance further attention (for evidence of the relationship between news decisions and editorial opinion stances, see Kahn & Kenney 2002).

Recall the variables helping to explain the occurrence of scandal cascades: the skill, power and motivations of the contending party elites; the decision-making heuristics or biases that shape news production; and the cultural congruence of the malfeasance. In 2007, while the Libby trial unfolded, Congress was controlled by the Democrats. The court proceedings offered them an opportunity to score political points against Bush and the Republican Party in advance of the 2008 election. Their passivity suggests that, for unknown reasons, Democrats' motivations to protect or expand their party's power were less intense than those of their Republican counterparts (see also Entman 2005). Democrats' skill at manipulating the scandal process also seemed inferior to the GOP's level of proficiency. Perhaps cultural congruence also played a part. Watergate was traumatic for the entire country, in major part because it told such a dissonant tale about the once-revered office of the presidency. It also unveiled the misleading public façades politicians often construct to obscure backstage realities. Ironically, after Watergate – generally seen as a triumph for both the Democrats and the "system" of constitutional checks and balances – the record shows Democrats hesitating, whether as the minority or majority in Congress, to pursue potential presidential scandals to their logical conclusions. Whereas Republicans consistently exploited presidential scandal opportunities under Clinton, Democrats held back, failing to establish Reagan and George H. W. Bush's responsibility in the Iran–Contra scandal (Fried 1997) for fear of another stressful impeachment crisis – and as we've seen throughout this book, forbearing from investigations of George W. Bush.

As with the non-scandal over WMD, these conditions meant information flowing from sources at Level 2 in the cascade hierarchy – political elites within and outside the administration – remained largely undifferentiated. The framing messages activated and channeled into news organizations at Level 3 were not organized into competing partisan narratives on Level 4, coherent stories that could serve as the template for high-magnitude scandal. Attention at and feedback from Level 5, public opinion, remained low and potential scandals occupied Path I.

Even in the age of independent news sites like *Huffington Post* and *Redstate*, of widely circulated ideological blogs such as those of Glenn Greenwald on the left and Michelle Malkin on the right, without government action, all that can happen at Level 3 is recirculation of scandalized discussion along specialized ideological and partisan sub-networks. For instance, Greenwald, Huffington or another blogger on the left might write in scalding detail of Bush's cynical undermining of national security for partisan gain when he outed Plame (see Gardner 2005; Greenwald 2005; Huffington 2005; "Remember what blogs were like before the Rove/Plame controversy? Nor do we" 2005). Occasionally, such information will be picked up by a reporter or, more likely, an editorialist. That writer will repeat the blog's allegations and some readers will be suitably outraged and pass along the item to their personal networks or post it to their own (barely read) blogs or Twitter feeds (see Hindman 2008). And there the information will reside, disregarded or derided by the administration's ideological defenders, added to the tally of complaints by its ideological opponents, and unknown by the moderates, independents, politically inattentive, and poorly informed citizens whose hearts and minds constitute the contestable ground of American politics.

9

Recalibrating Scandal and Silence

This concluding chapter first reviews and synthesizes the book's analysis of cases using the cascade model. Then it turns to normative matters, assessing how journalists might respond to potential scandals in ways more consistently supportive of democratic accountability. The key standard for all levels of misconduct, from the least costly (infidelity) through the moderately harmful (military records, financial malfeasance) to the most baleful (unjustified war), is *providing citizens the information needed for informed comparison of parties and candidates in presidential elections.* Anything less undermines America's already limited democracy (see Dahl 1989 on the necessity of some minimal level of voter information for an approximation of democracy; see also Entman 1989).

The book uses the cascade as a metaphor to illuminate the flows of information that possess the potential to initiate and sustain a politically significant scandal. Cascading activation is conceived as operating across a hierarchy of networks in which potentially scandalized responses from the lower-level networks (mediated communication texts and the public) must feed back to the upper levels (government elites and media organizations), with sufficient intensity and mass to ignite a politically meaningful scandal. Journalists and media observers sometimes assume that if a story has been covered somewhere once or twice, the information is out in the open, and the miscreant has been held to account. But a few reports of misconduct do not a politically meaningful scandal make.

As we've seen throughout the book, no presidential scandal of consequence occurs without repeated, resonant scandal framing in the mainstream media. Such scandals arise only when the media make information on misconduct readily accessible and easily interpretable by the public as scandalous. In the cascade model, it matters less for politics whether public opinion is actually outraged by the misdeeds than whether elites *believe* that there's widespread indignation, or a reasonable chance of public wrath in the future. Such perceptions can fulfill themselves as leaders move to exploit the political opportunity, setting off a cascading flow of opprobrium and further revelations, followed perhaps by government action that stimulates still more attention. Contrary to the implication of some observers, there's no guarantee that the political elites and journalists who jointly (though not in conscious collaboration) decide whether to magnify a scandal will accurately gauge public sentiments. Leaders may fail to seize any political opportunity offered by potential scandal, and media may take a pass on sensational revelations that could attract audiences. If so, the public will never have the chance to become incensed as they might have. When potential scandals are silenced, the power and authority of miscreants remain largely intact, and politics goes on as it did prior to the revelations.

The bulk of this book has been devoted to understanding how and why so many potential scandals remain dormant. In an attempt to understand the range of media responses to potential scandals in presidential politics, chapter 2 (figure 2.1) laid out a taxonomy based on two dimensions of variation: the realm and social costs of malfeasance. A simplified version is reproduced as figure 9.1 for the reader's convenience. The vertical spectrum starts from the essentially private arena; scandal can arise when politicians fail to uphold norms, ideals and laws that are supposed to guide the behavior of all respectable Americans. When such trespasses become public, politicians are exposed as violating (e.g. via marital infidelity) their symbolic/descriptive representational roles. At the second tier of actions that can spawn scandal are breaches of norms regulating social obligations and professional behavior outside politics (such as cooperating with the military draft or obeying insider trading laws). From the perspective of many Americans, failure on this score too constitutes symbolic or descriptive misrepresentation (Pitkin 1967). The top tier consists of violating norms and laws controlling political and governmental positions. Here we have reached substantive misrepresentation, as occurred when President George W. Bush failed to ensure citizens of the Gulf Coast were adequately protected before and after Hurricane Katrina (2005) or when his administration publicized the name of CIA agent Valerie Plame.

Scandalous misrepresentation can yield a range of consequences for other people. Along the horizontal axis in figure 9.1 is arrayed

Costs imposed on society →	Low	Substantial	High
Realm:			
Official			WMD
			Plame
Social			Insider trading
		National Guard	
		Draft evasion	
Private	Infidelity		

Figure 9.1 Simplified scandal taxonomy

a scale of social costs, from behavior that negatively affects only a handful of personal associates to malfeasance that seriously damages the public at large. Most potential scandals fall into one of the (loosely bounded) categories resulting when we combine these two axes.

Chapters 3 and 4 dealt with the contrast between scandals that happen and those that don't despite roughly similar breaches of norms governing the private realm. Scandals over politicians' marital lives occupy the lower left corner of figure 9.1, as their personal offenses impose costs on only a few people. Nonetheless, as displayed in the case of Bill Clinton, such scandals can develop high *magnitude* in the media and create major *political effects* – the third and fourth dimensions of scandal variation laid out in chapter 2. Chapter 3 explored the implicit rules governing the journalists' decision-making on scandals of personal misconduct, and finds them disjointed. Instead of following any consistent path of validating claims for truth or relevance to public office, the media produced – or didn't produce – personal scandals selectively, reflecting the media-friendly qualities of the information presented (e.g. simplicity, televisuality) and the skill and motivations of those sponsoring and attempting to block publicity.

The tacit knowledge that Washington journalists possessed about Clinton's sex life, based on widespread gossip and perceptions in Little Rock, combined with the poorly substantiated bombshells of Gennifer Flowers to create a salacious scandal that he survived politically in 1992. But it set the stage for later sex scandals to permanently degrade his moral image and his perceived fulfillment of ideals for symbolic representation. Meanwhile, the tacit knowledge insiders had about George H. W. Bush, Robert Dole and Newt Gingrich – the latter two arguably the dominant leaders of the Republican Party during the 1990s – went virtually unmentioned. And a completely unfounded claim about Michael Dukakis's personal (mental) health record was splashed all over the media, albeit briefly, after President Reagan promoted the rumor. Dukakis's presidential candidacy appears to have been damaged. Dole's was not, and Gingrich seriously pursued the 2012 Republican presidential nomination. Thus did chapter 3 demonstrate the uncalibrated nature and political impacts not merely of scandals covered but of potential scandals omitted.

Chapter 4 considered two sex scandals that did not occur in timely fashion during the 2008 presidential campaign despite the titillating evidence, and one that crashed immediately when the accused skillfully reframed it as a journalism scandal. National journalists chose to keep compromising information on the Clinton and Edwards families inside the beltway, and to accept John McCain's recasting of suspicions around his marital fidelity as a breach of journalistic ethics. Among other things, the chapter reveals the loopholes in the ability of the Internet to enhance transparency.

Even if it's true that Americans have grown more tolerant of sexual peccadilloes in their leaders, the energy that George H. W. Bush, Bob Dole and then John McCain devoted to squelching the threats of sex scandal testifies that fear of sexual exposure remains widespread among the political elite. Yet the Dole, McCain and other cases discussed in these chapters indicate that – contrary to legend – mainstream media between 1988 and 2008 were not especially eager to delve into the sexual activities of top-tier politicians, and readily detoured from such inquiry. The one time the mainstream media did expose a president's extramural sex life in prurient detail, it was because a highly motivated special prosecutor and opposition party kept pushing the matter. Like Watergate, Clinton–Lewinsky, the signature presidential sex scandal of this era, is a special case. Other sex scandals during these two decades immolated many political careers, but – with the spectacular but partial exception of Edwards, by then out of the race – only for lower-level politicians whose symbolic misrepresentation affected far fewer Americans than would that of a serious presidential contender.

In chapters 5 and 6 we considered cases falling into the middle range of the scandal taxonomy, behavior that violated social obligations and imposed costs on a somewhat wider scale. By evading the draft during Vietnam, Dan Quayle, George W. Bush and Bill Clinton transgressed the normative expectations Americans apparently held for young men eligible to serve. In these three cases, the scandals are classified as imposing costs on a segment of the public, because their actions did impinge slightly on all the males of draft age who did not have the resources or inclination to avoid getting drafted. Only a tiny number of federal office-holders ever served in Vietnam. Nearly all in that generation maneuvered to avoid the draft, as did most well-educated men (see Appy 1993). However, few have been subjected to the microscopic investigations and public opprobrium befalling Quayle and Clinton. In this respect, George W. Bush was fortunate. Using the cascade model and its key explanatory variables – elite skill, motivations, media decision biases and cultural congruence – chapter 5 explained why Quayle's and Clinton's draft evasion stimulated high-magnitude coverage compared with Bush's. Chapter 6 then extended the investigation by showing how George W. Bush managed to avoid a potentially even more damaging scandal over his privileged treatment by the National Guard. He and his advisors dodged scandal by reframing the reports to focus on CBS News, Dan Rather and their alleged journalistic malpractice as the real problems confronting the society. So successful was this reframing that, years later, serious writers assumed that the memos concerning Bush's Guard duties were certified forgeries or that Rather's journalism, instead of Bush's conduct, constituted the real scandal (e.g. Dugan 2008; Manjoo 2008, pp. 179–80; Maratea 2008).

By quashing the Guard scandal in 2004, the Bush campaign protected itself and the broad social interests allied to the president and his party. More subtly, one could argue that the ultimate scandal in this matter was indeed journalistic misbehavior – but not the kind alleged by critics of CBS. Instead, the prunent malfeasance was the media's cooperation in refocusing on Rather and CBS. Misleading coverage of the controversy over the memos imposed the social cost of ignorance about Bush's behavior. Knowledge of this could conceivably have affected the 2004 presidential election, in which Bush's opponent was a war hero. Bush won by an unusually close margin for an incumbent seeking his second term.[1] The unremarked journalistic scandal also imposed an additional social cost: a diminution in public trust of the media that was not warranted by CBS's failings in reporting on Bush's Guard service. Arguably what should have reduced public trust was the way most mainstream media responded to pressure from powerful, skilled political actors, abandoning concern with empirical facts of a politician's misconduct in his early adulthood to focus, perhaps in gleeful *Schadenfreude*, on purported malpractice by a journalistic competitor.

Chapter 7 turns to scandals involving alleged violations of norms *and* law in a politician's earlier professional life. George W. Bush's Harken Energy and Bill Clinton's alleged (and ultimately unsubstantiated) Whitewater misconduct therefore occupy a higher level in the scandal hierarchy of figure 9.1. Unlike the candidates' military records as young adults during Vietnam, or their private marital misconduct, breaching the law and ethics of business would appear indisputably relevant to their suitability for the presidency. Insider trading of the sort Bush apparently engaged in exacts tangible financial costs and threatens the integrity of the stock market. Here too we saw disparities in treatment of two politicians, with Clinton subjected to high-magnitude scandal publicity and Bush receiving barely any. Yet, after exhaustive probing, Clinton's financial activities were not found to have violated any law, whereas some of Bush's activities almost certainly breached laws and regulations. The Harken Energy case illuminates exactly how non-scandals such as this operate and how they are manifested in media texts.

Chapter 8 probes potential scandals of the highest level, where misconduct imposed the heaviest costs on the widest swath of the American public. Looking back on the United States' war with Iraq over weapons of mass destruction that did not exist, we found that the preponderance of media coverage supported the official White House line blaming faulty intelligence bureaucrats and deflecting President Bush's personal responsibility. The second silenced scandal involved the failure of news organizations to clarify and make widely available the inference that the outing of Valerie Plame in 2003 constituted presidential misconduct. The public record shows that the president and vice president jeopardized the fight against Iraqi weapons of mass destruction by publicizing Plame, the operations chief of the CIA's Joint Task Force for Iraq; at the very same time they were waging a war purportedly to eliminate Iraqi WMD. When Scooter Libby was tried and convicted in connection with the Plame affair, the news was never widely framed as a presidential or vice presidential scandal. Instead, journalists fingered Libby as the responsible actor. This followed the focus of governmental action (i.e.

the criminal proceedings against Libby) while distancing Bush and Cheney from the malfeasance. The top leaders' responsibility was functionally invisible to the larger citizenry. Their actions did not activate a scandal focused on them; the information never percolated up and down the communication hierarchy sufficiently to encourage government investigations focusing specifically on their roles. And lacking such intense governmental focus, media were unlikely to determine where the buck actually stopped.

What should the media do and when should they do it?

Critics often decry what they perceive as the rising trend of publicizing the personal histories and foibles of candidates (see Clemmitt 2011). Some observers (such as Sabato et al. 2000) suggested in essence limiting scandal coverage to illegal conduct or unethical behavior that adversely affects performance of official duties. However, by focusing on major scandals that happen, we can miss how much lawbreaking in and out of office, along with norm-violating behavior that breaches the trust of the presidency, never even comes close to scandal status. So, rather than a surfeit of scandal, we have a dysfunctional scandal system that misallocates scandalized attention.

For the purposes of democratic voting, what matters most about the scandal system is whether the majority would, if fully informed of who commits which malfeasance, have preferred different candidates from those elected. Even if scholars or Washington insiders believe the information irrelevant, it is far from clear that they possess a reasoned basis for arguing that journalists and elites have the right to decide which criteria the public is permitted to know and use. When it comes to a decision between the two alleged philanderers, Clinton and George H. W. Bush, or men with allegedly tainted military records, George W. Bush and Kerry in 2004, it seems unlikely that genuine democracy can be squared with the selective release of scandalizing information about one candidate but not the other. Particularly in the latter case, where Kerry indisputably served in a war that Bush avoided, it's difficult to justify news organizations' granting far more scandalized attention to unsubstantiated charges about Kerry's combat medals than to well-documented claims about Bush's draft avoidance and shoddy service in the National Guard.

Finally, the media's handling of the Plame and WMD issues suggests why *consistently* holding incumbent presidents to account for costly official misdeeds would benefit the US and perhaps the world. The remainder of this chapter contends that some unpublicized potential scandals may merit infusion into the mainstream of public discourse even if many others should be blocked, but all must be subjected to a standardized decision-making process designed to enhance democracy.

Character in sex scandals

In some ways, the toughest normative question revolves around scandalous allegations of private misconduct. Careful observers appear mostly to believe that journalists should ignore this realm. By examining this conventional position that a surfeit of attention to leaders' extra-marital sex lives corrodes American politics, we also begin to unpack the underlying values at stake in scandal journalism. What exactly does society lose when media expose such character flaws as infidelity, financial improprieties and other dodgy behavior before candidates assume the presidency? More generally, what are the costs of covering the misconduct of presidential candidates – as with most cases here – prior to their assumption of office? On the negative side of the ledger is infringement of individual politicians' privacy. We care about this because such invasions expose leaders and their families to hurt, which in turn may drive good people away from public life. Perhaps more distressing, scandals of personal behavior can distract the public from serious, substantive issues by highlighting the easily grasped, sensational and salacious. Consequences include obscuring presidents' more costly official wrongdoings. Finally, character scandals may encourage a naive standard for judging politicians. Holding presidents to impossibly strict requirements for behavior outside office reinforces a tendency for Americans to vote less on the basis of rational interest than on symbol and spectacle (see Edelman 1988). These are potent arguments on the costs side of the ledger (see Sabato 1991).

But consider two possible benefits: (1) exposing the real person and character behind the public mask; and (2) improving voters' decisions. First we have to identify just what "character" is, and what aspects of it are relevant to being a good leader. It isn't clear that adultery tells us much about a person's essential character, and similar reasoning might apply to hypocritical draft-evasion or shady but legal financial maneuvers. Judging both by history and by our knowledge of human psychology, any politician's real character is likely suffused with contradiction and paradox. If anything, a look back suggests that infidelity correlates with vigorous presidential performance. Examples include Jefferson, Franklin Roosevelt, Eisenhower, Kennedy and Lyndon Johnson (see Lichtenberg 1990). Moreover, insofar as Bush the elder's public character was defective, evidence was available in 1988 – such as the cynicism and dishonesty, if not criminality, he demonstrated in Iran–Contra (Walsh 1998, ch. 23). Thus one might argue that there was no need to publicize any marital straying by the senior Bush; the public had the data to reject him on other, better grounds.

On the other hand, most Americans did not see Bush's public character for what it was. The shortcomings of daily journalism predict that such a cognitively accessible portrait will not be available. Practices like objectivity, the distaste for context and history, and the focus on today's horserace and political game process obscure the totality of politicians' records (Patterson 1993; Jamieson & Waldman 2002). If public character remains murky, or of little interest to politically inattentive citizens, one might argue in favor of probing private character as a proxy, a heuristic for inattentive voters. Thus, if George H. W. Bush did have an unconventional marriage, just as Kennedy before him and Clinton afterward, citizens should learn about the distance between his actual behavior and Republican claims to represent traditional family values in opposition to Democrats' heedless hedonism. Otherwise, voters who themselves weighed Bush's guise of family man as a sign of his value commitments and proxy for his public integrity would be misled. Should journalism ever do a better job reporting the policy record and public character, however, the affirmative argument for personal unmasking as proxy would weaken considerably.

This brings us to the second benefit, enhancement of voting deliberation, and here the case for sometimes reporting infidelity, and generally for a journalism of private character, becomes stronger. All campaign news is at least implicitly comparative. For the purposes of democracy, the most important single role of journalism is helping the public decide whether to vote and which party's candidates to choose. This suggests the following three-part standard for highly publicizing politicians' private conduct: (1) Determine whether public policy issues relating to private character are on the campaign agenda or are significantly featured in a party's official platform and in a candidate's advertising; if so, (2) publicize evidence on personal behavior relevant to the agenda or platform of that party's candidate; but (3) publicize only if the evidence is compelling enough to convince large numbers of powerful, knowledgeable figures in Washington – some of whom are willing to be quoted anonymously or identified – of their veracity.

Journalists would be required to conduct a careful examination of *tacit* knowledge in Washington. Where significant numbers of elites subscribe to a story, its components would become fair game for publicity if the first two standards are met. The reported allegations should be clearly labeled and qualified: circumstantial evidence should be presented as such, political motivations behind its circulation disclosed, and inferences drawn from it subjected to scrutiny and debate by supporters and opponents of the accused. For instance, there is little doubt, as indicated in prior chapters and in Heilemann & Halperin's (2010) *Game Change*, that credible though not definitive information on the marital infidelity of George H. W. Bush, Bob Dole, John McCain, John Edwards and Bill Clinton (in 2008, impinging on Hillary's presidential campaign) was widely shared throughout the political and media elite in Washington. Sentiment inside the beltway varied from strong suspicion in the case of Bush to virtual certainty in the cases of Dole and Edwards. Mainstream media withheld this information even as they fulsomely conveyed far more trivial and poorly documented speculation about dissension among campaign advisors, political prospects in particular states, future campaign tactics, public responses to speeches and the like. Journalists don't apply ironclad distinctions between publishable news rooted in proven facts and news that arises from speculation and rough inference based on professional instinct, conversation with journalistic peers, claims of self-interested sources and other tenuous data. Indeed, some might say the latter traits characterize the vast bulk of campaign horserace reporting. In this light, it would seem to be the lesser of evils for journalists to consistently apply the three standards just laid out rather than continue haphazardly publicizing some evidence for personal misbehavior while hiding the evidence for other, similar misconduct.[2]

Following the suggested principles would help de-activate rumors with no standing, no claim to tacit acceptance among the knowled geable elite, and no relevance to the current issue agenda. But, when rumors *do* have significant standing, and they relate to issues one party has already placed on the agenda, material buttressing them would merit publicity. The suggested standards permit journalists to make *reasoned* choices while rendering participation in the public sphere more democratic and efficacious. Surely this is preferable to the external forces of scandal production explored here combining haphazardly to determine what private-realm information reaches the public and what remains confined to inner circles of power. The guidelines also avoid lumping together all claims that are not attested by on-the-record witnesses or 100 percent authenticated documentary evidence as "unsubstantiated rumor." The recommended practice protects journalists from being driven by the competitive newsmaking process to publicize rumors without foundation, such as those on Dukakis. And it would work against elitist concealment of allegations relevant to the agenda promoted by a party, so long as the charges enjoyed sufficient substantiation to generate acceptance among many insiders. Those conditions held with respect to George H. W. Bush, Gingrich, Dole, Edwards and McCain. Even less often would the guidelines permit journalists to overlook well-documented (non-sexual) misconduct of the type engaged in by George W. Bush before and after entering public office.

Scandal coverage should always include a sophisticated rather than superficial version of horserace journalism, one that traces out the political interests and individuals served by promoting the scandal, not just the electoral implications for the accused. In addition, where a candidate and party benefit from exposing an opponent's scandalous misconduct, news organizations must hold those benefiting to the same standard. It is important for news organizations to keep in mind their function as arbiters of the (limited) choice that Americans have in their polyarchy (Dahl 1989): between elites who are organized into two imperfectly competing political organizations, the Democrats and Republicans. Their competition takes the form of an *ongoing* contest between party narratives and partisan brands. Because of this, for instance, when House leaders are pursuing impeachment of a president for sexual or financial misconduct, journalistic probing of Congressional leaders' behaviors in these realms becomes not just permissible but mandatory. If the inquisitors are prosecuting misbe-havior that they themselves have engaged in, it demeans and distorts the democratic process to withhold this context – one that arguably renders the inquisition itself a scandalous abuse of power, since the prosecutors themselves would apparently belong in the dock along with the defendant.

In 1997–8, Newt Gingrich appeared all over the media saying he was shocked, shocked that a leader (Bill Clinton) would besmirch his office by committing adultery with a young staff member – without being asked why the same standard didn't apply to the House Speaker himself. If Party A's leaders are purveying a narrative that identifies Party B's leaders as morally deficient because the latter do not adhere to conventional marital norms, failing to investigate and clarify for citizens whether Party A's leaders actually conform to those norms and practices means intervening on A's side in the continuing parti-san competition. It's not merely lazy or cautious journalism when the media pounce on one side's alleged failings without probing energetically whether citizens actually have a choice between the parties on that criterion. Nor is it merely obscuring truths of scant relevance to rational voting, as some journalists might say (e.g. "We made a mistake in dogging Clinton on his sexual peccadilloes so we'll give a pass to Gingrich; after all, most citizens didn't care about Clinton, and they were right not to"). That decision allocated power to the side sponsoring the scandal; it helped one party sell a bill of goods to the citizenry. In this case, the falsehood is that by voting for Party A they are choosing a party led by persons who fulfill the criterion of traditional marital morality that Party A itself has promoted (in social science terms, primed) as a basis for voting. Since the scandal battleground is above all a partisan arena – as many have observed, politics by other means (see Lowi 2004; Feldstein 2006, 2010; Castells 2009) – failure to convey the full political and factual context is an unwarranted intrusion by the media in the partisan balance of power. Unlike much other news coverage, where slanted news is potentially visible to audiences, such partisan tilt by omission is undetectable by the public.

At the same time that they avoid unintentionally slanting the news, the suggested standards would create a disincentive to partisan manipulation. If Republican operatives had known that elevating infidelity to the forefront (by paying Gennifer Flowers to come forward and by campaigning on "family values") would also open the way to high publicity for allegations about George H. W. Bush's extra-marital activities, the whole matter might have remained off the campaign agenda, where it arguably belonged. These standards seem a reasonable compromise between the Scylla of encouraging the media to censor (while savoring in private) agenda-relevant information, and the Charybdis of letting them become tools of unscrupulous manipulators like those who targeted Dukakis in 1988.

Because the implications of George H. W. Bush's apparent marital misdeeds so drastically clashed with his public image and "family value" stands, publicizing that information simultaneously with the Flowers controversy could have damaged the president's chances for re-election. In an analogous way, high publicity for Newt Gingrich's apparent counter-cultural lifestyle could well have doomed his ambition to serve as leader of a resurgent GOP majority in Congress, let alone to flirt with presidential candidacy for the next 15 years. And indeed when Rep. Robert Livingston of Louisiana was elected by the GOP caucus to succeed Gingrich in the midst of the Lewinsky scandal (1998), publicity about Livingston's own extra-marital affairs was sufficient to induce his resignation from the speakership almost immediately. The threat that mainstream media would publicize John

Edwards's adultery did the public the great favor of removing him from presidential contention, and once the publicity actually came to pass, eliminated him from public life.

These standards do not merely work to expose hypocrisy. They help in uncovering misrepresentation. Contrary to what a House speaker and party leader like Gingrich was representing about himself, he did not actually support intensive investigation and public questioning and punishment of high-level public officials for committing adultery with staff members. If he did support such a scandalized response, he would have had to demand investigation and punishment of himself (and quite a few colleagues), or at least confess to his transgressions and seek forgiveness from his constituents (Brauer 2008).

In the light of the potential power in these sexual revelations, what are we saying if we decide nonetheless that the press was right to suppress the infidelity evidence on George H. W. Bush, Gingrich and Dole, old, flawed and incomplete though it might have been? And how would we justify ignoring the relatively fresh information on the Clinton, Edwards and McCain marriages? Bypassing the matters would be tantamount to deciding the public sphere must be functionally narrowed, knowledgeable deliberation confined to the elite few. The choices of the public would thereby be skewed, democracy itself corrupted. The benefits of this decision would be protecting the privacy of some politicians (but not all), and shielding them only from discovery by those outside Washington, i.e. their constituents, the very people being misrepresented. Insiders would still know or strongly suspect. At the same time, continued journalistic suppression of most infidelity among presidential aspirants would uphold standards of truth rooted more in operational convenience and skillful media manipulation than in consistent allegiance to well-considered rules for generating knowledge and holding power accountable.

Beyond hypocrisy

As already suggested, political agendas involve not just individual politicians but their parties in ongoing partisan competition to promote their own brand and derogate the other's. The politicians, especially leaders of the parties, represent – stand for and symbolize – the party, its platform and its dominant ideological, value and character appeals. Therefore their private behavior becomes publicly newsworthy, not because of any hypocrisy but because the

Republicans in particular have successfully made private-realm morality a core of their brand appeal (Hayes 2005). Reporting on private behavior is less intended to puncture hypocrisy than to reveal dishonesty.

One way to clarify matters is distinguishing between publicly defensible and publicly indefensible hypocrisy. When Republican free-market advocates support economically inefficient farm subsidies, that stand is publicly defensible as a principled and relatively minor deviation from core values, a tactical decision that pleasing a key constituency like agribusiness maintains Republicans' power to achieve what may be more important implementations of core values. To make that kind of argument is impossible when it comes to private sexual or financial shenanigans, not to mention failure to meet military obligations. So Newt Gingrich could perhaps reason privately: "I need to endorse family values to win power for Republicans so we can fight for even more important core values of the party, even though I do not in fact live my own life in accordance with traditional family values." But that stance is not publicly defensible on grounds of his own selfish needs for sex, or on grounds that it distributes useful benefits to a group of vital constituents (like farmers) and to other constituents who are served by the higher-priority values being fulfilled via this trade-off for the farm vote. Marital infidelity does not deliver benefits to anyone but the miscreant (and, perhaps, his lovers). It was in no way necessary for the fulfillment of the GOP agenda that Gingrich, Dole or McCain engage in infidelity.

There would be no real shame in admitting that political calculations went into decisions to subsidize farmers rather than relying on hallowed free-market principles for agriculture. And, of course, public records reveal when Republicans vote for farm subsidies. Understanding the pragmatics of electoral politics – even if they find it distasteful – very few voters would punish politicians for this kind of trade-off, but at least the public record allows voters to contemplate the information. Even if one argues (as moral philosophers do) that lying is sometimes justifiable in service to the greater good, those circumstances only apply when that action ultimately distributes values to the group rather than to the self. Journalists should give Gingrich and his ilk a pass only if, whenever playing the family values card, they are willing to include words to the following effect: "I endorse family values. Although I enjoy a life unbounded by those principles myself, I do believe it would be the best thing for society if everyone else lived that way." Then the hypocrisy would be transparent, and citizens would be able – as they are when their free-market-loving representative votes for subsidies or tariffs, or when their pro-integration legislator sends her own children to white, upper-class private schools – to assess it for themselves.

The complications here are plentiful. Republicans did not accuse Barack Obama of failing to live a traditional, faithful married life.[3] But they did allege he scandalously breached American values by "palling around with terrorists."[4] Do such attacks on character and values aside from sexual behavior raise the sex issue for McCain under the guidelines suggested here, particularly if the specific charge against Obama was baseless?[5] Or should the standards be limited to an eye for an eye, adultery for adultery? Either choice would be defensible. My core point is that journalists need to choose explicit standards and apply them across the board. In the end, it is not the revelation of true personal character that would justify privacy-invading reports, so much as the need for the voting public to assess truth claims in an accurate comparative context – even when the truth about alleged sexual misconduct is a probabilistic one (as most, important truth is), rather than a certainty.

The conventional argument is that private-realm information should be withheld unless the malfeasance demonstrably affects performance in public office. Yet proving a link between private conduct and official actions can be extraordinarily difficult. Journalists and fellow politicians (and scholars) would likely disagree about the matter, and if one or two media break the silence, a scandal cascade could well ensue in one instance, but not another, for no consistent or considered reason. In other words, following the "only if it affects official performance" standards would lead us back to where we started: neither truth nor relevance to citizen deliberation would determine the claims that reach the public, but rather televisuality, operational convenience, manipulative skill, and the party affiliation of the allegedly misbehaving candidate. If some damaging claims about politicians' private affairs *will* be covered, it appears best to establish consistent rules for processing them. It is well to recall in this context that the press was once a lively site for political thrust and parry over high-level hanky-panky. The extra-marital sexual affairs of Thomas Jefferson and Alexander Hamilton, among others, were widely publicized and debated. Whatever pain the news coverage caused them, both founders remained able to perform great public service, and citizens of that era did not apparently withdraw from politics in disgust either (see Gordon-Reed 2008; Flynt & Eisenbach 2011). Perhaps the sensibilities of 21st-century audiences are no more delicate than those of two centuries earlier.

Still, we must acknowledge that like any standard, this one has its own drawbacks. It could make the journalism of private-realm behavior a fixture in campaigns, institutionalizing distraction from more substantive misrepresentation. Political consultants and operatives could spread rumors inside the beltway, using convincing but misleading circumstantial evidence to establish tacit knowledge, thereby meeting the standard above. Of course this would be undesirable. Yet party operatives would sponsor sex scandals in the knowledge that the same could be done to them. If their manipulation succeeded in making the agenda, damaging information about their clients could also receive wide attention. And their own roles and interests in the matter, their orchestration of dishonest political communication, would become news as well.

There remain pitfalls and uncertainties with the standards proposed. Intra-party conflicts, such as primaries, could pose difficulties where, say, four candidates are running. If one of them spreads damaging innuendoes about another while posing as a true advocate of marital fidelity, military service or other ideal, it would be undesirable for the other two to endure investigation of their private lives also. The campaign could descend into a mudslinging of all against all. The proposal here works best in a two-person competition; any more and the identity of the rumor's beneficiary might be unclear. Furthermore, the case of John Edwards does not clearly fall within the guidelines since he did not explicitly run as a representative of traditional family ideals, or attack others for failing to do so. (Edwards did, however, play up his love and support for his wife Elizabeth who was dying of cancer; and Elizabeth went along with the charade even after finding out about his lover.) In suggesting these standards for the journalism of private behavior, I do not claim to have arrived at the final and comprehensive answer to the ethical and political dilemmas.

Calibrating scandals of the social realm

More troubling than the unpredictably inconsistent nature of the public's access to knowledge about their leaders' sexual conduct is the public's general vulnerability to a newsmaking process that circulates factual claims without fixed standards of rational judgment (reporters operating under the explicit mandate of investigative journalism are partial exceptions, see Ettema & Glasser 1998). Instead, statements are largely authenticated and judged worthy of high publicity if they happen to correspond with the interests and motivations of elites and news organizations. For all practical purposes, statements that do not conform, whatever the empirical evidence underlying them, however relevant they might be to citizen deliberation, may never attain the magnitude necessary for them to enter the wider public domain.

This problem becomes more important and itself adds to the societal costs of official misconduct when we move beyond the purely private to the social realm. For moderately serious misconduct, the evidence is less difficult to find and assess and the normative decision on whether the matters deserve publicity less complicated. With respect to the draft evasion of Clinton, Bush and Quayle, as well as Bush's unpunished disobedience of his National Guard obligations and insider trading, empirical validation is relatively straightforward. On the normative side, though, there remain some conundrums. Arguably, since the overwhelming majority of educated or affluent young men took steps to avoid the draft during Vietnam, the US really couldn't exclude such men from public service. The case for privacy on this sort of character blemish is somewhat analogous to that for sex – lots of leaders commit adultery, and we can't disqualify people from politics on that basis. Nor does such violation of norms and ideals typically affect the leaders' ability to serve the public.

The case for publicity would be similar as well: to tell the truth about who our leaders actually are. In the Vietnam era, evasion of service *was* the norm for men coming of age who possessed the highest probability of becoming leaders in journalism, government, corporations, academia and every other sphere except the military itself. That's a truth about US class relations that ought to be told. However, Vietnam probably had its last hurrah as an issue in 2008 when John McCain ran. With Obama, a younger generation took over US politics. So, as for infidelity, the main benefits of consistent coverage across all politicians guided by the standards outlined for private realm misconduct are: (1) exposing Americans to truths about how their leaders live and about the moralities they follow; and (2) ensuring no party gains political advantage over the other merely because they manipulate media into covering malfeasance by the opposing party while covering up their own similar misconduct.

Bush's transgressions while in the National Guard imposed a larger social cost than the others' draft evasions, and were certainly not the unstated norm for his peers in the military. The class privilege that got Bush (and Quayle) into the Guard is noteworthy, but more important is Bush's unsanctioned violation of military rules. There is little or no ambiguity about the facts. As noted in chapter 6 and can be confirmed in many sources cited there, Bush never produced convincing evidence (and hardly any unconvincing evidence for that matter) to support his version of his Guard service – beyond saying it must have been satisfactory because he wasn't dishonorably discharged. Yet, again, that very fact, combined with his seeming derelictions of duty, indicates that abuses of power took place. Therefore, if we have a journalistic scandal here, it would not revolve around the controversial memos reported in Dan Rather's *60 Minutes II* story. The scandal would be that due to flawed media coverage, the public's lasting impression centers on the purportedly fake memos rather than the likely truth that Bush flouted Guard rules during Vietnam, and got away with it because of his powerful connections. This case is another one that reveals the importance of external forces in determining what becomes a scandal and what doesn't. Not only here but generally, scandal magnitude is determined more by manipulative skill of sponsors and their opponents than by substantive judgments about the facts of malfeasance and their effects on society. Note that intimidation is an important component of skill in the cascade model. For example, Republicans used intimidation to pressure CBS to back down from its story. As recounted in chapter 6, CBS caved and submitted almost immediately, which squelched the Bush scandal and promoted Rathergate.

All that said, an argument could be made for the irrelevance of what Bush did as a privileged young man. Thirty years before running for president, in contravention of his duties, Bush failed to keep his pilot qualification current and refused the medical exams required to remain a pilot (exams that would have included drug testing). Then he essentially went AWOL to attend Harvard Business School. Arguably these moderately serious transgressions of young adulthood do not disqualify a man who has redeemed himself through good works since. However, it becomes much more relevant to the *comparison* that voters had to make during the 2004 election campaign. Bush escaped accountability for the WMD and Plame miscues in part through the media's allowing him to maintain his image as a macho, tough supporter of the military. As with sexual malfeasance, the key factor weighing on the side of publicizing facts of private and social realm misconduct is that knowing the information is necessary for an informed comparison. If the issue of macho toughness and military expertise is on the agenda, as in 2004, John Kerry should not have been the only one facing repeated questions and defending himself against resonant allegations involving deficiencies in his military service.

Journalists might argue that this reflects Kerry's and the Democrats' ineptitude at playing the political game, along with Bush's and the Republicans' skill. I have often heard journalists assert that it's not the media's job to make up for one candidate's campaign deficiencies.

They say journalists' duty is to report the candidates' campaign activities accurately, not to guarantee balanced reporting between the candidates. Yet this stance would seem to punish the victim: the *citizenry*. Good watchdogs stay vigilant and keep barking to alert their owners even if a burglar is clever and stealthy, and hands out treats to quiet the animals. The watchdog's duty is to calibrate the alarm to the danger, not to the skill, seductiveness or scariness of the perpetrator. Voters have no way of knowing the truths in these instances unless the media find and tell it for them, and it seems difficult to rest easy with the decision that citizens are simply out of luck if one of the candidates or parties is better than the other at sponsoring and blocking scandals.

That same principle holds for the most serious of the social-realm scandals, Bush's insider trading (and related malfeasance detailed in the sources cited by chapter 7). His actions violated laws and regulations but he went unpunished after withholding evidence from the SEC commissioners whom his father appointed. Thus there was evidence at least for a dual scandal, over abusing the SEC's rules and procedures as well as the illegal trading itself. If the public wanted to give Bush a pass on his insider trading and on Harken's Enron-like corporate inside dealing too, that would be up to them. But they should have been given that information in clear, memorable terms. There was no privacy right here. Quite the contrary, the SEC and its rules are designed to make the stock market transparent so that it will serve all Americans rather than a privileged, unethical network of insiders. And Bush's Harken activities occurred when he was not 22 but fully adult. It is difficult to conceive of any benefits to society in the media's lack of attention to Bush's financial investments, particularly in light of the high-magnitude publicity for Clinton's. American politics is a continuing partisan struggle for power conducted through ongoing competitive narratives that invoke and exploit certain norms and values. That makes it desirable for journalists to calibrate scandal coverage to ensure continuing, diachronic equity between the two parties' standard bearers.

In implementing this regime, there should be no statute of limitations. No matter how distant in the past, the accusations deserve a thorough airing if they meet the above three criteria. Any limitation based on elapsed time inevitably leads to such perversities as penalizing younger candidates and advantaging old candidates merely because the latter's sins are more likely to have occurred longer ago. If a candidate strayed from the bounds of marriage 30 years earlier, let the public decide if that is less of a character stain than adultery 30 hours before – assuming the candidate's or party's platform features marital conduct and traditional family values. If a party trumpets its candidate's superior qualifications for military leadership and its platform promises unrelenting toughness on defense or equates patriotism with unquestioning support of military action, and traditional masculinity with strong political leadership, the candidate's military service, whenever it occurred, should be newsworthy. And if a business deal of questionable legality occurred 5 or 25 years before the campaign, it's relevant as long as the candidate's party claims adherence to the rule of law; in other words, evidence of such socially costly misconduct virtually always merits thorough investigation and, if substantiated, reporting. If the electorate judges engaging in unethical or illegal business practices irrelevant to a candidate's qualifications, that is fine, but it should be the electorate's call.

Calibrating the most costly scandals

The normative implications of the cascade model for serious scandals of official misconduct are straightforward. In the interest of democratic accountability, news organizations should make a point of asking well-informed and well-documented questions until they are answered. Then they should publicize the answers, along with supporting and opposing evidence, repeatedly and with resonance. When one outlet initially uncovers a potential scandal, others should self-consciously seize on the information rather than ignoring their competitor's scoop, or waiting until there's a sufficient political reaction to make the scandal accusation worthwhile because of its impact on the political game. Any such hesitation will often lead the potential scandal onto Path I, political silence, where the media's failure to grant attention discourages elites who might otherwise demand answers and initiate remedial action.[6]

In addition, news outlets should ensure the buck stops where it should, as it did not in the Plame case. This can be difficult. As the cascade model suggests, if no government agencies (especially courts or legislatures) respond to allegations by seeking to trace responsibility as high as it might go, journalists are reduced – at best – to uncovering new evidence on their own. News organizations obviously do not have subpoena power or any other way to compel those possessing relevant information to disgorge it. Sometimes it's available nonetheless in court documents or other records, but investigating is a time-intensive, expensive proposition for which traditional news organizations have diminishing resources and motivations. And the powerful actors who are targeted will deploy the array of evasion tactics identified in chapter 7's discussion of Harken Energy and elsewhere in this book. Sometimes the information is publicly available, such as Bush and Cheney's responsibility for outing Plame. But as that case and others suggest, media alone cannot elevate a presidential-level scandal to propel a self-sustaining cascade that illuminates responsibility all the way to the top.

Even if it were true that news organizations are eager to seize on scandals and push them as far as they can, their fervency would not be all that relevant politically. As willing as they might be, journalists don't have the power to create and maintain scandals. In most cases, the path of least resistance politically and economically is Path I, meaning they will shift attention to newer events, perhaps after a token report or two and some discourse on the editorial pages or Sunday political talk shows.

Endemic corruption and partisan competition

When the scandal is substantively serious and the causes are structural and institutional, as in the financial crisis of 2008, there is no more important media goal than to uncover the deeper roots – rather than stopping once an individual demon like Bernard Madoff has been identified. He masterminded a $50 billion Ponzi scheme but was a relative piker compared to the large American financial institutions that imposed trillions of dollars in lost wealth on the world (see Sorkin 2009; M. Lewis 2010; S. Johnson & Kwak 2011; Martens 2011). As of 2011, none of the masterminds of those corporations or their putative government regulators had joined Madoff in prison, and most kept their jobs.

The US was by the twenty-first century arguably a polity suffused with subtle forms of corruption that rarely garner the kind of attention that would fit the definition of high-magnitude scandal offered in this book. Even after the meltdown of 2008, it was impossible for Congress to pass a financial regulatory act with real teeth (S. Johnson & Kwak 2011). Just one provision that Big Finance strongly opposed made it into the final bill (the Consumer Finance Protection Bureau) (CFPB) and this only because of enormous internal and external pressure on the administration and Congress (see Alter 2010). Although this agency could protect consumers against the worst depredations, the major provisions of the bill rendered the US financial system just about as vulnerable to systemic crisis as it was in 2007 (S. Johnson & Kwak 2011), and the CFPB was hobbled from its inception by bipartisan determination to limit its power and prevent its prime mover, Elizabeth Warren, from heading the agency.

The ability of the US government to make policy decisions based on optimal cost–benefit calculations continued to decline even after the transformative change promised by Obama's campaign in 2008. Indeed, the power of campaign contributors was likely to grow in the aftermath of a Supreme Court ruling (*Citizens United* vs. *Federal Election Commission*, 130 S.Ct. 876, 2010) that removed most restrictions on campaign spending and made it impossible to track the source of many donations. In these circumstances of deteriorating democracy and institutionalized corruption, it appears that properly calibrated political scandals are more vital than ever.

One of the primary symptoms of the deterioration is a structural difference in the ability of the two parties to sponsor and block scandals. Democrats are now beholden to conservative big-business interest groups and contributions, as suggested by the almost uncontested decisions of President Obama to block retrospective accountability for the Bush administration, and to oppose major substantive change in the Republican-initiated (and often Democratic co-sponsored) financial deregulations of the 1980s and onward. It is possible that the post-1980 decline of unions and other changes advantaging large corporations and the most affluent sliver of the American income and wealth pyramid (see Greenwald 2009; Hacker & Pierson 2010) moved the scandal production process into a new phase.

I don't mean to suggest that America reached a permanent situation that will look a lot like 2009–10, when rampant financial and governmental misconduct went unpunished as neither media nor officials targeted individual leaders in the sectors for investigations of scandalous malfeasance. Some observers believe there are cycles of scandal politics, with scandals periodically waxing then waning (Lowi 2004; Feldstein 2006). But both parties being closely linked to similar financial contributors after *Citizens United* would predictably make high-magnitude scandals less common than they were, even if corruption continues or grows worse. It would therefore make less sense than ever to generalize about news organizations craving and over-producing scandal. As shown throughout this book, journalists must depend on party competition for creation and sustenance of high-magnitude scandals. If both US parties need (for reasons including the Supreme Court's ruling) to raise increasing portions of their money from the same or similar wealthy individuals and interests, Democrats will not want to threaten the GOP too severely, for fear that some key Democratic contributors might take umbrage. If competition is replaced by a form of tacit collusion not to go after miscreants whose misdeeds were enabled by both parties – as was the case for the financial crash of 2008 – production of scandals over socially costly misdeeds could diminish. More generally, structural changes in the operation and competitive positions of the two parties will continue to affect the dynamics and outputs of the scandal process. That should make observers hesitant to proclaim permanent generalizations about scandal politics.

Here is an example of the need to take the larger partisan context into account. Nyhan (2008, pp. 7–8) assumes that the two parties operate more or less identically, that their utility functions are identical, and that each tends to act in unified fashion. He also assumes that both parties operate under a similarly strong "presumption of deference" to a president of their own party. He says this arises from members of both parties having similar motivations to maintain the party brand, which enables all to benefit from the voters' use of brand identity to guide voting decisions. In part because he assumes parties are similar in these respects, Nyhan seems surprised that he doesn't find any effect of divided government on the prevalence of scandal. However, such a finding would make sense if, as I believe, a divided government with Republicans in control of one branch and not the other doesn't yield the same politics as a divided government with Democrats in a similar position. If parties differ systematically, we wouldn't expect a significant effect of a divided government variable that does not take that difference into account. If as a minority party Republicans are more highly motivated and effective in promoting scandal, and Democrats as a majority are less so, no systematic impact of divided government should appear. And there is plenty of reason to expect Democrats and Republicans to differ in their skill and motivation to promote scandal against their opponents (see especially Jarvis 2005; A. Taylor 2005; Westen 2007; Lakoff 2008; Entman 2011).

Perhaps Republicans learned their lesson during Watergate: party unity is vital to blocking scandal. As Tiffen (1999, pp. 73–5) notes, "the cross fire of frontal [from opposite party] and flank [from own party] attacks makes defense doubly difficult" for those exposed to potential scandal. Republicans failed to put up a united front to block Watergate, the scandal actually toppled a presidency. It would appear that most leaders of the GOP learned to fight scandal charges against one of their own in virtual unison, rather than investigating them. This leaves Democrats in the position of seeming partisan, carping and cravenly political if they keep promoting a scandal. They need some Republican voices in the mix too. The same holds for the major national news organizations; they too are legitimized in pursuing a scandal when both parties have some important members supporting investigation. Otherwise they will be vulnerable to charges of bias, and Republicans will likely press that claim, as they did in reacting to the Bush – National Guard and McCain–lobbyist allegations. Meanwhile, research, as noted earlier, supports the assumption that Democratic leaders almost never defend against scandal allegations by attacking media for bias favoring conservatives and Republicans. Elite ideological pressure against media bias comes almost entirely from the right (Watts et al. 1999; Entman 2010a), and all else being equal, that would predictably skew the scandal production system to favor Republicans. Occasionally (Tiffen 1999, p. 118) the rest of the party may have different interests from the accused; the accused might want to fight it out to seek vindication while the rest of the party just wants to make it go away. But for the most part, especially among the disciplined Republicans, the goal of protecting the brand has tended to supersede any individual member's honor.

Beyond the partisan situation, the United States faces other structural limitations on scandal production. For one thing, the amount of potential attention by media audiences is almost constant. For another, in the twenty-first century, traditional broadcast network news programs focused increasingly on soft news even as their audience shrank in size and its composition skewed toward the older demographic (average age of audiences: about 53; Pew Project for Excellence in Journalism 2011). Earnings of traditional print newspapers, sources of most investigative journalism, also declined as the Internet drew off classified advertising and other revenues – as well as the attention of younger demographics. The Internet, along with a choice among hundreds of cable channels, combined to diffuse audiences over larger numbers of news sources, and to channel people into polarized ideological sub-cultures. The former tight linkage among the levels of the traditional political communication system hierarchy could loosen. That means the general public may have a harder time learning in common about scandal allegations. One implication is that it becomes more difficult to create an impression of widespread concern and outrage in the public, the sort of perceived public opinion that motivates elites to investigate allegations of scandalous misconduct. The segmentation and diffusion of the audience into ever narrower niches makes it more likely that scandalizing information will circulate forcefully in some niches but only fleetingly in many others.

All this would portend a diminution of scandalized coverage of socially costly misconduct at the highest levels of the political power structure. Stable or rising tendencies toward corruption would predictably coexist with declining abilities and motivations of media and elites to ferret it out, or of the wider public to learn about it. Such conditions in turn could engender a rising proportion of potential scandals that remain just that – and would threaten still further increases of scandalous misconduct as the odds of getting caught and punished continue to decrease.

Next steps

There is one small ameliorative step that might boost the media's capacity to act more independently of the partisan context, and in particular to guide scandals onto Path II when merited: establishing the position of scandal editor. Scandal editors would monitor their own outlet's investigations and others' for appropriate calibration and follow-up. Scandal editors would search for patterns and under-publicized information pointing to official misconduct or related corruption. In an epoch of ProPublica, *Huffington Post*, Wikileaks and blog revelations, traditional news organizations should more self-consciously monitor and follow them up. Such systematic scandal calibration as enforced by this editor not only holds potential value for democratic politics but also could augment news organizations' bottom lines (see Entman 2010b). Occupants of this position could provide considerable added value for paying audiences coping with endemic information overload intensified by the Internet.

Scandal editors would also enable news organizations to transcend the limitations imposed by the 24/7 news cycle. One analogy would be with the way Jon Stewart's *The Daily Show* has connected actors and actions that are not necessarily synchronous in time. Overcoming the tendency of traditional news organizations to focus on what happened in the past few days or hours (or what will happen soon) – which usually winds up conveying what powerful leaders said or did publicly within that time period – enabled Stewart's show to link what officials say now to what they said or did a month, year or decade before. Breaking free from the constraints of timeliness led *The Daily Show* to uncover and pointedly satirize patterns of deception, irresponsibility and, occasionally, structural corruption. For instance, in 2010, Stewart revealed politicians of both parties limning the heroics of first responders on September 11, 2001 even while they were failing to seriously consider a bill providing health care to the very people injured in responding to 9/11 (see episodes of August 4 and December 17, 2010). The ensuing cascade of condemnation encouraged passage of the bill and led some to label

Stewart the Edward R. Murrow of the twenty-first century.[7] A scandal editor could similarly break the bonds of time to arrange narratives in a sequence that would clarify action (and inaction) for which officials should be held to account.[8]

Conclusion

Between 1988 and 2008, high scandal magnitude seemed to be most common when revealing private, norm-violating, symbolic/descriptive misrepresentation of the sort that imposed low social costs. Yet the normative ideal for scholars and journalists, and the frequent perception empirically, was that the most publicized and most damaging to those implicated were scandals that involved public-realm violation of law, substantive misrepresentation and high social cost. As the book shows, there has been no relationship between the societal cost or nature of misrepresentation on the one hand and media output or political outcome on the other. Unfortunately, there's no guarantee of punishment for official misdeeds or for the second-order malfeasance embodied in cover-ups.

This point returns us to the core problem of disproportionality: the media's seeming inability to calibrate their attention so that the public can, for instance, focus less on Bill Clinton's "$200 haircut" or his love life than on how his coziness with Wall Street led to the repeal of the Glass–Steagall Act, predictably paving the way for the 2008 economic crash (Krugman 2009). Whether for grand or trivial misdeeds, democratic leaders' malfeasance demands coherent and consistent treatment by news organizations. Consistency in these affairs is no hobgoblin or vice. Journalists can and should work mindfully and continuously to align politicians' motivations with the highest needs of democracy rather than unintentionally enabling them to do whatever they can get away with.

Notes

1 High Crimes or Misdemeanors?

1 "D-CO" signifies Hart was a Democrat who represented Colorado in the Senate; "R" is used similarly to denote Republican members of the House or Senate.

2 Among those offering parallel treatments are Canel & Sanders (2006, pp. 34–7), who boil Thompson's perspective down to its essence, defining scandals as abuses of the public trust that, once widely known, stimulate indignation. Williams (1998, pp. 6–7) writes that "Scandals are events which provoke public concern, indignation or even outrage" when they become known because they breach common expectations for officials' behavior. In Garrard & Newell's (2006, p. 5) convergent definition, scandals are significant but deliberately concealed breaches of standards for correct behavior brought suddenly to light, stimulating an audience beyond those immediately involved to outrage.

3 Many Americans were angrier at the Republicans and news organizations for flogging the scandal than at Clinton for philandering and lying. Clinton's reputation improved over time. With a favorability rating from 55 to 67 percent, depending on the specific poll, Clinton in 2010–11 was one of the most popular political figures in the country, up from 34 percent in 2001. See survey data at http://www. pollingreport.com/clinton1.htm and http://blogs.wsj.com/washwire/ 2010/09/28/wsjnbc-poll-president-clinton-gets-top-rating/ (all websites cited in this volume were accessed during 2010–11). Many forces probably contributed to this change, including nostalgia for better economic times, admiration for Clinton's post-White House accomplishments, forgiveness – and simple generational replacement

(by 2010, those under 30 had little memory of the scandal and many senior citizens who disapproved of Clinton in 1996 had passed on).

4 Although large majorities of the public appeared to reject torture in the abstract, most said it did not affect their support for the Bush administration's handling of the war on terror (worldpublicopinion. org 2004). And of course the Bush–Cheney ticket did win the 2004 election despite the Abu Ghraib revelations that year.

5 Think Progress Poll released July 31, 2009, http://thinkprogress.org/2009/07/31/poll-birther/.

6 The major exception to this generalization involves sex scandals, and therein lies an important qualification: scandals arising from sexual impropriety cannot be fully equated with those arising from illegal, incompetent or unethical uses of political position and influence. More on critical distinctions among scandals will follow shortly.

7 A minority of scholars (see Groseclose & Milyo 2005), and much of the public, believe the major national media (except Fox) exhibit a consistent liberal bias traceable to the Democratic sympathies of their reporters and editors. Most political communication scholars see little evidence for such a generalization (see Niven 2002; Bennett & Iyengar 2008; Covert & Wasburn 2008; Entman 2010c).

8 The title of perhaps the most influential American book on scandals (Sabato 1991), which offers a more nuanced account than most who have used the term since.

9 See, for a statement of this common refrain, Fritz, Keefer & Nyhan (2004, p. 36). As noted in the text, Nyhan at least has modified this earlier view.

10 Earlier in 2011, Rep. Chris Lee (R-NY) experienced a similar scandal. Like Weiner, Lee, a married congressman, engaged in online flirtation, allowing suggestive pictures to leak out on the Internet. He too resigned under pressure. Both scandals were activated and spread through online sources such as Twitter and the website Gawker.com. Judging by these and other examples, the rise of the Internet media modified the scandal production process in some respects (discussed in chapter 4) but did not alter the hypothesized inverse relationship between substantive seriousness and magnitude of scandal publicity. If anything, Internet media reinforce that relationship as vehicles like Twitter, with its 140-character instant messages, are especially suited to highly efficient communication of superficial and entertaining information.

11 Although Tiffen acknowledges more clearly than most that scandals possess no inexorable momentum that will lead to full disclosure and accountability, he nonetheless asserts (1999, p. 129) that cover-ups can't last in the long term if legislative or judicial officials are suffi-

ciently determined to pursue the matter. However, more often than not in the US, official determination is lacking and scandals end in *effective* secrecy, generating publicity that is too obscure, complex or fleeting to affect much.

12 See Alter (2001); cf. Rutenberg (2001).

13 See Greenwald (2009).

14 For which there is no credible evidence; see *The 9/11 Commission Report* (www.9-11commission.gov/report/911Report.pdf), pp. 58, 162, 470.

15 The Rockefeller Report (Rockefeller 2009, p. 41) contains testimony to the effect that there was great pressure on analysts to come up with links between 9/11 and Saddam Hussein, which led to heightened pressure for application of torture techniques. Other testimony reported pressure to get tougher but not necessarily because of a desire to incriminate the Iraqi government. The point is not that politically motivated torture was proved, only that this explosive allegation of torture for political purposes did not ignite even a minor scandal targeting Bush.

16 An example of journalistic faith in the scandal system's effectiveness in holding presidents accountable is Rich (2009).

17 Note that from here on, to eliminate clutter, I will not qualify observations by inserting "American" or "US," but this is the political system readers should infer unless explicitly stated otherwise.

18 A simple LexisNexis search in the *New York Times*, *Washington Post*, *USA Today*, ABC, CBS and NBC for the word *scandal* within 15 words of *Katrina* for the six months starting the day of the New Orleans flood yields 35 stories calling the administration's handling of the hurricane's effects scandalous.

19 More than enough has been written about the Lewinsky imbroglio and its roots in an unusually intense partisan campaign to ensnare Bill Clinton in scandal (Conason & Lyons 2000; Kalb 2001; Brock 2002; Blumenthal 2003). This anti-Clinton effort included pressure to replace the original Independent Counsel investigating the Whitewater scandal, Robert Fiske (a relatively non-partisan Republican), with Kenneth Starr. A Republican political activist who once advised counsel for Paula Jones in her sexual harassment lawsuit against Clinton, Starr would seem to have a conflict of interest since the Jones case became entangled with Whitewater, the original target of the Independent Counsel's investigation. Clinton's perjury about his relationship with Lewinsky occurred in his Jones case testimony, and Starr energetically pursued the Lewinsky–Jones issue when he was unable to find evidence of lawbreaking in the Clintons' Whitewater investment.

20   Edwards apparently dropped out of the presidential chase earlier than he might have as a result of the brewing sex scandal, so in this sense Internet discussions, along with the *National Enquirer* (a venerable weekly tabloid with a circulation in excess of 1 million) arguably did have some impact. The tawdry situation, however, was not covered in mainstream media until August 2008 and presumably few citizens knew about it until then.

21   See Conason (2000); Ivins (2000); Phillips (2004); Baker (2009).

2 Analyzing Media and Presidential Scandal

1   See Walsh (1998); see also Kornbluh & Byrne (1993), and the "Final Report of the Independent Counsel for Iran-Contra Matters" (August 4, 1993) at www.fas.org/irp/offdocs/walsh/.

2   Another scandal, sometimes labeled "Iraqgate," actually did occur during the administration of the first President Bush. It involved a truly Byzantine mixture of financial corruption, abuse of power and international intrigue that included US assistance to Saddam Hussein during the 1980s. George H. W. Bush managed to avoid serious political damage. Dispositive evidence for the failure of Iraqgate or Iran–Contra to become more than minor scandals for Bush is that he – like Reagan but unlike Clinton – garnered many governmental honors after leaving office. Among these are receiving the Medal of Freedom, and having both Houston's major airport and the CIA's headquarters rechristened in his name.

3   Allegations that the Johnson and George W. Bush administrations violated US and international law are numerous. A contemporary report (Falk & American Society of International Law 1968) details the international legal and American constitutional aspects of the Vietnam war, including such issues as Johnson's failure to formally declare war and the operation's contravention of the UN Charter's Chapter 1, prohibiting war unless authorized by the UN Security Council. George W. Bush faced legal scrutiny for his authorization of torture, approval of domestic surveillance in breach of the FISA (1978) and, like LBJ, for launching a war without UN approval. For an in-depth discussion of these and other legal issues arising during the Bush administration, see Sarat & Hussein (2010).

4   Technically, laws against adultery and homosexual acts remain on the books in many jurisdictions, but prosecutions are rare.

5   We should also remain cognizant that the cultural norms for personal behavior are honored mostly in the breach. Anyone who has worked in Washington knows that high-level officials, politicians and

their staffs engage in behavior quite at odds with public personae emphasizing their personal conformity and commitment to traditional values. The documentary film *Outrage* (Dick 2009) exposes homosexual or bisexual lifestyles practiced by many avowedly "family values" politicians, most of them conservative supporters of anti-gay legislation. For instance, Dana Milbank reported that "No fewer than 15 of the 73 elected in the landslide that year [1994] have entertained the nation with flaps that include messy divorces and a suspicious car accident" (Milbank 2010). An earlier *Politico* article stated that "in the 14 years since that star-crossed 1994 class arrived in Washington espousing an agenda that placed family values at its core, no less than a dozen of its members have been caught up in affairs, sex scandals or in messy separations and divorces from their spouses that, in more than a few instances, led to their political downfalls" (Falcone 2009, July 2).

6   The matter gets complicated since such a scandal could also provide a "teachable moment" leading to constructive dialogue that on balance improves interracial understanding.

7   Bush's deep involvement in Iran–Contra is detailed by Lawrence Walsh (1998, pp. 194–6). Some believe Bush's re-election quest was damaged by the indictment of former Defense Secretary Caspar Weinberger on October 31, 1992, by Special Prosecutor Walsh (see Kevin Phillips 2004, p. 303). However, it's difficult to imagine this was decisive, given Bill Clinton's margin, aided by the strong third-party candidacy of Ross Perot who won 18.9 percent of the vote, and Bush's low approval ratings (dipping to 29 percent in July 1992). Just before leaving the White House, on Christmas Eve, 1992, Bush pardoned Weinberger and five others. Intentionally or not, the pardon protected him from damaging revelations that might have been produced in a Weinberger trial. In fact, Walsh charged at the time that Bush's pardoning of Weinberger "completed" the Iran–Contra cover-up (see Johnston 1992; Kornbluh & Byrne 1993).

8   Arguably the cable news networks Fox and MSNBC belong in this group, along with NPR, the national public radio service that enjoys a large audience. Fox is predictably conservative, MSNBC somewhat liberal, and NPR adheres like the television broadcast networks to the non-partisan middle, so little should be lost by excluding them from this study of the national media that follow the dominant "objectivity" norms (essentially, partisan balance and removal of substantive personal judgments; see Entman 1989).

9   This explanation was also consistent with stereotypes of Reagan. He was known for communication and higher-level vision, not being a detail-oriented policy geek.

10   As to more general ratings of the two presidents, a 2004 *USA Today* poll found 83% saying they had a favorable view of Reagan as a person, twice as many as for Clinton (41%) (see "Poll: most rate Reagan over Clinton" 2004). Retrospective Gallup job approval ratings in 2002 were 73% for Reagan, 51% for Clinton (see "Ronald Reagan from the people's perspective: a Gallup Poll review" 2004). As time passed, memories of both softened, but polls suggest Reagan's greater success in fighting off the taint of scandal.

11   The line between partisan spokesperson and journalist eroded by the turn of the twenty-first century. It became difficult to distinguish between party operations, interest group communication campaigns and news. Not only was one cable news network, Fox, largely devoted to promoting the Republican Party's positions (see Harmon & Muenchen 2009; Aday 2010); another, MSNBC, allocated disproportionate airtime to Democratic Party loyalists. Many news talk shows, including influential Sunday morning broadcast network programs like *Meet the Press* and *This Week*, regularly featured guests and correspondents with long partisan histories (e.g., George Stephanopoulos, former Clinton communication director, and George Will, who advised Ronald Reagan). In addition, interest groups perfected the practice of "Astroturf" politics, through which they promoted self-serving policies in the guise of grass-roots citizens' organizations (W. Potter 2010). Spokespersons presented as disinterested experts or as concerned citizens frequently were paid flacks for established interest groups. All this made the boundaries between networks of elites, journalists and citizens more permeable than previously. Nonetheless, the distinctions in the text are useful conceptually.

12   Perhaps Obama sincerely believed what he said, or perhaps he was merely trying to appeal beyond the liberal Democratic base that never liked Reagan. Either way, Obama's endorsement provides evidence for the bipartisan rehabilitation of Reagan's legacy.

13   Moore (2008) documents the close interdependence between the commercial needs of news organizations and pollsters' selection of specific questions, wording and other choices that shape survey data that purport to scientifically reflect public opinion itself.

14   In many cases the event is unplanned and uncontrolled, and actors must react afterwards to protect their interests through promoting a frame (see Molotch & Lester 1973). This is why the model distinguishes Time 1 and Time 2. When rolling out a new candidate or policy proposal in a planned fashion, the political actor controls timing and initial framing, making Time 1 and Time 2 essentially simultaneous.

15   Despite his fall-guy role, North escaped permanent damage from the scandal. Throughout the summer of 1987 North's overall favorability ratings hovered around 60 percent in nearly every national poll. Although the public's attitudes toward him were more ambiguous when ratings of his personal traits were considered alongside attitudes toward his actions in this affair (Corry 1987; Fried 1997, pp. 80–90), he developed a lucrative career as a conservative pundit building on the name recognition and perceived popularity garnered during Iran–Contra, and ran as Virginia's Republican nominee for the US Senate in 1994.

16   If we're concerned with, say, drunk-driving, there will be more interest in a transgression involving a presidential candidate than one committed by an under- secretary of commerce or random citizen. Yet such episodes of relatively minor private misconduct are not contagious – they don't spread to the vice presidential candidate, to the presidential nominee's supporters and advisors, or to the party at large.

3 Private Lives in the Public Sphere: What Do Journalists Know, and When Do They Tell It?

1   Adultery is illegal in many of the US states, but violations are rarely punished.

2   Among the useful references on sex scandals are: Hart, Smith-Howell & Llewellyn (1991), Sabato (1991) and Jamieson (1993) on the growth of character journalism; Gross (1991) and Goldstein (2009) for related case studies of "outing" gay politicians; and cf. Axford, Madgwick & Turner (1992); Renshon (1992); Rollberg, Sanders & Rutherford (1993); Williams & Apostolidis (2004); Adut (2008); Bower (2008); Rosen (2009).

3   The sources available on LexisNexis in 1992 which referred to the *Vanity Fair* flap are the following, including the page numbers for some of the most influential newspapers: *Newsday*, Gannett News Service, *ABC World News*, UPI, *Minneapolis Star Tribune*, *New York Times* (p. 22; another p. 1 story on April 1 refers only to Hillary's "outspokenness in a *Vanity Fair* magazine interview"), *Los Angeles Times* (p. 31), *Chicago Tribune*, *Boston Globe* (p. 15 and p. 16), *San Francisco Chronicle*, *USA Today*, *Washington Times*, *Hartford Courant*, *Washington Post* (p. 8). Some of these stories consist of brief mentions of Barbara Bush dismissing Hillary Clinton's charges as "baloney."

4   One Bush biography discussed suspicions of Bush's infidelity without reaching a conclusive judgment on its veracity; see Parmet (1997).

5   Felker told me this in a private conversation. He was one of America's most prominent and respected magazine publishers; his wife was Gail Sheehy, who 25 years later wrote the *Vanity Fair* article quoting Hillary Clinton on Bush and his marriage.

6   This exchange is documented on video of C-SPAN for that date.

7   See "False rumor of Post story batters stocks," *Washington Post*, October 20, 1988, p. E1. Also see Randolph (1988), documenting the media's reluctance to dig into the story despite having earlier that year pounced on Gary Hart's womanizing. Of course, Hart did some of his cavorting in public, which made available incriminating pictures of Donna Rice sitting on his lap (published initially by the *National Enquirer*).

8   See "Dukakis aide resigns over remark on Bush," *New York Times*, October 21, 1988, p. A17; "Fallout from remarks on Bush," *Washington Post*, October 21, 1988, p. A-10.

9   When the new president named Fitzgerald to the State Department in 1989, the *Washington Post* reported that she had "served President-elect George Bush in a variety of positions" (Schwartz, Devroy & Ifill 1989). This *double entendre* was widely interpreted as an inside joke.

10   Herbert Gans suggested in a personal communication that one reason for the inability to come up with evidence on Fitzgerald or other possible Bush lovers is their social class membership. In the old-line upper classes, Gans suggests, the culture of discretion and secrecy is considerably more rigid and inviolable than among those allegedly involved with Gary Hart or Bill Clinton.

11   At a forum on "Campaign '92 and Race" in Washington, DC on October 22, 1992, John Dinges of National Public Radio (NPR) observed that, as a medium relying on audio recordings, NPR immediately recognized that Flowers's tape had been altered and decided not to air it. He also said NPR decided not to report this discovery and decision.

12   For discussion of how widely known Clinton's womanizing was among Arkansas elites, see Stewart (1996).

13   Referred to in Rosenstiel (1993, p. 61).

14   Only in the aftermath of the Lewinsky affair did Clinton finally admit he had indeed committed adultery with Flowers.

15   The stories are: "Dukakis releases medical details to stop rumors on mental health," *New York Times*, August 4, 1988, pp. A1, D20; "The psychology barrier," *New York Times*, August 5, 1988, p. A24; "Dukakis acts to kill rumor: doctor says nominee in 'excellent

health,'" *Washington Post*, August 4, 1988, pp. A-1, A-6; "The rumors about Gov. Dukakis," *Washington Post*, August 5, 1988, p. A-22.

16   After Gingrich divorced a second time and married Bistek, he did confess to having an affair with her long before his divorce (see Gillon 2008, pp. 248–50). In announcing his entry into the 2012 nomination campaign, Gingrich represented himself as a new, repenting convert to Catholicism (Tumulty 2010).

17   See Benen (2011, March 9).

18   Research by the Pew Center's Project for Excellence in Journalism shows that despite ongoing audience erosion, television remained America's most popular news medium. In fact when asked where they got their news "yesterday," more than 60 percent of respondents in 2010 said television, with radio and online lagging 20 percentage points behind. Similarly, although the evening newscasts had lost more than half of their viewers since about 1980, even in 2010 almost twice as many people watched the lowest-rated broadcast evening news program as watched the highest-rated cable news show. (On television news audiences, see Pew Project for Excellence in Journalism 2011.)

19   NPR is one of the few news outlets that showed substantial gains in audience during the 2000s. It averaged over 27 million listeners a week and the flagship morning news show garnered an average audience around 8 million. That figure put it on a par with the ABC, CBS and NBC evening newscast (Pew Project for Excellence in Journalism 2011; also Farhi 2009). On the other hand, the newsweeklies were on shaky financial ground by 2010, and the Washington Post Company actually sold *Newsweek* to the *Daily Beast*, an Internet site.

20   Note that journalists defended the stake-out of Hart's townhouse and publication of damaging information on his private behavior on the grounds he had denied the adultery charge and urged reporters to follow him to check his veracity. One might argue that Gingrich's longstanding public devotion to family values and his attack on Clinton and other Democrats for violating them might have been interpreted as a similar kind of challenge – a sort of taunt. But journalists did not rise to Gingrich's more implicit bait.

4 Secret Sins of 2008: The McCain, Edwards and Clinton Families' Values

1   The authors agreed to exchange broad access behind the scenes of the campaigns for withholding information until after the election.

2   The lack of attention to Schecter's book is another indication of the hierarchy hypothesized in figure 3.1. A book by Washington insider journalists can apparently garner more attention from the mainstream media than one by an outsider like Schecter. The distinction being made might make sense, as the outsider hasn't been vetted as an insider has. On the other hand, we've seen that inside-the-beltway culture can include a tacit decision to withhold information that insiders believe true.

3   A biography of Sarah Palin published in the run-up to the 2012 presidential campaign (McGinniss 2011) received similar, scandal-avoiding rather than scandal-seeking treatment by the mainstream media. The book contained charges that Palin, a vociferous advocate of traditional family values, engaged in marital infidelity with her husband's business partner. A search in the LexisNexis category of "All News (English)" found few references to the matter in US media outlets, most of them brief snippets. The search terms were *McGinniss* and *Palin* and *(infidelity* or *adulter!* or *unfaithful!* or *extramarital!* or *betray!* or *cheat!)* (exclamation point retrieves all possible suffixes, such as *-ing* or *-ed*). The most important national media, such as the *New York Times*, *Washington Post*, ABC and CBS never used the search terms. The Associated Press wire service ran a piece – "Palin camp denounces racy bio of former governor" – that, like most coverage, focused on denying the charge and disparaging McGinniss for shoddy journalism. A similar theme characterized NPR's one story ("Methods of Palin book author draw ire") and *USA Today*'s single article (NBC transcripts were unavailable). The mainstream media's tepid response to McGinniss's allegations offers yet another illustration of their disinclination by 2008 to exploit potentially sensational sex scandals involving upper-tier politicians.

4   The staff was responding to the threat manifested in the *Enquirer*'s coverage. Thus the Edwards case offers an example of indirect influence exerted by a medium outside the mainstream. By encouraging Edwards to cease campaigning in anticipation that the mainstream media would otherwise take up the matter, the tabloid's earlier reporting affected politics in a pre-emptive way, without a scandal cascade.

5   As noted in chapter 2, high-magnitude scandal involves "alleged misconduct by government officials or politicians that is saliently framed by virtually all mainstream media as a problem for society demanding intense scrutiny and extraordinary remedial action."

6   Mainstream national media for these purposes included the *New York Times*, *Washington Post*, *USA Today* and the three broadcast networks' evening newscasts and Sunday morning talk shows.

7   ProPublica earned its 2010 Pulitzer Prize for a story by doctor and ProPublica writer Sheri Fink on the challenges of medical treatment at a hospital during Hurricane Katrina. It was published jointly on ProPublica.org and in the *New York Times Magazine.*

8   While readily admitting that he, like other editors, incorporated online reader data into the decision-making process, then-WashingtonPost.com executive editor Jim Brady also affirmed his belief in the essential intermediary function of the press: "people still want the *Washington Post*, the *New York Times*, the *Wall Street Journal* and other papers to play a gatekeeper role. If we start letting real-time traffic drive our home-page promotion, for example, we're on the path to becoming Digg [a service that allows stories to be shared and voted up or down in rank by users]" (Brady 2009).

9   Still another potentially scandalous element of the Foggo saga: he was instrumental in setting up some of the CIA's controversial secret war-on-terror prisons (Johnston & Mazzetti 2009). Nonetheless, searching on Academic Search Premier and ABI Inform / Complete Plus revealed no academic studies of the Foggo scandal, aside from two law review articles that mention Foggo in passing.

5 Dodging Scandals – and the Draft

1   About 1 percent of Guard members who served in Vietnam died, compared with about 3 percent of regular military.

2   As Shanto Iyengar and others have shown, by focusing attention on certain problems and ignoring others, media can alter the criteria that citizens use to evaluate candidates and public servants. Known as priming, this is a closely related but narrower concept than framing. Specifically:

> Priming presumes that when evaluating complex political objects – the performance of an incumbent president, or the promises of a presidential contender – citizens do not take into account all that they know. They cannot, even if they were motivated to do so. What they do consider is what comes to mind, those bits and pieces of political memory that are accessible. And television news is a most powerful force determining what springs to the citizens' mind and what does not. (Iyengar & Kinder 1987, p. 4)

See also Brewer, Graf & Willnat (2003); Althaus & Kim (2006).

3 The *Times* was chosen because it offers the most extensive and influential print coverage of presidential candidates. It is unlikely that less thorough media outlets treated Quayle and Bush much differently, an inference supported by the public opinion data cited later.

4 Calculating the costs with any precision is impossible. Even conceptualizing them is a challenge. One might argue that the cost was limited to the two men who perhaps went to Vietnam because Quayle and Bush chose not to, but of course then Quayle and Bush would have borne the cost so the net social cost difference would be zero. Or perhaps the true social cost would be the marginal difference in war-fighting effectiveness that Quayle and Bush, as well-educated and self-confident men, might have contributed, as opposed to two random recruits. But that is pushing things into an almost purely speculative realm. I refer to the larger, less tangible costs to society of exploiting a rigged system like the Vietnam-era Selective Service process (Appy 1993; MacPherson 2002).

5 To be sure, some of the items for all three men are likely to be false hits (e.g., because they mentioned draft in reference to a preliminary text of a speech or proposal). But there's little reason to think correcting for this would change the relative positions of the candidates, with the greatest absolute volume of attention given Clinton's military-related record.

6 As an example of the way connections enabled evasion of Vietnam service: no child of a member of Congress died in Vietnam, and only one was even wounded (MacPherson 2002).

7 Although Vietnam naturally recedes ever further into the past, right up through the 2008 presidential campaign, it retained political potency. Politicians who were Vietnam vets continued to use their service as a core selling point, preeminently candidates John Kerry (2004) and John McCain (2008).

8 See the polls collected at www.pollingreport.com/wh2gen1.htm.

6 Rathergate: From a Scandal of Politics to a Scandal of Journalism

1 For instance, George Will admitted to helping Ronald Reagan prepare for a debate with Jimmy Carter in 1980 – a debate for which he served as an ABC News commentator. Will praised Reagan's performance on the air without disclosing his association with the campaign. Thirty years later, Will was still a featured commentator on ABC's *This Week*.

2   Some of the Swift Boat damage should be traced to the Kerry campaign's weak defense. For instance, when an independent political group, Moveon.org, ran a TV ad attacking Bush's National Guard record, Kerry actually demanded that the organization pull the spot – which it did.

3   In practice, only a tiny number of Guard units were ever sent to Vietnam, so even checking this box would have subjected Bush to a nearly infinitesimal chance of serving there. According to the Guard, a total of 8,700 Army and Air National Guard personnel were deployed to Vietnam (www.ngb.army.mil/About/default.aspx). These included a "token" of four ANG squadrons, and their service ended in 1969, before Bush would have been qualified on the F-102 aircraft used there (www.globalsecurity.org/military/agency/usaf/ang.htm).

4   For the poll data see: www.usatoday.com/news/politicselections/nation/polls/usatodaypolls.htm?loc=interstitialskip. On the Bush campaign's links to the Swift Boat Veterans and the weakness of the evidence for their attacks on Kerry, see Zernike & Rutenberg (2004).

5   For instance, Lt. Colonel Killian claimed in the allegedly forged memo that he was being pressured by Brigadier General Walter B. Staudt, head of the Texas Air National Guard, to "sugar coat" his evaluation of Bush. Confronted with this claim, Staudt himself refused to comment for a week, then spoke to his local (New Braunfels, TX) newspaper. AP picked up that story (Sept. 22, 2004), in which Staudt merely denied that he'd been pressured to provide (or gave) Bush special treatment in admitting him to the Guard. The story did not quote Staudt as denying *he* had pressured Killian.

6   The search chose stories in which the words *Bush* and *Massachusetts* appeared within the same paragraph as *National Guard*.

7   Published by the Cox News Service, *Atlanta Journal-Constitution* and *Philadelphia Daily News*.

8   The sample period encompasses the day of the *60 Minutes II* broadcast and goes through the weekend after the fourth anniversary of the last *CBS Evening News* program that Rather anchored (March 9, 2005).

9   Clift also quotes an astute observation by the head of the Nieman Foundation at Harvard:

> "I'm troubled by the lack of transparency on the part of CBS," says [Bill] Kovach. A former *New York Times* Washington bureau chief and former editor of the *Atlanta Journal-Constitution*, Kovach thinks CBS should have said at the very beginning that it believed the documents to be accurate but

couldn't be sure, but that people on the scene at the time say they adequately reflect the perceptions of Bush's squadron commander, Lt. Col. Jerry B. Killian, who died in 1984. "Be honest about what you've got and you wouldn't be in as much jeopardy," says Kovach.

It seems CBS would have been better served to admit the continued uncertainties especially when there was so much supporting evidence independent of the memos.

10   Wrote Gibbs et al. 2004:

John Kerry supporters were so frustrated. . . . How could their guy, a decorated war hero, have dropped in the polls after being slimed for a month by unsubstantiated charges about his Vietnam record, while Bush, who has never fully answered questions about whether he performed his duties during five years in the Air National Guard, looked as if he would escape any damage just because CBS had screwed up its fact checking?

11   These data were collected and analyzed under my supervision by my research assistant, Eric Walker, then a junior at George Washington University.

12   The search terms were *Mapes* for the first analysis and *Dan Rather* plus *lawsuit/sue/suit* for the second.

13   News consumption has other "uses and gratifications" (Hartmann 2009).

14   A good account of the latter can be found in *Fear and Favor in the Newsroom*, a documentary film (Sanders 1996). See also memoirs of Raymond Bonner (1984), Morton Mintz (1985), Arthur Kent (1997), Daniel Schorr (1978) and many other mainstream journalists.

15   On the widespread perception of liberal bias dominating the mainstream media, and the ways those organizations actually support that perception, see Entman (2010c).

7 Harkening to Other Matters: What News Looks Like When a Scandal is Silenced

1   Because this is a book on media and scandal, not on the details of presidential misconduct, and because Bush's and Harken's activities were arcane and complex, the list in the text highlights only a selection of aspects that possessed scandal potential. Sources on Bush's activities at Harken include Corn (2003), Ivins (2000), Phillips (2004)

and other writings cited throughout those books. The Center for Public Integrity published a series of reports on Bush and Harken along with some documents relevant to the case. Links to these can be found at www.publicintegrity.org/articles/entry/432/?utm_source=publicintegrity&utm_medium=related_heds&utm_campaign=side_v1.

2   The *New York Daily News* ran a series of stories on the Bahrain deal that was not picked up by the mainstream media. One of them, "Harken board notes contradict W's claims" (Burger 2002), reads as follows:

> WASHINGTON – President Bush said Wednesday that he opposed a foreign drilling contract while serving as a director of Harken Energy Corp. – but newly disclosed board minutes suggest that he voted for the deal.
>
> "I opposed, as you may recall, when I was a director of the company" the deal with the government of Bahrain, Bush said on Wednesday, when questioned about the Daily News' disclosure of the offshore Harken Bahrain Oil Co. subsidiary set up to limit U.S. taxes.
>
> But minutes of a Dec. 6, 1989, meeting of Harken's board list Bush as present for discussion of – and suggest he voted for – the company's deal with Bahrain, an oil-poor Arab island nation.
>
> After discussion, "the board unanimously approved . . . proceeding toward finalization of a formal agreement with the State of Bahrain," according to the minutes, disclosed Thursday on the Center for Public Integrity Web site.
>
> White House Communications Director Dan Bartlett told The News yesterday that Bush "opposed the Bahrain deal" during deliberations – but apparently followed a Harken "tradition of board members having unanimous votes on most major matters involving the company."

   The December 1989 minutes do not reflect Bush opposing the deal.
3   For an account of the Enron scandal, see McLean & Elkind (2003).
4   The SEC's general counsel at the time it issued its report on Harken (August 21, 1991) was James R. Doty, who had served as George W. Bush's private lawyer when he acquired his stake in the Texas Rangers, and SEC Chairman Richard Breeden was an appointee and major political supporter of President Bush.

5   One investigative story alleges even worse corruption beneath the surface, suggesting connections between George H. W. Bush, Harken, the Gulf war of 1991 and the corrupt international financial institution, BCCI (Pizzo 1992; on the Bush family's entanglements with international finance and oil-industry intrigue, see also Kevin Phillips 2004). Regardless of these allegations' veracity, their sensational nature could have led to far more journalistic interest in the Harken scandal than was directed to the entirely domestic and small-time charges about Clinton's Whitewater investment – and that comparison reinforces the usefulness of the Harken story for empirically understanding stillborn scandals.

6   This was before the Iraq war, during which Halliburton became even more controversial as one of the leading private contractors. The company earned billions of dollars because of the war, and, according to a Congressional Research Service (CRS) investigation, Cheney retained a financial interest in its prosperity. In 2003, *CBS News* reported that the CRS document "undermines Vice President Dick Cheney's denial of a continuing relationship with Halliburton Co. . . . The report says a public official's unexercised stock options and deferred salary fall within the definition of 'retained ties' to his former company" (Murphy 2003, February 25).

7   A 10 percent reliability sample of articles showed 96 percent agreement and a Scott's Pi of .74 across the variables.

8   The quantitative content analysis was a joint venture by Dr. Carole V. Bell, Post-doctoral Research Scientist at George Washington University, and the author, based on the blocked scandal trait list developed through the qualitative analysis. Lauren Martens, a graduate of the George Washington University (GWU) School of Media and Public Affairs (MA, 2011), and Morgan Dibble, a graduate of GWU's Elliott School of International Affairs (MA 2009), conducted the coding.

9   There was hardly any variation in framing the Harken story among the TV outlets, and just slightly more in the newspapers (data not shown).

10 See Hindman (2008) on blogs and polarization. Brock (2002) offers a full description of this apparatus on the Republican side (see also Conason 2003; Domke 2004; Rampton & Strauber 2004; Entman 2005; M. Smith 2007; Jamieson & Cappella 2008).

11 On Enron, which among other things helped trigger an economic downturn in California by manipulating electricity production and newly deregulated markets, see McLean & Elkind (2003), and see especially pp. 87–9 on the Bush family's connections to the company; see also Kevin Phillips (2004, pp. 154–8).

8 Silenced Scandals of Grave Misconduct

1   Available at www.harrisinteractive.com/Insights/HarrisVault.aspx.
2   This study was carried out with Dr. Carole V. Bell, Abby Jones (a GWU Ph.D. student in public policy) and Lauren Martens.
3   The argument that the Iraq war actually fulfilled Osama bin Laden's strategic goals (perhaps his wildest dreams) while increasing al Qaeda's strength and boosting its recruitment efforts is supported by a variety of analysts across the political spectrum, including Mueller (2006) and Bacevich (2010); cf. J. A. Baker, Hamilton & Eagleburger (2006).
4   Almost all the available survey questions asked about whether the *Bush administration* deliberately misled, or in a few polls, "lied." The "Bush administration" covers a great many potential culprits. Also, wording often failed to ask about the specific issue of WMD, instead inquiring more generally about the administration misleading the public on Iraq. That is the case for the survey cited in the text (Kull 2004), which asked whether Bush decided to go to war on the basis of "assumptions about Iraq" that were correct or incorrect. It did not specify WMD. Kull's data also showed a wide partisan divide in answering this question. Among Bush supporters (surveyed just before the 2004 election), only 2 percent said Bush knew the assumptions were incorrect; among Kerry supporters, 48 percent felt the president acted in bad faith. But again, the wording, though it does ask about Bush himself, doesn't focus on WMD. These shortcomings further limit the usefulness of surveys in trying to assess public sentiments on whether George W. Bush, personally, knowingly lied.
    Most dispositive for this book's purposes are the majorities of Americans in various polls who rated Bush as honest or moral. These data tell us that the fundamental requirement for a scandal of high political impact as described in chapter 2 – evidence that charges of corruption or incompetence critically damaged a politician's standing – did not occur for Bush, at least in the moral/trustworthy dimension (which presumably would reflect assessments of whether Bush was a liar).
5   Also see the National Security Archive for an extensive selection of documents related to the war and intelligence, at www.gwu.edu/~nsarchiv/.
6   The US and UK withdrew their pro-war resolution from the UN Security Council when it became apparent they could count on only 4 of 15 votes (their own, Spain's and Bulgaria's) (R. Bennett 2008). The defeat of such a resolution would have made the Iraq invasion a more transparent violation of international law. Removing the

resolution allowed the US to claim that the earlier one (#1441) implicitly endorsed war.

7   Spoken by John Humphrys, interviewing BBC defense correspondent Andrew Gilligan on the Radio Four *Today* program (May 29, 2003).

8   On June 28, nearly two months after the Downing Street memo surfaced, the *Post* finally ran "a full, in-depth news story" on its front page (Schiffer 2006, p. 503).

9   See Benoit (2006) for a rhetorical analysis. On both the WMD and Plame matters, see: Blumenthal (2006) for a Democratic political operative's perspective, and Rich (2006) for a liberal *New York Times* op-ed columnist's dissection; and see Gill & Phythian (2006) and Pfiffner (2004) on the WMD intelligence.

10 The most powerful administration figures in national security, former Vice President Cheney and Defense Secretary Donald Rumsfeld, were influenced by the political philosophy of Leo Strauss at the University of Chicago. The Straussian approach justifies strong leadership that is not necessarily bound by adherence to facts (see Bok 1978, pp. 168–9; see also Shorris 2004).

11 George H. W. Bush had enjoyed a similar lightning victory in the Gulf war, only to see his extraordinary war-time popularity evaporate as attention turned to domestic matters. He lost his 1992 re-election bid, a family trauma his son shared in and would want to avoid repeating.

12 Along with Deputy Secretary of State Richard Armitage, who asserted that his own Plame leak was an unplanned, unknowing slip.

13 Libby's denial to investigators that Cheney and he had discussed leaking Plame's identity was one reason for his indictment and conviction on perjury. As Fitzgerald notes and the jury's verdict indicates, it strains credulity to believe that, on a matter which Libby admitted speaking about with the vice president several times a day for a week, the two men did not cooperate in plotting the leak. In any case, what's at issue here, as throughout the chapter, is whether there was enough evidence to constitute a potential high-magnitude scandal centering on Cheney and Bush. On Bush's role, see Waas (2006).

14 The proximity analysis was carried out by Abby Jones under the guidance of the author, with great technical assistance from Normand Péladeau, developer of the MAXQDA content analysis program.

15 After a careful reading of 200 paragraphs that included *Cheney* or *Vice President*, we decided to exclude the following phrases from counting as mentions of Cheney himself: *Vice President's Chief of Staff*, *Former Cheney Advisor*, *Top Aide to Vice President Dick*

Cheney, Former Cheney, Former Chief of Staff to Vice President Dick Cheney, Former Aide, Ex-Cheney Aide and *Ex-Aide*. Our judgment was that the listed terms did not imply any direct responsibility on the part of Cheney for the Plame incident. These adjectival uses of *Cheney* were not counted as textual connections suggesting a causal relationship between the vice president and Plame. The coding dictionary similarly distinguished *Bush* from the terms "Bush Administration" and "Bush White House."

16   The sample consists of the following numbers of stories or editorial commentaries in each outlet:

Outlet	# of items
Washington Post	457
New York Times	317
USA Today	85
AP Wire	656
Newsweek	45
CBS	32
ABC	18
NBC	29
FOX News	157
CNN	194

17   According to the WordStat manual:

the proximity plot is the most accurate way to graphically represent the distance between objects by displaying the measured distance from one or several target objects to all other objects. It is not a data reduction technique but a visualization tool to help one extract information from the huge amount of data stored in the distance matrix. . . . The Jaccard coefficient is a statistical measurement of asymmetric information on binary (and non-binary) variables. Given two objects, each with *n* attributes, the Jaccard coefficient can gauge the overlap of their attributes.

18   Note that some commentaries were syndicated columns appearing in several papers, so the total number of negative (and supportive) voices on editorial pages is lower than the number (125) of items in the sample. For instance, an identical column by David Broder appeared in multiple papers.

19   This count includes 2 stories that were published in multiple outlets; the total number of separate stories was 37.

20   Factors outside those encompassed by the cascade model contributed to this result. One was that another scandal occurred around the same time. Attorney General Alberto Gonzales oversaw dismissal of some eight US district attorneys whom the administration felt were insufficiently responsive to its political needs. Bush was pressured to fire Gonzales and eventually accepted Gonzales's resignation, but once the latter left office, Congress dropped the matter (Stephen 2007; Rozel & Sollenberger 2008). Further on Gonzales's politicization of his office, see Horton (2008).

9 Recalibrating Scandal and Silence

1   In terms of electoral votes, George W. Bush's margin of 286 to 251 was the thinnest for a re-elected president since Woodrow Wilson's in 1916.

2   This brings up the problem of proof. Few sex scandals are conclusively proven; they only offer degrees of credibility. Arguably, the public has a right to weigh all evidence. DNA finally confirmed Bill Clinton and John Edwards as adulterers. But, had Clinton and Edwards been a bit more careful, only circumstantial evidence would be available – information not much different from that available on George H. W. Bush and Jennifer Fitzgerald, or John McCain and Vicki Iseman. Hardly any cases will offer the equivalent of the semen-stained dress that unwound Clinton's cover-up. Where there's no evidence at all, journalists can report that this is the case, along with the political sources and motivations for the allegations, and the public can probably be trusted to dismiss truly unfounded charges – if, that is, the public believes that media are consistently holding everyone to the same standard.

3   The exception, an accusation that arose and died quickly online, involved allegations of an affair with an aide on his 2004 US Senate campaign. Obama and the Democrats never promoted marital fidelity or traditional family ideals as a theme of their platforms, nor did they try to get the press to investigate McCain's or Palin's sexual habits. Therefore the mainstream media were correct to ignore the accusations against Obama's private behavior, which were neither substantiated nor disproved conclusively.

4   For contemporaneous accounts of Palin's initial use of that accusation, see Kate Phillips (2008); M. Stewart (2008).

5   Obama had some peripheral interactions in the 1990s with William Ayers, a professor of education who had been a violent 1960s radical. Most of these interactions came in the context of an educational

reform commission on which such establishment figures as the Republican philanthropist Leonore Annenberg – wife of Reagan's former ambassador to the UK, Walter Annenberg – also sat.

6   In some instances, minimizing initial attention to a potential scandal might actually boost investigations by keeping the miscreant in the dark. Not knowing he or she is under suspicion, a politician might be less likely to initiate a cover-up (e.g. shredding documents or pressuring witnesses). It also takes time to document a case, even if there is no attempt to cover up. Therefore, delay is not always undesirable. On the other hand, more often, too much delay is likely to render the potentially scandalous news stale or to discourage scandal sponsors, sources and journalists who have tried and failed on their initial attempt to spark wide media interest.

7   Murrow was a legendary *CBS News* correspondent who occasionally spoke truth to power and created pressure for reform. See the biography by Edwards (2004).

8   Although it might be assumed that high levels of scandal news could turn citizens off from politics, research shows that scandals can actually motivate people to pay closer attention to candidates and to retain more substantive information on them (Miller 2010).

References

ACLU. (2005). Autopsy reports reveal homicides of detainees in U.S. custody. http://action.aclu.org/torturefoia/released/102405/.

ACLU. (2011). The torture report: an investigation into rendition, detention and interrogation under the Bush administration. www.thetorturereport. org.

Adamic, L. & Glance, N. (2005). The political blogosphere and the 2004 U.S. election: divided they blog. www.blogpulse.com/papers/2005/ AdamicGlanceBlogWWW.pdf.

Aday, S. (2010). Chasing the bad news: an analysis of 2005 Iraq and Afghanistan war coverage on NBC and Fox News Channel. *Journal of Communication*, 60(1), 144–64.

Aday, S., Farrell, H., Lynch, M., Sides, J., Kelly, J. & Zuckerman, E. (2010). *Blogs and Bullets: New Media in Contentious Politics*. Washington, DC: United States Institute of Peace.

Adut, A. (2008). *On Scandal: Moral Disturbances in Society, Politics, and Art*. New York: Cambridge University Press.

Allen, M. (2002, July 3). Memo cited Bush's late SEC filings: White House dismisses suggestions of wrongdoing in Bush's time in oil business, *The Washington Post*, p. A-4.

Alter, J. (2001). Time to think about torture. *Newsweek*. www.newsweek. com/2001/11/04/time-to-think-about-torture.html.

Alter, J. (2010). *The Promise: President Obama, Year One*. New York: Simon & Schuster.

Alterman, E. (2003). *What Liberal Media? The Truth about Bias and the News*. New York: Basic Books.

Althaus, S. L. & Kim, Y. M. (2006). Priming effects in complex information environments: reassessing the impact of news discourse on presidential approval. *Journal of Politics*, 68(4), 960–76.

Ambinder, M. (2008). McCain/lobbyist story in The New York Times finally drops.www.theatlantic.com/politics/archive/2008/02/mccain-lobbyist-story-in-the-new-york-times-finally-drops/52029/.

The American National Election Studies. (2008). Palo Alto, CA, and Ann Arbor, MI: Stanford University and the University of Michigan.

Ames, C. (2011, June 26). Memo reveals intelligence chief's bid to fuel fears of Iraqi WMDs: Sir John Scarlett wanted dossier to strengthen case for war. www.guardian.co.uk/uk/2011/jun/26/intelligence-chief-iraqi-wmds.

Ames, C. & Doward, J. (2010, September 5). Iraq WMD dossier was "reviewed" to match Labour spin, memo reveals, *The Observer*. www.guardian.co.uk/uk/2010/sep/05/iraq-war-inquiry-iraq.

Appy, C. G. (1993). *Working-Class War: American Combat Soldiers and Vietnam*. Chapel Hill, NC: University of North Carolina Press.

Are "No Strings Attached" and "Friends With Benefits" the same movie? (2010). *The Wall Street Journal*. http://blogs.wsj.com/speakeasy/2010/11/05/no-strings-attached-trailer-makes-us-root-for-natalie-portman-and-ashton-kutcher/.

Arts, humanities cut by a third in Senate. (1995, August 10). *USA Today*, p. 4A.

Axford, B., Madgewick, P. & Turner, J. (1992). Image management, stunts and dirty tricks: the marketing of political brands in television campaigns. *Media, Culture and Society*, 14(4), 637–51.

Bacevich, A. (2010). *Washington Rules: America's Path to Permanent War*. New York: Metropolitan Books.

Baker, J. A., Hamilton, L. & Eagleburger, L. S. (2006). *The Iraq Study Group Report*. New York: Vintage Books.

Baker, R. (2004, September 27). Why Bush left Texas. *The Nation*, 279.

Baker, R. (2009). *Family of Secrets: The Bush Dynasty, the Powerful Forces that Put it in the White House, and What Their Influence Means for America*. New York: Bloomsbury Press.

Balz, D. (2002, August 4). Gore takes issue with Lieberman: ex-running mates at odds over message of 2000 campaign, *The Washington Post*, p. A-4.

Bates, M. J. (1996). *The Wars We Took to Vietnam: Cultural Conflict and Storytelling*. Berkeley: University of California Press.

Battle plans for Iraq. (2002, July 6). Editorial, *The New York Times*, p. A12.

Behr, P. (2002, November 1). Bush sold stock after lawyers' warning: SEC closed probe before receiving letter from Harken's outside attorneys, *The Washington Post*, p. A-4. www.washingtonpost.com/ac2/wp-dyn?pagename=article&node=&contentId=A49309-2002Oct31&notFound=true.

Benen, S. (2011, March 9). Political animal. *Washington Monthly*. www.washingtonmonthly.com/archives/individual/2011_03/028355.php.

Bennett, R. (2008, March 8). Ten days to war, *Guardian*. www.guardian.co.uk/world/2008/mar/08/iraq.unitednations.

Bennett, W. L. & Iyengar, S. (2008). A new era of minimal effects? The changing foundations of political communication. *Journal of Communication*, 58(4), 707–31.

Bennett, W. L., Lawrence, R. G. & Livingston, S. (2007). *When the Press Fails: Political Power and the News Media from Iraq to Katrina*. Chicago: University of Chicago Press.

Benoit, W. L. (2006). President Bush's image repair effort on Meet the Press: the complexities of defeasibility. *Journal of Applied Communication Research*, 34(3), 285–306.

Berkowitz, B. (2001, June 26). Is the Ronald Reagan legacy project heading for your town? *AlterNet*. www.alternet.org/story/11107/.

Bicket, D. & Wall, M. (2007). Circling the wagons: containing the Downing Street memo's impact in America. *Journal of Communication Inquiry*, 31(3), 206–21.

Birnbaum, J. H. & Shear, M. D. (2008, February 21). McCain's ties to lobbyist worried aides, *The Washington Post*. www.washingtonpost.com/wp-dyn/content/article/2008/02/20/AR2008022002898.html.

Bishin, B. G., Stevens, D. & Wilson, C. (2005). Truth or consequences? Character and swing voters in the 2000 election. *Public Integrity*, 7(2), 129–46.

Bishin, B. G., Stevens, D. & Wilson, C. (2006). Character counts? Honesty and fairness in election 2000. *Public Opinion Quarterly*, 70(2), 235–48.

Blumenthal, S. (1992). *Pledging Allegiance: The Last Campaign of the Cold War*. New York: HarperCollins.

Blumenthal, S. (2003). *The Clinton Wars*. New York: Farrar, Straus and Giroux.

Blumenthal, S. (2006). *How Bush Rules: Chronicles of a Radical Regime*. Princeton, NJ: Princeton University Press.

Blumenthal, S. (2007). Libby and the White House book club, *Salon*. www.salon.com/news/opinion/blumenthal/2007/03/08/scooter_libby/index.html.

Bode, K. (1992). Pull the plug: we have the power to say no, to abandon our photo-op addiction. *The Quill*, 80, 10–13.

Bok, S. (1978). *Lying: Moral Choice in Public and Private Life*. New York: Pantheon Books.

Bonner, R. (1984). *Weakness & Deceit: U.S. Policy and El Salvador*. New York: Crown.

Bower, S. W. (2008). *The Art of the Public Grovel: Sexual Sin and Public Confession in America*. Princeton, NJ: Princeton University Press.

Brewer, P. R., Graf, J. & Willnat, L. (2003). Priming or framing. *Gazette: International Journal for Communication Studies*, 65(6), 493–508.

Brock, D. (2002). *Blinded by the Right: The Conscience of an Ex-Conservative*. New York: Crown.

Brock, D. (2004). *The Republican Noise Machine: Right-Wing Media and How It Corrupts Democracy*. New York: Crown.

Bucy, E. P. & Grabe, M. E. (2008). Happy warriors revisited: hedonic and agonic display repertoires of presidential candidates on the evening news. *Politics and the Life Sciences*, 27(1), 24–44.

Bunch, W. (2009). *Tear Down This Myth: How the Reagan Legacy has Distorted Our Politics and Haunts Our Future*. New York: Free Press.

Burger, T. J. (2002, August 3). Harken board notes contradict W's claim, *New York Daily News*. www.nydailynews.com/archives/news/2002/08/03/2002-08-03_harken_board_notes_contradic.html.

Bush, B. (1994). *Barbara Bush: A Memoir*. New York: Scribner.

Bush, G. W. (2010). *Decision Points*. New York: Crown.

Calhoun, C. (1992). *Habermas and the Public Sphere*. Cambridge, MA: MIT Press.

Canel, M. J. & Sanders, K. (2006). *Morality Tales: Political Scandals and Journalism in Britain and Spain in the 1990s*. Creskill, NJ: Hampton Press.

Carr, D. (2002, June 20). Reassessing Martha Stewart, the brand, *The New York Times*. www.nytimes.com/2002/06/20/business/the-media-business-advertising-reassessing-martha-stewart-the-brand.html.

Carter, G., Kalogerakis, G. & Anderson, K. (2006). *Spy: The Funny Years*. New York: Miramax.

Castells, M. (2009). *Communication Power*. Oxford: Oxford University Press.

Chadwick, A. (2010). The political information cycle in a hybrid news system: the British prime minister and the "Bullygate" affair. *International Journal of Press/Politics*, 16(1), 3–29.

Chandrasekaran, R. (2006). *Imperial Life in the Emerald City*. New York: Alfred A. Knopf.

Chestnut, B. M. (1996). The narrative construction of Iran–Contra: the failure of Congress and the press to hold Reagan accountable. Ph.D., Northwestern University, Evanston, IL.

Chong, D. & Druckman, J. N. (2007). Framing theory. *Annual Review of Political Science*, 10, 103–26.

Christians, C. G., Ferré, J. P. & Fackler, M. (1993). *Good News: Social Ethics and the Press*. Oxford: Oxford University Press.

Chulov, M. & Pidd, H. (2011, February 15). Defector admits to WMD lies that triggered Iraq war, *The Guardian*. www.guardian.co.uk/world/2011/feb/15/defector-admits-wmd-lies-iraq-war.

Citizens United vs. *Federal Election Commission*, 130 S.Ct. 876. (2010).

Clarke, R. A. (2004). *Against All Enemies: Inside America's War on Terror*. New York: Free Press.

Clemmitt, M. (2011). Lies and politics: do politicians lie more today? *CQ Researcher*, 21(7), 145–68. www.cqpress.com/product/Researcher-Lies-and-Politics-v21-7.html.

Clift, E. (2004, September 24). Rhetoric vs. reality. *Newsweek*. www.newsweek.com/2004/09/23/rhetoric-vs-reality.html.

Conason, J. (1992, July/August). 1,000 reasons not to vote for George Bush, No. 1: he cheats on his wife. *Spy*, 29–38.

Conason, J. (2000, February). The George W. Bush success story: a heartwarming tale about baseball, $1.7 billion, and a lot of swell friends. *Harper's*, 39–53.

Conason, J. (2003). *Big Lies: The Right-Wing Propaganda Machine and How It Distorts the Truth*. New York: Thomas Dunne Books.

Conason, J. & Lyons, G. (2000). *The Hunting of the President: The Ten-Year Campaign to Destroy Bill and Hillary Clinton.* New York: St. Martin's Press.

Cooper, M. & Isikoff, M. (1997, March 17). With friends like these. *Newsweek*, 21.

Corn, D. (2003). *The Lies of George W. Bush: Mastering the Politics of Deception.* New York: Crown.

Corry, J. (1987, July 16). Poindexter testimony: a decrease in drama, *The New York Times*, p. C–26.

Cosgrove, K. M. (2007). *Branded Conservatives: How the Brand Brought the Right from the Fringes to the Center of American Politics.* New York: Peter Lang.

Covert, T. J. & Wasburn, P. (2008). *Media Bias? A Comparative Study of* Time, Newsweek, *the* National Review, *and the* Progressive, *1975–2000.* Lanham, MD: Lexington Books.

D'Alessio, D. & Allen, M. (2000). Media bias in presidential elections: a meta-analysis. *Journal of Communication*, 50(4), 133–56.

Dahl, R. (1989). *Democracy and Its Critics.* New Haven, CT: Yale University Press.

Davis, L. (2007). *Scandal: How "Gotcha" Politics is Destroying America.* New York: Palgrave Macmillan.

Dean, J. (2007). *Broken Government: How Republican Rule Destroyed the Legislative, Executive, and Judicial Branches.* New York: Viking Press.

Dick, K. (writer). (2009). *Outrage.* USA: Magnolia Pictures.

Domke, D. S. (2004). *God Willing? Political Fundamentalism in the White House, the "War on Terror," and the Echoing Press.* Ann Arbor, MI: Pluto Press.

Don't look now. (1996, November 18). *Newsweek*, 106. www.newsweek.com/1996/11/17/don-t-look-now.html#.

Dowd, M. (2011, February 12). Simply the worst, *The New York Times.* www.nytimes.com/2011/02/13/opinion/13dowd.html.

Downie, L., Jr. & Kaiser, R. G. (2003). *The News About the News: American Journalism in Peril.* New York: Knopf.

Dreier, P. & Martin, C. R. (2010). How ACORN was framed: political controversy and media agenda setting. *Perspectives on Politics*, 8(03), 761–92.

Dugan, M. A. (2008). Journalism ethics and the independent journalist. *McGeorge Law Review*, 39, 801–11.

Edelman, M. (1988). *Constructing the Political Spectacle.* Chicago: University of Chicago Press.

Edwards, B. (2004). *Edward R. Murrow and The Birth of Broadcast Journalism.* Hoboken, NJ: Wiley.

Entman, R. M. (1989). *Democracy Without Citizens: Media and the Decay of American Politics.* New York: Oxford University Press.

Entman, R. M. (1991). Framing U.S. coverage of international news: contrasts in narratives of the KAL and Iran Air incidents. *Journal of Communication*, 41(4), 6–27.

Entman, R. M. (1993). Framing: toward clarification of a fractured paradigm. *Journal of Communication*, 43(4), 51–8.

Entman, R. M. (2004). *Projections of Power: Framing News, Public Opinion, and U.S. Foreign Policy*. Chicago: University of Chicago Press.

Entman, R. M. (2005). The nature and sources of news. In G. Overholser & K. H. Jamieson (eds.), *The Press* (pp. 48–65). New York: Oxford University Press.

Entman, R. M. (2007). Framing bias: media in the distribution of power. *Journal of Communication*, 57(1), 163–73.

Entman, R. M. (2008). Theorizing mediated public diplomacy: the U.S. case. *International Journal of Press/Politics*, 13(2), 87–102.

Entman, R. M. (2010a). Framing media power. In P. D'Angelo & J. A. Kuypers (eds.), *Doing News Framing Analysis: Empirical and Theoretical Perspectives* (pp. 332–55). New York: Routledge.

Entman, R. M. (2010b). Improving newspapers' economic prospects by augmenting their contributions to democracy. *International Journal of Press/Politics*, 15(1), 104–25.

Entman, R. M. (2010c). Media framing biases and political power: explaining slant in news of campaign 2008. *Journalism*, 11(4), 389–408.

Entman, R. M. (2011, March 28–29). Incivility and asymmetric partisan warfare. Paper presented at the Conference "In the Name of Democracy: Political Communication Reseach and Practice in a Polarized Media Environment," Louisiana State University.

Entman, R. M., Livingston, S., Aday, S. & Kim, J. (2010). Condemned to repeat: the media and the accountability gap in Iraq war policy. In S. Koch-Baumgarten & K. Voltmer (eds.), *Public Policy and Mass Media: The Interplay of Mass Communication and Political Decision Making* (pp. 194–214). New York: Routledge.

Entman, R. M., Livingston, S. & Kim, J. (2009). Doomed to repeat: Iraq news, 2002–2007. *American Behavioral Scientist*, 52(5), 689–708.

Entman, R. M., Matthes, J. & Pellicano, L. (2009). Nature, sources, and effects of news framing. In K. Wahl-Jorgensen & T. Hanitzsch (eds.), *The Handbook of Journalism Studies*. New York: Taylor & Francis, pp. 175–90.

Esser, F. & Hartung, U. (2004). Nazis, pollution, and no sex. *American Behavioral Scientist*, 47(8), 1040–71.

Ettema, J. S. & Glasser, T. L. (1998). *Custodians of Conscience: Investigative Journalism and Public Virtue*. New York: Columbia University Press.

FAIR. (2005, June 17). Justifying the silence on Downing Street memos. www.fair.org/index.php?page=2556.

Falcone, M. (2009, July 2). The Republican class of 1994 plagued with scandal. *Politico*. www.politico.com/news/stories/0709/24435.html.

Falk, R. A. & American Society of International Law (eds.). (1968). *The Vietnam War and International Law*. Princeton, NJ: Princeton University Press.

Fallows, J. M. (1997). *Breaking the News: How the Media Undermine American Democracy*. New York: Vintage Books.

Farhi, P. (2009, March 24). Consider this: NPR achieves record ratings, *The Washington Post*, p. C-01.

FCC. (2011). *Internet*. http://transition.fcc.gov/osp/inc-report/INoC-4-Internet.pdf.

Feldstein, M. (2006). A muckraking model: investigative reporting cycles in American history. *International Journal of Press/Politics*, 11(2), 105–20.

Feldstein, M. (2010). *Poisoning the Press: Richard Nixon, Jack Anderson, and the Rise of Washington's Scandal Culture*. New York: Farrar, Straus and Giroux.

Fineman, H. (1997, March 3). Collision course. *Newsweek*, 50.

Fineman, H. & Isikoff, M. (2004, September 20). Slime time live. *Newsweek*, 144, 18–21.

Fink, S. (2009, August 29). The deadly choices at memorial, *The New York Times*, p. 28. www.nytimes.com/2009/09/13/magazine/13letters-t-THEDEADLYCHO_LETTERS.html.

Fitzgerald, P. (2006). *Government's Response to Defendant's Third Motion to Compel Recovery in* US *vs.* I. Lewis Libby. (Case 1:05-cr-00394-RBW Document 80). Washington, DC: Department of Justice www.justice.gov/usao/iln/osc/documents/2006_04_06_governments_response_to_third_motion_to_compel.pdf.

Flynt, L. & Eisenbach, D. (2011). *One Nation under Sex*. New York: Palgrave Macmillan.

Fournier, S. (2004, January 26). *Martha Stewart and the ImClone Scandal*. Hanover, NH: Tuck School of Business at Dartmouth.

The Freedom Forum Media Studies Center. (1993). *Top-Ten Campaign Names and Phrases from the Campaign Trail*. Washington, DC: The Freedom Forum.

Fried, A. (1997). *Muffled Echoes: Oliver North and the Politics of Public Opinion*. New York: Columbia University Press.

Fritz, B., Keefer, B. & Nyhan, B. (2004). *All the President's Spin: George W. Bush, The Media, and the Truth*. New York: Simon and Schuster.

Froomkin, D. (2009, April 22). Torturing for propaganda purposes, *The Washington Post*. http://voices.washingtonpost.com/white-house-watch/2009/04/torturing_for_propaganda_purpo/pf.html.

Gans, H. J. (1979). *Deciding What's News: A Study of CBS Evening News, NBC Nightly News, Newsweek, and Time*. New York: Pantheon.

Gardner, S. (2005, April 25). Ambassador Wilson: White House operatives are traitors [blog post]. www.dailykos.com/story/2005/04/25/109548/-Ambassador-Wilson:-White-House-Operatives-Are-Traitors.

Garment, S. (1992). *Scandal*. New York: Anchor Books.

Garrard, J. & Newell, J. (2006). *Scandals in Past and Contemporary Politics*. Manchester: Manchester University Press.

Germond, J. & Witcover, J. (1989). *Whose Broad Stripes and Bright Stars? The Trivial Pursuit of the Presidency, 1988.* New York: Warner Books.

Gibbs, N., Bacon, P., Jr., Cooper, M., et al. (2004, September 27). Blue truth, red truth. *Time,* 24–34.

Gill, P. & Phythian, M. (2006). *Intelligence in an Insecure World.* Cambridge: Polity.

Gillon, S. M. (2008). *The Pact: Bill Clinton, Newt Gingrich, and the Rivalry that Defined a Generation.* New York: Oxford University Press.

Ginsberg, B. & Shefter, M. (2002). *Politics by Other Means: Politicians, Prosecutors, and the Press from Watergate to Whitewater* (3rd edn.). New York: W.W. Norton.

Gitlin, T. (1992). Blips, bites and savvy talk: television's impact on American politics. In D. Shimkin, H. Stolerman & H. O'Connor (eds.), *State of the Art: Issues in Contemporary Mass Communication* (pp. 213–22). New York: St. Martin's Press.

Gitlin, T. (1998). The Clinton–Lewinsky obsession. *The Washington Monthly,* 30(12). www.washingtonmonthly.com/features/1998/9812.gitlin.obsession. html.

Goldstein, P. (2009). Outrage: Kirby Dick kicks open Washington's closet door, *Los Angeles Times.* http://latimesblogs.latimes.com/the_big_picture/ 2009/04/outraged-kirby-dick-kicks-open-washingtons-closet-door-.html.

Gordon-Reed, A. (2008). *The Hemmingses of Monticello.* New York: Norton.

Gore discusses fundraising, his role in the campaign. (1997). *Congressional Quarterly Weekly Report,* 55(14), 811.

Goss: CIA resignation "one of those mysteries." (2006, May 6). *CNN.* http:// articles.cnn.com/2006-05-06/politics/goss.resignation_1_goss-and- negroponte-cia-post-nsa-director?_s=PM:POLITICS.

Grabell, M. (2009, October 25). Stimulus contracts go to companies under criminal investigation. *ProPublica.* www.propublica.org/article/stimulus- contracts-go-to-companies-under-criminal-investigation-1023.

Grabell, M. (2010, March 22). New investigations of stimulus waste, fraud and abuse. *ProPublica.* www.propublica.org/article/new-investigations-of- stimulus-waste-fraud-and-abuse-322.

Greenwald, G. (2005, December 15). Allowing Bush to breach his Plame vows [blog post]. http://glenngreenwald.blogspot.com/2005/12/allowing- bush-to-breach-his-plame-vows.html.

Greenwald, G. (2009). What the new Jim Comey emails actually reveal. *Salon.* www.salon.com/opinion/greenwald/2009/06/07/torture_memos/ index.html.

Groseclose, T. & Milyo, J. (2005). A measure of media bias. *Quarterly Journal of Economics,* 120(4), 1191–237.

Gross, L. (1991). The contested closet: the ethics and politics of outing. *Critical Studies in Mass Communication,* 8(3), 352.

Grossman, J. (2002, June 21). Martha envy, *The Wall Street Journal,* p. A8.

Habermas, J. (1989). *The Structural Transformation of the Public Sphere: An Inquiry into a Category of Bourgeois Society.* Cambridge, MA: MIT Press.

Hacker, J. S. & Pierson, P. (2010). *Winner-Take-All Politics: How Washington Made the Rich Richer and Turned Its Back on the Middle Class.* New York: Simon & Schuster.

Hallin, D. C. (1986). *The "Uncensored War": The Media and Vietnam.* New York: Oxford University Press.

Halper, S. A. & Clarke, J. (2005). *America Alone: The Neo-Conservatives and the Global Order.* Cambridge: Cambridge University Press.

Hamilton, J. T. (2004). *All the News That's Fit to Sell: How the Market Transforms Information Into News.* Princeton, NJ: Princeton University Press.

Hamilton, J. T. (2009). *Subsidizing the Watchdog: What Would it Cost to Support Investigative Journalism at a Large Metropolitan Daily Newspaper?* http://sanford.duke.edu/nonprofitmedia/documents/dwchamiltonfinal.pdf.

Hanley, C. J. (2006, August 7). Half of U.S. still believes Iraq had WMD, *The Washington Post.* www.washingtonpost.com/wp-dyn/content/article/2006/08/07/AR2006080700189.html.

Harmon, M. & Muenchen, R. (2009). Semantic framing in the build-up to the Iraq War: Fox v. CNN and other U. S. broadcast news programs. *ETC: A Review of General Semantics*, 66(1), 12–26.

Hartmann, T. (2009). *Media Choice: A Theoretical and Empirical Overview.* New York: Routledge.

Hatfield, J. (2001). *Fortunate Son: George W. Bush and the Making of an American President.* New York: Soft Skull Press.

Hayes, D. (2005). Candidate qualities through a partisan lens: a theory of trait ownership. *American Journal of Political Science*, 49(4), 908–23.

Hayes, D. (2008). Party reputations, journalistic expectations: how issue ownership influences election news. *Political Communication*, 25(4), 377–400.

Hayes, D. & Guardino, M. (2010). Whose views made the news? Media coverage and the march to war in Iraq. *Political Communication*, 27(1), 59–87.

Heilemann, J. & Halperin, M. (2010). *Game Change: Obama and the Clintons, McCain and Palin, and the Race of a Lifetime.* New York: Harper.

Hertsgaard, M. (1989). *On Bended Knee: The Press and the Reagan Presidency.* New York: Schocken.

Hillygus, D. S. & Shields, T. G. (2008). *The Persuadable Voter: Wedge Issues in Presidential Campaigns.* Princeton, NJ: Princeton University Press.

Hindman, M. S. (2008). *The Myth of Digital Democracy.* Princeton, NJ: Princeton University Press.

Holmes, S. (2010). The spider's web: how government lawbreakers routinely elude the law. In A. Sarat & N. Hussain (eds.), *When Governments Break the Law: The Rule of Law and the Prosecution of the Bush Administration.* New York: New York University Press.

Horton, S. (2008, March). The Spitzer sex sting: a few more questions. *Harper's.* www.harpers.org/archive/2008/03/hbc-90002589.

Hosenball, M., Isikoff, M. & Gesalman, A. B. (2004, September 27). A source of contention. *Newsweek*, 6.

Hoyt, C. (2008, August 8). Sometimes, there's news in the gutter. *New York Times*, p. WK–10.

Huffington, A. (2005, October 25). Plamegate: worse than Watergate [blog post]. www.huffingtonpost.com/arianna-huffington/plamegate-worse-than-wate_b_9522.html.

Hunter. (2004). TANG typewriter follies; wingnuts wrong. *Daily Kos*. www.dailykos.com/story/2004/9/10/213416/348.

Inter-University Consortium for Political and Social Research. (1984). *American National Election Study, 1984: 1983 Pilot Survey*. http://dx.doi.org/10.3886/ICPSR08178.

Isikoff, M. (2000, June 12). A very close call for Al. *Newsweek*, 36.

Isikoff, M. & Corn, D. (2006). *Hubris: The Inside Story of Spin, Scandal, and the Selling of the Iraq War*. New York: Three Rivers Press.

Isikoff, M. & Hosenball, M. (2004, September 23). The story that didn't run. *MSNBC/Newsweek*. www.commondreams.org/headlines04/0923-02.htm.

Ivins, M. (2000). *Shrub: The Short but Happy Political Life of George W. Bush*. New York: Vintage.

Ivins, M. & Dubose, L. (2003). *Bushwhacked: Life in George W. Bush's America*. New York: Random House.

Iyengar, S. (1990). The accessibility bias in politics: television news and public opinion. *International Journal of Public Opinion Research*, 2(1), 1–15.

Iyengar, S. & Kinder, D. R. (1987). *News That Matters: Television and American Opinion*. Chicago: University of Chicago Press.

Iyengar, S., Peters, M. D. & Kinder, D. R. (1982). Experimental demonstrations of the "not-so-minimal" consequences of television news programs. *American Political Science Review*, 76(4), 848–58.

Jackson, D. (2002, November 1). The wild, wild Bush boyz, *The Boston Globe*, p. A23. http://pqasb.pqarchiver.com/boston/access/229589351.html?FMT=ABS&date=Nov%201,%202002.

Jacobsson, K. & Löfmarck, E. (2008). A sociology of scandal and moral transgression: the Swedish "nannygate" scandal. *Acta Sociologica*, 51(3), 203–16.

Jacoby, M. (2004). George W. Bush's missing year. *Salon*. http://dir.salon.com/story/news/feature/2004/09/02/allison/print.html.

Jamieson, K. H. (1993). The subversive effects of a focus on strategy in news coverage of presidential campaigns. In K. H. Jamieson, K. Auletta & T. E. Patterson (eds.), *1–800-President: Report of the Twentieth Century Fund Task Force on Television and the Campaign of 1992* (pp. 35–61). New York: Twentieth Century Fund Press.

Jamieson, K. H. & Cappella, J. N. (2008). *Echo Chamber: Rush Limbaugh and the Conservative Media Establishment*. New York: Oxford University Press.

Jamieson, K. H. & Waldman, P. (2002). *The Press Effect: Politicians, Journalists, and the Stories That Shape the Political World*. New York: Oxford University Press.

Jarvis, S. E. (2005). *The Talk of the Party: Political Labels, Symbolic Capital, and American Life*. Lanham, MD: Rowman & Littlefield.

John Edwards's docudrama: the anatomy of innuendo. (2007, January 14). http://nymag.com/daily/intel/2007/10/john_edwards_docudrama_the_ana. html.

Johnson, R., Hagen, M. G. & Jamieson, K. H. (2004). *The 2000 Presidential Election and the Foundations of Party Politics*. New York: Cambridge University Press.

Johnson, S. & Kwak, J. (2011). *13 Bankers: The Wall Street Takeover and the Next Financial Meltdown*. New York: Vintage Books.

Johnston, D. (1992, December 25). Bush pardons 6 in Iran affair, aborting a Weinberger trial; prosecutor assails "cover-up," *The New York Times*. www.nytimes.com/books/97/06/29/reviews/iran-pardon.html.

Johnston, D. & Mazzetti, M. (2009, August 14). Rise and fall of C.I.A.'s go-to guy for secret jails; agent's story is a glimpse of how prisons were built and what they were like, *The International Herald Tribune*, p. 1.

Johnston, D. & Savage, C. (2009, January 11). Obama reluctant to look into Bush programs, *The New York Times*. www.nytimes.com/2009/01/12/us/politics/12inquire.html?_r=1.

Jones, J. M. (2003, January 17). Bush second-year approval rating one of best ever; post-Sept. 11 decline evident in latest quarterly ratings. www.gallup.com/poll/7600/bush-secondyear-approval-rating-one-best-ever.aspx.

Kahn, K. F. & Kenney, P. J. (2002). The slant of the news: how editorial endorsements influence campaign coverage and citizens' views of candidates. *American Political Science Review*, 96, 381–94.

Kalb, M. L. (2001). *One Scandalous Story: Clinton, Lewinsky, and Thirteen Days that Tarnished American Journalism*. New York: Free Press.

Karpf, D. (2008). Understanding blogspace. *Journal of Information Technology & Politics*, 5(4), 369–85.

Karpf, D. (2010). Macaca moments reconsidered: electoral panopticon or netroots mobilization? *Journal of Information Technology & Politics*, 7(2/3), 143–62.

Kelly, M. (2002, July 17). Two-edged weapon, *The Washington Post*, p. A23.

Kent, A. (1997). *Risk & Redemption: Surviving the Network News Wars*. London: Interstellar.

Key Players in the CIA leak investigation. (2007, July 3). *The Washington Post*. www.washingtonpost.com/wp-srv/politics/special/plame/Plame_KeyPlayers.html.

Klaidman, D. & Breslau, K. (1997, September 22). The trouble with Al. *Newsweek*, 39.

Kornbluh, P. & Byrne, M. (1993). *The Iran–Contra Scandal: The Declassified History*. New York: New Press.

Kramer, M. (1987, February 2). State of the scandal. *New York Magazine*, 20.

Kranish, M. & Healy, B. (2002, October 30). Board was told of risks before Bush stock sale: Harken memo went to SEC after probe, *The Boston Globe*, p. A1.

Krugman, P. (2002, October 2). Moles at work, *The New York Times*, p. A33.

Krugman, P. (2009). *The Return of Depression Economics and the Crisis of 2008*. New York: W.W. Norton.

Kull, S. (2004, January). *PIPA / Knowledge Networks Poll: Americans and Iraq on the Eve of the Presidential Election*. www.pipa.org/OnlineReports/Iraq/IraqPresElect_Oct04/IraqPresElect_Oct04_quaire.pdf.

Kurtz, H. (1998). *Spin Cycle: How the White House and the Media Manipulate the News*. New York: Free Press.

Lakoff, G. (2004). *Don't Think of an Elephant: Know Your Values and Frame the Debate – The Essential Guide for Progressives*. New York: Chelsea Green Publishing.

Lakoff, G. (2008). *The Political Mind: Why You Can't Understand 21st-Century American Politics with an 18th-Century Brain*. New York: Penguin Group.

Landay, J. S. (2009, April 21). Report: abusive tactics used to seek Iraq – al Qaida link, *McClatchy*. www.mcclatchydc.com/2009/04/21/66622/report-abusive-tactics-used-to.html.

Lang, G. & Lang, K. (1983). *The Battle for Public Opinion: The President, the Press, and the Polls During Watergate*. New York: Columbia University Press.

Lawrence, J. (2000, July 28). The evolution of George W. Bush, *USA Today*, p. 8A.

Lawrence, R. G. & Bennett, W. L. (2000). Civic engagement in the era of big stories. *Political Communication*, 17(4), 377–82.

Leebaert, D. (2003). *The Fifty-Year Wound: How America's Cold War Victory Shapes Our World*. Boston: Back Bay Books.

Leopold, J. (2007, January 31). Cheney's handwritten notes implicate Bush in Plame affair. *The Public Record*. http://pubrecord.org/nation/345/cheneys-handwritten-notes-implicate-bush-in-plame-affair/.

Lewis, M. (2010). *The Big Short: Inside the Doomsday Machine*. New York: W.W. Norton.

Lewis, N. A. (2007, January 24). Libby defense portrays client as a scapegoat, *The New York Times*, p. A1.

Lichtenberg, J. (ed.). (1990). *Democracy and the Mass Media*. Cambridge: Cambridge University Press.

Linzer, D. (2005, October 29). CIA yet to assess harm from Plame's exposure, *The Washington Post*. www.washingtonpost.com/wp-dyn/content/article/2005/10/28/AR2005102801988.html.

Loftus, E. (1996). *Eyewitness Testimony*. Cambridge, MA: Harvard University Press.

Longley, K., Mayer, J. D., Schaller, M. & Sloan, J. W. (2007). *Deconstructing Reagan: Conservative Mythology and America's Fortieth President*. New York: M. E. Sharpe.

Lowi, T. (2004). Power and corruption: political competition and the scandal market. In P. Apostolidis & J. Williams (eds.), *Public Affairs: Politics in the Age of Sex Scandals* (pp. 69–100). Durham, NC: Duke University Press.

Lull, J. & Hinerman, S. (1997). *Media Scandals: Morality and Desire in the Popular Culture Marketplace*. New York: Columbia University Press.

MacPherson, M. (2002). *Long Time Passing: Vietnam and the Haunted Generation*. Bloomington: University of Indiana Press.

Mallaby, S. (2002, July 29). Bush's credibility gap, *The Washington Post*, p. A-19. www.washingtonpost.com/ac2/wp-dyn/A14367-2002Jul28?language=printer.

Manjoo, F. (2008). *True Enough: Learning to Live in a Post-Fact Society*. Hoboken, NJ: John Wiley & Sons.

Manning, D. (2005, May 1). The secret Downing Street memo, *The Sunday Times*. www.timesonline.co.uk/tol/news/uk/article387374.ece.

Mapes, M. (2005). *Truth and Duty: The Press, the President, and the Privilege of Power*. New York: St. Martin's Press.

Maratea, R. (2008). The e-rise and fall of social problems: the blogosphere as a public arena. *Social Problems*, 55(1), 139–60.

Martens, L. (2011). Self-fulfilling policy: a constructivist study of elite crisis management and its implications for scandal politics. Unpublished Master's thesis, George Washington University, Washington, DC.

Mason, J. (2001). Approval nears for ambassador to Saudi Arabia, *Houston Chronicle*, p. A16.

Matthes, J. & Kohring, M. (2008). The content analysis of media frames: toward improving reliability and validity. *Journal of Communication*, 58(2), 258–79.

Mayer, J. (2008). *The Dark Side: The Inside Story of How The War on Terror Turned into a War on American Ideals*. New York: Doubleday.

Mayer, W. G. (2007). *The Swing Voter in American Politics*. Washington, DC: Brookings Institution.

McClellan, S. (2008). *What Happened: Inside the Bush White House and Washington's Culture of Deception*. New York: Public Affairs.

McGinniss, J. (2011). *The Rogue: Searching for the Real Sarah Palin*. New York: Crown.

McInerney, J. (1988). *Story of My Life: A Novel*. New York: Atlantic Monthly Press.

McLean, B. & Elkind, P. (2003). *The Smartest Guys in the Room: The Amazing Rise and Scandalous Fall of Enron*. New York: Portfolio.

McLeary, P. (2005, May 20). The Downing Street memo: it's no runaway bride. *Columbia Journalism Review*. http://64.130.24.93/politics/the_downing_street_memo_its_no.php?page=all.

Meyrowitz, J. (1985). *No Sense of Place: The Impact of Electronic Media on Social Behavior*. New York: Oxford University Press.

Mezey, M. L. (2008). *Representative Democracy: Legislators and their Constituents*. Lanham, MD: Rowman & Littlefield.

Milbank, D. (2010, May 19). Scandals in the House Republican class of 1994, *The Washington Post*. www.washingtonpost.com/wp-dyn/content/article/2010/05/18/AR2010051803985.html.

Miller, B. (2010). The effects of scandalous information on recall of policy-related information. *Political Psychology*, 31(6), 897–914.

Mintz, M. (1985). *At Any Cost: Corporate Greed, Women, and the Dalkon Shield*. New York: Pantheon.

Moeller, S. (2004). *Media Coverage of Weapons of Mass Destruction*. College Park, MD: Center for International and Security Studies at Maryland.

Molotch, H. & Lester, M. (1973). News as purposive behavior: on the strategic use of routine events, accidents and scandals. *American Sociological Review*, 39(1), 101–12.

Montopoli, B., Roth, Z. & Lang, T. (2004). Ambush politics. *Columbia Journalism Review*. www.alternet.org/story/19665/ambush_politics/?page= entire.

Moore, D. W. (2008). *The Opinion Makers: An Insider Exposes the Truth Behind the Polls*. Boston: Beacon Press.

Morris, N. (2009, March 13). Secret emails show Iraq dossier was "sexed up," *The Independent*. www.independent.co.uk/news/uk/politics/secret-emails-show-iraq-dossier-uwasu-sexed-up-1643960.html.

Mueller, J. E. (2006). *Towel Snapping the Press: Bush's Journey From Locker-Room Antics to Message Control*. Lanham, MD: Rowman & Littlefield.

Murphy, J. (2003, February 25). Cheney's Halliburton ties remain. *CBS News*. www.cbsnews.com/stories/2003/09/26/politics/main575356.shtml.

National Commission on Terrorist Attacks Upon the United States. (2004). *The 9/11 Commission Report*. http://govinfo.library.unt.edu/911/report/911Report.pdf.

Niven, D. (2002). *Tilt? The Search for Media Bias*. Westport, CT: Praeger.

Nyhan, B. (2008). Breeding ground: when presidents are more vulnerable to political scandal. Unpublished manuscript. www-personal.umich.edu/~bnyhan/breeding-ground.pdf.

Nyhan, B. (2009). Strategic outrage: the politics of presidential scandal. Doctoral dissertation, Duke University, Durham, NC. www-personal.umich.edu/~bnyhan/dissertation-final.pdf.

Nyhan, B. (2011, May 9). Scandal potential: how political and media context affect the president's vulnerability to allegations of misconduct. www.dartmouth.edu/~nyhan/scandal-potential.pdf.

Office of Special Counsel. (2005). *White House Official I. Lewis Libby Indicted on Obstruction of Justice, False Statement and Perjury Charges Relating to Leak of Classified Information Revealing CIA Officer's Identity*. Washington, DC: US Department of Justice.

Packer, G. (2005). *The Assassins' Gate: America in Iraq*. New York: Farrar, Straus and Giroux.

Page, B. I. (1996). *Who Deliberates? Mass Media in Modern Democracy*. Chicago: University of Chicago Press.

Parmet, H. S. (1997). *George Bush: The Life of a Lone Star Yankee*. New York: Scribner.

Paterno, S. (1997). An affair to ignore. *American Journalism Review*, 19, 31–3.

Patterson, T. E. (1993). Let the press be the press: principles of campaign reform. *Report of the Twentieth Century Task Force on Television and the Campaign of 1992* (pp. 91–109). New York: Twentieth Century Fund Press.

Payne, G. J. & Mercuri, K. (1993). Private lives, public officials. *American Behavioral Scientist*, 37(2), 291–301.

Pelosi, A. & Lubarsky, A. (writers). (2002). *Journeys with George*. USA: HBO Films.

Perel, D. (2011, February 1). The never-before-revealed details of why John Edwards finally confessed to his affair. *The Huffington Post*. www.huffingtonpost.com/david-perel/john-edwards-affair_b_816599.html.

Peretz, E. (2005, November). High noon in Crawford. *Vanity Fair*. www.vanityfair.com/politics/features/2005/11/crawford200511.

Pershing, B. (2008, June 11). Kucinich forces vote on Bush's impeachment, *The Washington Post*. www.washingtonpost.com/wp-dyn/content/article/2008/06/10/AR2008061003087.html.

Pew Project for Excellence in Journalism. (2010). *The State of the News Media 2010*. Washington, DC: Pew Project for Excellence in Journalism.

Pew Project for Excellence in Journalism. (2011). Network news: durability and decline. In *The State of the News Media 2011*. Washington, DC: Pew Project for Excellence in Journalism. http://stateofthemedia.org/2011/network-essay.

Pew Research Center. (2007). *The Invisible Primary – Invisible No Longer: A First Look at Coverage of the 2008 Presidential Campaign*. Washington, DC: Pew Research Center Project for Excellence in Journalism.

Pfiffner, J. (2004). Did President Bush mislead the country in his arguments for war with Iraq? *Presidential Studies Quarterly*, 34(1), 25–46.

Pfiffner, J. (2007). Intelligence and decision making before the war with Iraq. In G. C. Edwards III & D. S. King (eds.), *The Polarized Presidency of George W. Bush*. Oxford: Oxford University Press.

Phillips, Kate (2008, October 4). Palin: Obama is "palling around with terrorists" [blog post]. http://thecaucus.blogs.nytimes.com/2008/10/04/palin-obama-is-palling-around-with-terrorists/.

Phillips, Kevin (2004). *American Dynasty: Aristocracy, Fortune, and the Politics of Deceit in the House of Bush*. New York: Viking Books.

Pillar, P. R. (2006). Intelligence, policy, and the war in Iraq. *Foreign Affairs*, 85(2), 15–27.

Pincus, W. & Priest, D. (2003). Some Iraq analysts felt pressure from Cheney visits, *The Washington Post*. www.washingtonpost.com/ac2/wp-dyn?pagename=article&contentId=A15019-2003Jun4.

Pitkin, H. F. (1967). *The Concept of Representation*. Berkeley: University of California Press.

Pizzo, S. (1992, September/October). Bush family value$. *Mother Jones*. http://motherjones.com/politics/1992/09/bush-family-value.

Plame Hearing Transcript. (2007, March 16). http://rawstory.com/news/2007/Plame_hearing_transcript_0316.html.

Poll: most rate Reagan over Clinton. (2004, June 21). *USA Today*. www.usatoday.com/news/politicselections/nation/president/2004-06-21-reagan-clinton_x.htm.

Portland DA: criminal prosecution possible in the Al Gore sex scandal. (2010, June 23). *National Enquirer*. www.nationalenquirer.com/al_gore_sex_scandal_police_confidential_report/celebrity/68876.

Potter, P. B. K. & Baum, M. A. (2010). Democratic peace, domestic audience costs, and political communication. *Political Communication*, 27(4), 453–70.

Potter, W. (2010). *Deadly Spin: An Insurance Company Insider Speaks Out on How Corporate PR is Killing Health Care and Deceiving Americans*. New York: Bloomsbury Press.

Presidential cheating scandal! Alleged affair could wreck John Edwards' campaign bid (2007). www.nationalenquirer.com/celebrity/presidential-cheating-scandal-alleged-affair-could-wreck-john-edwards-campaign-bid.

Price, J. F. (2007). *Martha Stewart: A Biography*. New York: Greenwood Publishing Group.

Priest, D. & Gellman, B. (2002, December 26). US decries abuse but defends interrogations, *The Washington Post*, p. A-01.

ProPublica journalism in the public interest: how we do it. (2010, September 20). *ProPublica*. www.propublica.org/about/how-we-do-it/.

Protess, D. L., Cook, F. L., Doppelt, J. C., et al. (1991). *The Journalism of Outrage: Investigative Reporting and Agenda Building in America*. New York: Guilford.

Rampton, S. & Strauber, J. (2004). *Banana Republicans: How the Right-Wing is Turning America into a One-Party State*. New York: Jeremy P. Tarcher.

Randolph, E. (1988, October 22). Bush rumor created dilemma for media. *The Washington Post*, p. A-09.

Rather, D. (1994). *The Camera Never Blinks Twice: The Further Adventures of a TV Journalist*. New York: William Morrow & Co.

Ray, R. W. (2001). *Final Report of the Independent Counsel In* Re: Madison Guaranty Savings & Loan Association – *The Clintons, The McDougals, and the Whitewater Development Company*. Washington, DC: Superintendent of Documents, US Government Printing Office.

Reese, S. D., Gandy, O. H., Jr. & Grant, A. E. (2001). *Framing Public Life: Perspectives on Media and Our Understanding of the Social World*. New York: Taylor & Francis.

Regan, D. T. (1988). *For the Record: From Wall Street to Washington*. San Diego, CA: Harcourt Brace Jovanovich.

Remember what blogs were like before the Rove/Plame controversy? Nor do we. (2005, July 18). [Blog post.] http://blogometer.nationaljournal.com/archives/2005/07/718_remember_wh.php.

Rich, F. (2006). *The Greatest Story Ever Sold: The Decline and Fall of Truth from 9/11 to Katrina*. New York: Penguin Press.

Rich, F. (2009, May 17). Obama can't turn the page on Bush, *The New York Times*. www.nytimes.com/2009/05/17/opinion/17rich-5.html.

Ricks, T. E. (2006). *Fiasco: The American Military Adventure in Iraq*. New York: Penguin.

Rieder, R. (2005). Asleep at the wheel. *American Journalism Review*, 27(4), 6.

Rimer, S. (2004, September 20). Portrait of George Bush in '72: unanchored in turbulent time, *The New York Times*. www.nytimes.com/2004/09/20/politics/campaign/20bama.html.

Ripley, A., Macias Aguayo, A., Dickerson, J. F., et al. (2004, September 27). Campaign '04: how did Dan Rather get in this fix? *Time*, 28–9.

Risen, J. (2006). *State of War: The Secret History of the CIA and the Bush Administration*. New York: Free Press.

Roberts, J. L. (2004). Media mogul maelstrom. *Newsweek*. www.newsweek.com/id/55035.

Robertson, L. R. (1989). After such knowledge: the rhetoric of the Iran–Contra fiasco. *Rhetoric Society Quarterly*, 19(1), 3–14.

Robinson, P., Goddard, P., Parry, K., Murray, C. & Taylor, P. (2010). *Pockets of Resistance: British News Media, War and Theory in the 2003 Invasion of Iraq*. Manchester: Manchester University Press.

Robinson, W. (2004, September 8). Bush fell short on duty at Guard: records show pledges unmet, *The Boston Globe*, p. A1. www.boston.com/news/nation/articles/2004/09/08/bush_fell_short_on_duty_at_guard/.

Rockefeller, S. J. (2009). *Whether Public Statements Regarding Iraq by U.S. Government Officials Were Substantiated by Intelligence Information* (110th Congress). Washington, DC: United States Senate.

Rogers, R. A. (1988). *Assurance through Performance: The Iran–Contra Hearings as Celebration*. www.eric.ed.gov/PDFS/ED299605.pdf.

Rollberg, J. N., Sanders, L. W. & Rutherford, B. (1993). The "Bimbo primaries": a comparison of how the major television networks covered charges of womanizing against Bill Clinton and Gary Hart. Paper presented at the Annual Meeting of the Association for Education in Journalism and Mass Communication (Kansas City, MO). www.eric.ed.gov/PDFS/ED362919.pdf.

Romano, L. & Lardner, G. (1999, July 28). At height of Vietnam, Bush picks Guard, *The Washington Post*, p. A-1. www.washingtonpost.com/wp-srv/politics/campaigns/wh2000/stories/bush072899.htm.

Ronald Reagan from the people's perspective: a Gallup Poll review (2004). www.gallup.com/poll/11887/ronald-reagan-from-peoples-perspective-gallup-poll-review.aspx.

Rosen, D. (2009). *Sex Scandal America: Politics and the Ritual of Public Shaming*. Toronto: Key Publishing House.

Rosenstiel, T. (1993). *Strange Bedfellows: How Television and the Presidential Candidates Changed American Politics*. New York: Hyperion.

Rosenthal, A. (1992, April 12). THE 1992 CAMPAIGN: political memo; Bush may get more scrutiny after what Clinton endured, *The New York Times*, p. A1. www.nytimes.com/1992/04/13/us/1992-campaign-political-memo-bush-may-get-more-scrutiny-after-what-clinton.html.

Rozel, M. J. & Sollenberger, M. (2008). The contemporary presidency executive privilege and the U.S. attorneys firings. *Presidential Studies Quarterly*, 38(2), 315–28.

Russakoff, D. & Balz, D. (1994, December 19). After political victory, a personal revolution, *The Washington Post*, p. A-1.

Rutenberg, J. (2001, November 5). Media stoke debate on torture as US option, *The New York Times*, p. A1.

Rutenberg, J., Thompson, M. W., Kirkpatrick, D. D. & Labaton, S. (2008, February 21). For McCain, self-confidence on ethics poses its own risk, *The New York Times*. www.nytimes.com/2008/02/21/us/politics/21mccain.html?pagewanted=all.

Sabato, L. (1991). *Feeding Frenzy: Attack Journalism and American Politics*. New York: Free Press.

Sabato, L., Stencil, M. & Lichter, R. (2000). *Peep Show: Media and Politics in an Age of Scandal*. Lanham, MD: Rowman and Littlefield.

Sanders, B. (writer) & Sanders, B. & Baker, R. (directors). (1996). *Fear and Favor in the Newsroom*. USA: Northwest Passage Productions.

Sanger, D. E. & Johnston, D. (2006, April 11). With one filing, prosecutor puts Bush in the spotlight, *The New York Times*. www.nytimes.com/2006/04/11/washington/11leak.html.

Sarat, A. & Hussain, N. (2010). *When Governments Break the Law: The Rule of Law and the Prosecution of the Bush Administration*. New York: New York University Press.

Schaller, T. F. (2006). *Whistling Past Dixie: How Democrats Can Win Without the South*. New York: Simon & Schuster.

Schattschneider, E. E. (1960). *The Semisovereign People: A Realist's View of Democracy in America*. New York: Holt.

Schecter, C. (2008). *The Real McCain: Why Conservatives Don't Trust Him and Why Independents Shouldn't*. Sausalito, CA: PoliPoint Press.

Schiffer, A. J. (2006). Blogswarms and press norms: news coverage of the Downing Street memo controversy. *Journalism & Mass Communication Quarterly*, 83(3), 494–510.

Schmitt, E. (2002, July 5). U.S. plan for Iraq is said to include attack on 3 sides, *The New York Times*, p. A1. www.nytimes.com/2002/07/05/world/us-plan-for-iraq-is-said-to-include-attack-on-3-sides.html.

Schorr, D. (2008). *Clearing the Air*. Boston Houghton Mifflin.

Schudson, M. (1992). *Watergate in American Memory: How We Remember, Forget and Reconstruct the Past*. New York: Basic Books.

Schudson, M. (1998). *The Good Citizen: A History of American Civic Life*. Cambridge, MA: MIT Press.

Schwartz, M., Devroy, A. & Ifill, G. (1989, January 10). Bush office aide expected to get a protocol post, *The Washington Post*, p. A-21.

Serrano, R. A. & Vartabedian, R. (2008, July 11). McCain's broken marriage and fractured Reagan friendship, *Los Angeles Times*. http://articles.latimes.com/2008/jul/11/nation/na-divorce11.

Sheehy, G. (1992, May). What Hillary wants. *Vanity Fair*, 55.

Sheehy, G. (1995, September). The inner quest of Newt Gingrich. *Vanity Fair*, 147.

Sheppard, M. (2008). How close were the presidential elections? www.mit.edu/~mi22295/elections.html#2000.

Shorris, E. (2004, June). Ignoble liars: Leo Straus, George Bush and the philosophy of mass deception. *Harper's*, 308, 65–71.

Sifry, M. L. (2004). The rise of open-source politics. *Nation*, 14–20. http://proxygw.wrlc.org/login?url=http://search.ebscohost.com/login.aspx?direct=true&db=aph&AN=14978810&site=ehost-live.

Sifry, M. L. (2009). A see-through society. *Columbia Journalism Review*, 47(5), 43–7.

Sifton, J. (2009). The Bush administration homicides. *The Daily Beast*. www.thedailybeast.com/blogs-and-stories/2009-05-05/how-many-were-tortured-to-death/.

Silver, N. (2011, March 24). A note to our readers on the Times pay model and the economics of reporting, *The New York Times*. http://fivethirtyeight.blogs.nytimes.com/2011/03/24/a-note-to-our-readers-on-the-times-pay-model-and-the-economics-of-reporting/#more-7393.

Smith, M. (2007). *The Right Talk: How Conservatives Transformed the Great Society into the Economic Society*. Princeton, NJ: Princeton University Press.

Sorkin, A. R. (2009). *Too Big to Fail: The Inside Story of How Wall Street and Washington Fought to Save the Financial System – and Themselves*. New York: Viking.

Spillius, A. (2007, September 21). George Bush the Texan is "scared of horses," *The Telegraph* [UK]. www.telegraph.co.uk/news/worldnews/1563773/George-Bush-the-Texan-is-scared-of-horses.html.

Stephen, A. (2007). The murk and dirt of the White House. *New Statesman*, 136(4837), 28–9.

Stern, M., Kammer, J., Calbraith, D. & Condon, G. E. J. (2007). *The Wrong Stuff: The Extraordinary Saga of Randy "Duke" Cunningham, The Most Corrupt Congressman Ever Caught*. New York: PublicAffairs.

Stewart, J. B. (1996). *Blood Sport: The President and His Adversaries*. New York: Simon & Schuster.

Stewart, M. (2008, October 5). Palin hits Obama for "terrorist" connection. *CNN*. www.cnn.com/2008/POLITICS/10/04/palin.obama/index.html.

Stiglitz, J. E. (2010). *Freefall: America, Free Markets, and the Sinking of the World Economy*. New York: W.W. Norton.

Stiglitz, J. E. & Bilmes, L. J. (2010, September 5). The true cost of the Iraq war: $3 trillion and beyond, *The Washington Post*. www.washingtonpost.com/wp-dyn/content/article/2010/09/03/AR2010090302200.html.

Sullivan, A. (2009). Palin puts the Trig question back on the table. *The Daily Dish*. http://andrewsullivan.theatlantic.com/the_daily_dish/2009/12/sarah-

palin-has-now-made-two-very-clear-public-statements-in-the-last-day.
html.

Suskind, R. (2004). *The Price of Loyalty: George W. Bush, the White House, and the Education of Paul O'Neill*. New York: Simon & Schuster.

Suskind, R. (2006). *The One Percent Doctrine: Deep Inside America's Pursuit of Its Enemies Since 9/11*. New York: Simon and Schuster.

't Hart, P. & Tindall, K. (2011). Understanding crisis exploitation. In P. t' Hart and K. Tindall (eds.), *Framing the Global Economic Downturn: Crisis Rhetoric and the Politics of Recessions* (pp. 21–42). Canberra, Australia: ANU-E Press.

Taranto, J. (2008, February 21). The Iseman cometh, *The Wall Street Journal*. http://online.wsj.com/article/SB120361267441083195.html.

Taylor, A. (2005). *Elephant's Edge: The Republicans as a Ruling Party*. New York: Praeger.

Taylor, J. (2006). *Where Did the Party Go? William Jennings Bryan, Hubert Humphrey, and the Jeffersonian Legacy*. Columbia, MO: University of Missouri Press.

Think Progress. (2006, May 5). Breaking: CIA director Porter Goss resigns. http://thinkprogress.org/2006/05/05/breaking-cia-director-porter-goss-resigns/.

Thomas, E. & Breslau, K. (1996, November 18). Don't look now: at a critical stage of the race, Dole was preoccupied by a newspaper story that never ran. *Newsweek*, 106.

Thomas, E., Breslau, K., Rosenberg, D., Kaufman, L. & Kennerly, D. (1997). *Back from the Dead: How Clinton Survived the Republican Revolution*. New York: Grove/Atlantic.

Thompson, J. (2000). *Political Scandal: Power and Visibility in the Media Age*. Cambridge: Polity Press.

Tiffen, R. (1999). *Scandals: Media, Politics and Corruption in Contemporary Australia*. Sydney: University of New South Wales Press.

Time. (1992, August 24). A turbulent approach coming into Houston. www.time.com/time/magazine/article/0,9171,976294,00.html.

Trento, S. B. (1992). *The Power House: Robert Keith Gray and the Selling of Access and Influence in Washington*. New York: St. Martin's Press.

Trippi, J. (2004). *The Revolution Will Not Be Televised: Democracy, the Internet, and the Overthrow of Everything*. New York: Regan Books.

Tuchman, G. (1978). *Making News: A Study in the Construction of Reality*. New York: Free Press.

Tumber, H. & Waisbord, S. (2004). Political scandals and media across democracies. *American Behavioral Scientist*, 47(7), 1143–52.

Tumulty, K. (2010, October 29). Newt Gingrich: out of the wilderness and into the mix for 2012, *The Washington Post*. www.washingtonpost.com/wp-dyn/content/article/2010/10/28/AR2010102807414.html.

Tyler, P. (2002, July 5). The warpath: pressures build on Iraq, *The New York Times*, p. A6. www.nytimes.com/2002/07/05/world/the-warpath-pressures-build-on-iraq.html.

United Nations. (1984). Convention Against Torture and Other Cruel, Inhuman or Degrading Treatment or Punishment. http://untreaty.un.org/cod/avl/ha/catcidtp/catcidtp.html.

United States Financial Crisis Inquiry Commission. (2011). *The Financial Crisis Inquiry Report: Final Report of the National Commission on the Causes of the Financial and Economic Crisis in the United State.* Washington, DC: Superintendent of Documents, US Government Printing Office.

United States of America vs. *I. Lewis Libby* (2005, October 28). United States District Court, District of Columbia.

Vavreck, L. (2009). *The Message Matters: The Economy and Presidential Campaigns.* Princeton, NJ: Princeton University Press.

Waas, M. (2006, July 3). Bush directed Cheney to counter war critic. *National Journal.* www.sourcewatch.org/index.php?title=Murray_Waas/External_Links_2005–2008.

Waisbord, S. (2000). *Watchdog Journalism in South America: News, Accountability, and Democracy.* New York: Columbia University Press.

Waisbord, S. (2004). Scandals, media, and citizenship in contemporary Argentina. *American Behavioral Scientist*, 47(8), 1072–98.

Wallison, P. J. (2003). *Ronald Reagan: The Power of Conviction and the Success of his Presidency.* Boulder, CO: Westview Press.

Wallsten, K. Agenda setting and the blogosphere: an analysis of the relationship between mainstream media and political blogs. *Review of Policy Research*, 24(6), 567–87.

Wallsten, P. (2004, September 18). GOP activist made allegations on CBS memos, *Los Angeles Times.* http://articles.latimes.com/2004/sep/18/nation/na-buckhead18.

Walsh, L. (1998). *Firewall: The Iran–Contra Conspiracy and Cover-up.* New York: W.W. Norton.

The Washington Post (producer). (2011). *Ronald Reagan: Actor, President, Statesman.* www.washingtonpost.com/wp-dyn/content/gallery/2011/02/02/GA2011020207200.html#photo=5.

Watts, M. D., Domke, D., Shah, D. V. & Fan, D. P. (1999). Elite cues and media bias: explaining public perceptions of a liberal press. *Communication Research*, 26, 144–75.

Weigel, D. (2010, July 13). Believing Sarah Palin. *The Daily Dish.* http://andrewsullivan.theatlantic.com/the_daily_dish/2010/07/believing-sarah-palin.html.

Westen, D. (2007). *The Political Brain: The Role of Emotion in Deciding the Fate of the Nation.* New York: Public Affairs.

White House 2000: comparing the candidates. (2000). *The Polling Report.* www.pollingreport.com/wh2cand.htm.

Williams, I. (2004). *Deserter: Bush's War on Military Families, Veterans, and His Past.* New York: Nation Books.

Williams, J. & Apostolidis, P. (2004). *Public Affairs: Politics in the Age of Sex Scandals*. Durham, NC: Duke University Press.

Williams, R. (1998). *Political Scandals in the USA*. Edinburgh: Edinburgh University Press.

Wilson, J. C. (2004). *The Politics of Truth: Inside the Lies that Led to War and Betrayed My Wife's CIA Identity: A Diplomat's Memoir*. New York: Carroll & Graf Publishers.

Wilson, T. C. (1995). Vietnam-era military service: a test of the class-bias thesis. *Armed Forces & Society*, 21(3), 461–71.

Wilson, V. P. (2008). *Fair Game: How a Top Spy Was Betrayed by Her Own Government*. New York: Simon & Schuster

Wines, M. (1993, December 24). Troopers who accuse the president are questioned on their own pasts, *The New York Times*, p. A18. www.nytimes.com/1993/12/24/us/troopers-who-accuse-the-president-are-questioned-on-their-own-pasts.html.

Woodward, B. (2002). *Bush at War*. New York: Simon & Schuster.

Woodward, B. (2006). *State of Denial: Bush at War, Part III*. New York: Simon & Schuster.

Woodward, B. (2010). *Obama's Wars*. New York: Simon & Schuster.

Woodward, B. & Bernstein, C. (1974). *All the President's Men*. New York: Simon and Schuster.

Zaller, J. (2001). Monica Lewinsky and the mainsprings of American politics. In W. L. Bennett & R. M. Entman (eds.), *Mediated Politics: Communication in the Future of Democracy* (pp. 252–78). Cambridge: Cambridge University Press.

Zaller, J. (2003). A new standard for news quality: burglar alarms for the monitorial citizen. *Political Communication*, 20, 109–30.

Zernike, K. & Rutenberg, J. (2004, August 20). Friendly fire: the birth of an anti-Kerry ad, *The New York Times*, p. A1. www.nytimes.com/2004/08/20/politics/campaign/20swift.html.

Index